Education Redux

How to Make Schools Relevant to Our Children and Our Future

Education Redux

How to Make Schools Relevant to Our Children and Our Future

by

Eli Fishman

Lightning Smart®

Information Age Publishing, Inc.
Charlotte, North Carolina • www.infoagepub.com

Library of Congress Cataloging-in-Publication Data

Fishman, Eli.
  Education redux : how to make schools relevant to our children and our
future / by Eli Fishman.
      p. cm.
  Includes bibliographical references.
  ISBN 978-1-60752-404-5 (pbk.) -- ISBN 978-1-60752-405-2 (hardcover) --
ISBN 978-1-60752-406-9 (e-book)
  1. Public schools--United States. 2. Education--Aims and
objectives--United States. 3. Educational change--United States. I. Title.

  LA217.2.F566 2010
  370.973--dc22

                                                                    2009048053

Printed in the United States of America

CONTENTS

CHAPTER 1

INTRODUCTION

The challenges facing twenty-first century America are numerous and complex. Some of the crises include a housing/subprime crisis, the financial institution crisis, the oil crisis, the environmental and global warming crisis, the job crisis, obesity crisis, the loss of the middle class crisis, the violence crisis, poverty crisis and the school crisis. This is a limited list of current crises. The solutions lie in looking past all the posturing and the rhetoric.

U.S. political leaders at all levels of government are officially charged with identifying intelligent responses and initiating measures likely to achieve a positive resolution of each predicament. Needless to say, these objectives and processes have to be unambiguous and easily communicated in order to attain consensus—the plainer and simpler, the better. Unfortunately, in the interest of efficiency, pedestrian sound bites are generally substituted for thoughtful discourse.

However, none of the problems are simple. Consequently, the solutions will have to be both complex and will require remedial actions that are long term, even generational. Unfortunately, long term, strategic cures are always trumped by feel-good, you-can-have-it-now undemanding reactions. Appeals to immediate gratification prevail, no matter how futile the solutions may be. For example, even though both political leaders and ordinary citizens recognize that a recent program sending each taxpayer a check for a few hundred dollars will have little effect in stimulating a

Education Redux: How to Make Schools Relevant to Our Children and Our Future, pp. 1–9

sluggish economy, and will result in an ever-increasing budget deficit, everyone is happy to get some "free" money regardless of the amount.

The most popular and comprehensive resolution to the nation's disquiet over the myriad of crises is a proclamation of the need for better educational opportunities for the country's young people, who are the future. This is a response with guaranteed universal acceptance. Voters in all categories have been inculcated to embrace the legitimacy of an education agenda. Being an "education" candidate for virtually any public office affirms a potential officeholder's credentials. At the same time, the "education" designation precludes the need for a political figure to define a new and innovative plan capable of tackling complex challenges.

A belief in the importance of education is warranted. However, it is essential that the wider concept of education be deconstructed to further an understanding of what education is to achieve and how those objectives will be attained. The mere notion of education must be operationalized.

What are children supposed to be learning? Why are those subjects important? Why doesn't our present school system seem to be working? What is the problem with all those school reform efforts like charter schools, vouchers and merit pay that we always hear about? Who is supposed to establish an effective education agenda? What will it look like? What exactly are we training children to do? These questions are never asked, let alone answered. Thus, it is important to get beyond the gratuitous oratory. What specifically do political leaders mean by "improving education" and how exactly will that help the economy?

The second component of the typical education agenda is to suggest a means for providing better educational opportunities. Once again, a universal solution is readily available. It is always "spend more money." Since money fixes everything, it is only reasonable to believe that our educational system is ineffectual because it is underfunded and some incremental cash injection is all that is needed to get the job done. No one has expressed a need to explore any structural lack of effectiveness in America's contemporary education system. The existing educational bureaucracy is presumed capable of making needed improvements if adequate financial resources are forthcoming, and teachers and administrators are held to account. An unremitting history of their inability to produce acceptable results seems irrelevant.

In September, 2008 a Black pastor of a church on the Chicago's South Side organized a boycott for the first week of the public school year. Rev. Meeks arranged for school children to board dozens of school buses and drive to New Trier High School in an affluent North Shore suburb where they would register to attend. This gesture was purely symbolic since the children were not eligible to enroll because they lived outside the school district. The stated purpose of the boycott and the trip to the Winnetka school was to suggest that the reason for poor performance of students in South Side schools compared to those in the suburban school was a lack of adequate funding. However, a closer look at the funding differences would not suggest that any funding differences, which are minimal at best, remotely relate to the huge disparity in academic performance. The real purpose of the boycott was political theater.[1]

At any given time there are probably hundreds and maybe thousands of publicly funded education studies in progress. The mere existence of these efforts, regardless of their ultimate merit, seems sufficient to satiate the need for actual improvements. For the most part, these studies are nothing more that restatements of work that has been done over the past 60 years. The solutions, which have already proven to be unsuccessful, are tirelessly reiterated in an unending variety of configurations. It seems people have a preference for being told what they already know, even though it doesn't work.

Understandably, the primary job of all politicians is to get elected. Comforting constituents with predictable remedial activity is an effective strategy toward that end. Since schooling is a governmental responsibility, it is important to understand that governments have a different standard for rational behavior. Political entities are not subjected to the same rules for economic conduct that are applied by consumers and producers. Rational behavior for those two groups is usually defined as the pursuit of reasonable objectives using the least amount of scarce resources. Rationality will triumph over irrationality since efficiency will always surmount inefficiency in a pure economic model. In the realm of governmental activity, however, acting rationally means maximizing political support. Political strength is established by appealing to ideologies. The "spend more money to make schools better" ideology is a sure bet for politicians.[2]

The insipid iterations of half century old dogma are remarkably durable. Developing a radically new and innovative program that is sufficiently different from dependably useless solutions would frighten educational establishment stakeholders, disturb the comfort level of voters and threaten the electability of any politicians promoting revolutionary ideas that have any outside chance of working. Needless to say, sound new approaches are critical if any success is to be realized.

Currently, spending on American K-12 education exceeds one-half trillion dollars annually. At 50 million students, that is about $10,000+ for each student. The portion of these funds spent on teacher salaries varies somewhat, but is usually estimated at 40% of the total. This means that there is about $300 billion spent each year on materials, facilities, and administrators charged with assuring adequately performing schools.

U.S. schools are governed by 15,000 local districts, each with its own budget. There is no nationally endorsed curriculum or instructional method. Virtually every other enterprise has realized the benefits of pursuing both national and global strategies. The benefits include spreading fixed costs, such as research and development and corporate management costs over a larger number of outlets. In addition, increasing purchasing power with vendors by buying large quantities, and tried and tested processes that enable companies to deliver a cost effective product with consistent quality encourage large-scale tactics.

Once local industries realizing the advantages of national arrangements are the restaurant industry (McDonalds, Applebee's, Denny's, etc.), department stores (Wal-Mart, Macy's, Nordstrom's, etc.), office supplies (Staples and Office Depot), home improvement (Home Depot and Lowes), movie theaters (AMC and General Cinema), electronics stores (Best Buy and Circuit City), shoe stores (Foot Locker and Payless) grocery stores (Trader Joe's and Whole Foods), and even used cars (Car Max and Auto Nation).

Using any one of the thousands of interstate highway off-ramps practically anywhere in America will deposit an individual in a sea of flotsam consisting of buildings and businesses indistinguishable from those at any other interstate off-ramp. As mind-numbing and boring as this ambience may be, it does enable a traveler to acquire familiar product with dependable quality and price points almost anywhere. Similarly, schools will be more effective adopting the benefits of a national strategy rather than just reflecting the impulses of a local school board.

The consequence of such a fragmented educational system is the expenditure of massive financial resources in the development of duplicative bureaucracies and a limitless supply of instructional and curriculum programs that are reviewed and purchased individually by the various districts. Due to the vast sums being spent on programming and the sheer quantity of potential customers, the number of introductions of new and purportedly effective educational programs is incessant.

Educational solutions come from a myriad of research studies that may be publicly funded, and from a relatively small number of well-known companies producing academic resources. The duration of *curriculum-based* programs appears to evolve through a predetermined cycle. Initially, the programs are proposed in a popular professional periodical. They are then introduced in an innovative school district. The program expands rapidly. Once the program is widely disseminated, controlled evaluations are performed. Critical comments appear in trade publications. Preliminary evaluations may produce disappointing results and interest in the program diminishes. Thus, the new program introductions tend to behave like a pendulum from being the "answer" to being another boondoggle to generate cash for the major academic providers. They all have a limited longevity based on the amount of time it takes to chronicle their deficiencies.[3]

The commonality in the new program submissions is that they represent only modified versions of conventional formats. Yet the unrelenting introductions of the 'next big thing' provide both enduring hope and a justification for the existence of the various bureaucratic players and their work.

Instruction-based methodology follows a slightly different pattern. There are essentially two dichotomous perspectives that have had considerable theoretical and pragmatic durability. They are teacher-centered or behaviorist methods and student-centered or constructivist practices. The two approaches can be conceived as opposite ends of a continuum or as a dialectic. In any dialectic where there is a thesis, an antithesis and a synthesis, most activity occurs somewhere in between while being more or less inclined toward one side or the other.

Teacher-centered procedures are based on instituting a variety of rewards and punishments to shape student behavior. This method is a traditional means of getting students, children or employees to conduct themselves in a predetermined manner. It is a generally accepted principle that rewarding people or animals for good behavior and punishing or withholding rewards for undesirable behavior will foster consistent good behavior.

On the other hand, student-centered teaching is described as a scaffolding process. Teachers begin with the student's prior education and experience and provide a support structure using inquiry techniques to expand the students' knowledge base. By maximizing the use of that which a student already knows, their interests and innate curiosity, the teacher assists in the expansion of the learner's range of knowledge.

Both approaches have their legions of advocates and detractors. Once again, there is no certain route. Neither has proven to be a definitive methodology. All of the supposed new and innovative approaches to instruction are simply options located on differing points along the teacher-centered/student-centered continuum.

Aside from curriculum and instruction issues, a critical problem endemic to American education is student concern over school relevance. Those responsible for our education system—politicians, school board members, school administrators and teachers—tend to perceive schools as isolated institutions that are disconnected from the vicissitudes of the social, political, and economic order. This notion is not shared by students.

Children from a young age are keenly attuned to their adult prospects. The types and quantity of jobs likely to be available, speculation regarding the prospects for financial security and the nature of anticipated familial relationships are of paramount concern. Globalization, outsourcing, loss of the U.S. manufacturing sector, widening income disparity, wage compression, job insecurity, and diminished health care and retirement options are universal concerns not limited to adults.

Children's exposure to all types of electronic media will assure these issues remain prominent. Teachers and administrators can't keep whistling through the graveyard expecting children to respond to the lessons left over from a bygone era that fail to acknowledge new realities. To allay students' anxieties, education programming must address a broad range of school based activities responsive to the genuine needs of the future.

Efforts that have been made to manage the school crisis are similar to those expended in the fight against cancer. Remedial activity to end the unacceptably high incidence of cancer in the United States is directed at treating symptoms rather than addressing underlying causes. Research to find a cure for cancer began in earnest in 1971 with a particular emphasis placed on illnesses related to tobacco use. Other hazardous materials known to produce cancer at the time, such as radiation, asbestos and benzene were not included.

Since 1971 the government has spent more than $69 billion on cancer research. Yet, the rates of several forms of cancer are on the rise while tobacco use is declining. Fifty years ago, 1 in 20 women got breast cancer in her lifetime. Currently, one in seven women will suffer from breast cancer. Cancer is the number one cause of death of middle-aged persons, as well as the number two killer, after accidents, of children.[4]

Generously funded and connected political lobbying, manipulative scientific spin and misleading advertising created by major industries have derailed appropriate governmental corrective action. Although any industrial and environmental producers of cancer have been well documented, research continues its commitment to finding a cure rather than eliminating the sources. Reasons for this imprudent course of action are based on the priorities of industrial and health-care stakeholders.

Industrial producers of otherwise useful items that are known cancer causing agents or engender cancer causing conditions in their manufacture insist on the importance of assuring the availability of the product, as well as stressing the need for creating and maintaining jobs. Health care providers and drug companies depend on the revenue streams generated by millions of cancer patients using their products and services.

These groups dominate the political agenda and are inclined to promote their own interests despite evidence it is not the most prudent course of action. In a similar vein, the education industry, from teachers and administrators to textbook and educational research providers, have a considerable stake in sustaining the existing school system regardless of its effectiveness. Attempts to deal with symptoms, like poor test performance, without an examination of their macro-environmental origins will lead to limited success in improving the overall health of our school system.

The elemental egg-crate configuration omnipresent in contemporary schools is a remnant of the industrial era. This arrangement was developed more than a century ago to conform to an assembly line culture that was dominant in the late 1800s. One room, one teacher, one lesson plan and multiple students is a formula for failure in the twenty-first century.

The principle that "children are children" is a fiction that continues to guide our education system. Except for their similar ages and sizes, there are a variety of reasons that indicate today's *New Kids* do not remotely resemble their predecessors for whom schools were designed. New schools must be established on the model of the e-OneRoom Schoolhouse. The e-OneRoom Schoolhouse model is based on an individualized educational experience for each student using state of the art technologies that provide a relevant curriculum.

The need for reinforcement is a principle from the behaviorist camp that has a degree of broad support. The origins of the effectiveness of reinforcement techniques date to experiments in the late 1940s where pigeons learned to rotate levers in order to receive food. These experiments were conducted by American psychologist, B. F. Skinner. Skinner asserted that teaching consists of a teacher transmitting knowledge, a student acquiring that knowledge and retaining the acquired knowledge by grasping the structure of facts and ideas. Knowledge is retained through a process of reinforcement.

The three contingencies of reinforcement that lead to behavioral changes are: learning by doing or playing an active role in acquiring information; learning from experience which may involve some type of simulation; and learning by trial and error which highlights the consequences of specific behavior. There is behavior and there are consequences resulting from that behavior. Thus, dynamic participation in knowledge acquisition is important to the student's ability to absorb and retain that knowledge.[5]

The contingencies of reinforcement are best effectuated through the use of technology. Mechanical devices used to facilitate individualized learning appeared beginning in the 1920s. This primitive apparatus consisted of four keys that corresponded to multiple choice answers on a test. The student could not proceed until the correct response was entered. The post-World War II era brought advanced teaching machines operating electrically using motors and lights. It was also based on identifying the correct answer to a set of questions.

Since the 1960s and 1970s, as computer technology became more widely accessible, there have been many adaptations for computer use in individualized instruction. As computer power continued to improve and expand through the beginning of the twenty-first century, its use for educational purposes has become common. However, the widening gap between rapidly progressing computer development and the ability of teachers to fully utilize the computer's potential has severely limited the extent to which computers are employed for educational purposes. Computers are largely used for remedial purposes and software is predicated on the concept of "skill and drill," a repetitious and boring means of reinforcing very specific skill sets.

Individualized learning does allow students to proceed at their own pace. They should be able to interact with material in a manner that will nourish their interest, which is a goal that is consistently supported by virtually all theories of instruction. Many innovative and exciting technologies currently employed in the video game industry are readily transferable for use in schools. It is essential that a relatively small portion of the $300 billion already is being spent on school administration and retread academic programs be utilized for the development of first rate educational computer-based programming. In addition, teacher training is necessary to facilitate these programs.

From a broader perspective, schools, in addition to providing students with essential academic skills, must also consider a strategy for preparing children to solve America's economic, social, political and environmental crises. A major contributor to the problems we encounter daily is the loss of a sense of community. This phenomenon is largely the result of a focus on the individual by companies seeking to expand consumerist behaviors and by increased entertainment options indulging individual tastes— from cable TV to iPods.

Having adults maintain important bonds in their respective communities, as well as encouraging a strong sense of national identity and concern for fellow citizens, must be inculcated into current learners. It should be done through a formal academic process. The *e-OneRoom Schoolhouse* will provide students with important training in group involvement. This training will also be implemented using state of the art technologies offering projects that can only be completed by individuals interacting with a group making their contributions to the project.

Another significant issue facing the United States is the seeming insoluble problem of the ballooning trade deficit which is expected to reach more than 1 trillion dollars annually in the near term. This crisis can only be alleviated by restoring our manufacturing sector. Bringing back manufacturing to the United States may appear to be an unrealistic objective, but developing student interest in industry will guarantee its return.

Developing video games based on the challenges of designing and producing the goods we see every day using both individual and group efforts will create a fascination with manufacturing. Improving student interest in school means keeping them actively engaged. It is also necessary to cultivate a sense of the importance of a formal education as it relates to a student's future prospects. This is a more difficult task. However, both objectives are achievable through a carefully crafted video game curriculum in the *e-OneRoom Schoolhouse*.

CHAPTER 2

THE SCHOOL PROBLEM

The U.S. Secretary of Education, William Bennett, came to Chicago in 1988 and declared its schools to be the worst in the country. In 1992 the Council of Great City Schools ranked Chicago last, based on student test results in the 47 largest school districts. After a series of disclosures about millions of dollars in waste and fraud in the Chicago school system, the State Legislature permitted the city's mayor to take over the system in 1995. The mayor initiated a series of reforms that included placing underperforming schools on probation, discharging poor teachers and principals, eliminating social graduations where students were automatically sent through each successive grade regardless of their academic performance, and working with the unions to assure good labor relations.

Many of the worst schools were closed and several new charter schools were created. The charter schools were run independently from union and central school district administrations. Some of the newly created schools had a specific focus, such as college prep, military academies, arts, language, math or science centers. An outcome of these initiatives plus an investment of tens of millions of additional dollars from both public and private sources, is increased graduation and attendance rates, and test results that have shown improvement.[1]

However, as of 2006, only 6.5% of Chicago public school (CPS) students complete college by their mid-20s. For Black and Latino male ninth-graders, only 3% graduate college within 6 years of their high school graduations, although about 80% of CPS high school seniors say

Education Redux: How to Make Schools Relevant to Our Children and Our Future,
pp. 11–17

they want at least a bachelor's degree.[2] Despite moderate progress since the 1988 declaration by the secretary of education, the lack of compelling solutions for ostensibly intractable problems is evident.

Charter schools, teacher accountability, and a myriad of additional measures have resulted in minimal improvements, although no steady rate of progress is anticipated.

A consensus endures that to properly address the enormous scope of the problem educational spending must continue to be dramatically expanded. Currently, education spending in the United States for K-12 exceeds one-half trillion dollars a year for about 50 million students or more than $10 thousand annually for each child. Over the last 25 years, educational expenditures have steadily grown at a rate of 7% annually, or more than double the rate of inflation.[3]

At the end of World War II, according to the U.S. Department of Education, spending per pupil (in constant 2001-2002 dollars) for public elementary and secondary schools was $1,214 per student annually. That amount doubled by the middle of the 1950s to $2,345 per student, doubled again to $4,479 by the early 1970s and doubled again in 2001-2002 to $8,745 per student. The total spending increase in constant dollars during this period is over 700%.[4] Needless to say, student performance during this period has not responded proportionately, if at all.

Beginning in the early 1970s the National Assessment of Educational Progress (NAEP) began random classroom testing across the country. The average reading score for 12th grade students in 1971 was 285. Their average reading score in 1999 was 288. During the same period math scores for 12th graders went from 304 to 308. The average improvement was slightly over 1% during a 30-year period where school funding doubled. Not much of a return on investment.

In this same time span, high school graduation rates for all 17-years-olds actually dropped from 75.6% to 72.5% according to U.S. Department of Education statistics. Considering the increased funding devoted to education, there is no evidence that the higher spending levels yield any improvement in student performance. Despite clear evidence that spending increases do not produce concomitant improvements in student performance, political leaders, experts and educators continue to advocate in favor of this solution as an educational panacea.

Further, they continue to reinforce the notion that the simple solution to all societal challenges is improving education, and to improve education, it is only necessary to increase expenditures. The argument goes round and round without any acknowledgment of real outcomes. Both of these assertions are, at face value, false. More money does not automatically result in better student performance, and the failure to identify useful educational objectives will also miss the target.

To begin, deciding the best approach to how the ever-increasing funds should be spent continues to be an elusive. The visibility of new school buildings and publicly funded charter schools are a popular recourse. More and better teachers, which may require some salary increases, are also a popular solution. Yet, according to the U.S. Department of Education, in 1959 teacher salaries were 56% of the average school budget. By 1989 the teacher salary portion had dropped to 40% of the school budget due to increases in special personnel and administrators. Relative investment in actual teaching is being reduced in favor of bureaucratic priorities.

In any case, there is no persistent evidence to suggest that new school buildings or minor teacher salary increases will have a positive effect on student academic performance. Throughout the more education and more money conversation, elemental investment in research and development in education is reliably overlooked. The reason is that research funds are committed to the bureaucratic priorities of the educational establishment which continues to reinforce the present anemic system.

The 1983 report, *A Nation at Risk*, by the National Commission on Excellence in Education warned that the educational foundations of our society were being eroded by a rising tide of mediocrity.[5] Having squandered gains in student achievement resulting from the Sputnik Challenge, we have lost sight of the basic purposes of schooling. Knowledge, information and skilled intelligence are the new materials of international commerce. Further, a high level of shared education is essential to a free, democratic society.

To combat declining student performance, the Commission recommended strengthening the curriculum in basic subject matter, adopting more rigorous standards, increasing homework and time-on-task in classrooms, improving teacher preparation and salaries, and holding educators and elected officials responsible for educational performance. Although this mom-and-apple-pie remediation seems perfectly reasonable, the prescriptions are far too broad to have any utility. What is "basic subject matter" in the twenty-first century? How does increased time-on-task in the classroom get implemented? How is teacher preparation to be improved, and what are reasonable salary levels?

The upshot is that a quarter century after this dire warning was issued, no progress by any standard has been made. In many districts, student achievement has dropped since *A Nation at Risk* was introduced. *A Nation at Risk* is representative of educational research and development activities. It only restates what has been known for a long time. For the most part, the findings are intuitive. Yet vast sums continue to be consigned to academic research that offers the same worn-out, ineffectual platitudes.

Though pointless exercises appear to be the standard approach to educational research and development, a one-time incident that demanded immediate and specific action precipitated a much less ambiguous response. On October 4, 1957 the Soviet Union launched the first man-made object into space. The satellite, called Sputnik 1, weighed 184 pounds, was silver and about the size of a beach ball. It contained only a radio transmitter which emitted a chirp from outer space in the key of A-Flat. As Sputnik orbited the Earth at 18,000 miles per hour, that sound was described as separating the old from the new.

The impact of Sputnik was massive and unparalleled in its effect on the American populace. It was the source of a "dread" that re-ordered American priorities. The immediate reaction was passage of the National Defense Education Act (NDEA) in September, 1958. The NDEA provided billions over several years for language labs, instruction in new math, PhD. Fellowships and improvements in a science heavy curriculum, as well as the purchase of scientific equipment. As a partial consequence of these efforts, by May, 1961 President Kennedy addressing a joint session of Congress was able to announce the goal of landing Americans on the moon by the close of the decade.[6]

Earlier in the 50s decade, federal aid to education was limited by Southern legislators who believed the funds would be used to force deseg-regation, fundamentalists concerned with the teaching of Darwinism, and Catholics disturbed that parochial schools would receive no benefit.

The Southern contingent was well-represented on September 4, 1957, exactly one month prior to the Sputnik saga, when the story of the Little Rock Nine began. In response to the *Brown v. Board of Education* Supreme Court decision of 1954 which desegregated all schools, nine Black stu-dents enrolled at the all-White Central High School in Little Rock, Arkan-sas. These nine students were selected on the basis of their superior grades and attendance records. When the nine students arrived at the school, Arkansas governor Orval Faubus ordered soldiers from the Arkan-sas National Guard to block their entry.

On September 20th the U.S. Justice Department obtained an injunc-tion allowing the students to enter the school. The injunction was enforced on September 25 when President Eisenhower sent the 101st Air-borne Division of the United States Army to take positions at the school permitting the nine students to attend Central High.[7] For Southern poli-ticians, providing all children with solid academic credentials was and continues to be secondary to the need to reinforce racial boundaries.

There are a couple of reasons for the failure of educational research in its present form. These include issues of relevance and consideration of student priorities and dispositions. Relevance is a problem in school ame-liorative schemes to the extent that they treat schools as isolated entities disconnected from economic, social, and political realities. Therein lays a fatal flaw with all school reform agendas. School is a subclass of our social, political, and economic institutions. To nourish student interest, schools must be reflective of both current and future priorities in society. There cannot be a divide between schools and, not only the experiences and preferences of childhood, but also between school and the application of its lessons to potential adulthood experience.

Children are concerned about their adult prospects. Thus, new directions in curriculum and instruction must be contextualized in expected student-as-adult requirements. The contextualization is critical. If an individual goes to a physician for a headache, the doctor does not immediately order a brain scan to see what is inside the patient's head. Initially, the physician checks other vital signs, such as temperature, blood pressure, cholesterol and various organ functions. The headache is more likely to be a symptom of a bodily malfunction outside the brain. Similarly, school reform requires an analysis of the universe in which the student will participate, not just the school. The school is only part of a larger societal organism.

The significance of adult employment prospects and a young person's eventual ability to successfully participate in the economy can be understood within the context of the work of Karl Marx. Marx describes the relationship between people and the material forces of production. He suggests that this relationship is independent of an individual's will. It is the totality of the relations of production—the interaction between capital and labor—that determine the economic structure of society. The economic structure, or the nature of the relationship between individuals and the forces of production, is the foundation upon which a legal and political superstructure is based. Further, an individual's existence is not determined by their personal consciousness. All social consciousness corresponds to the economic structure.

Periodically, according to Marx, changes to the relations of production, or the economic structure, will lead to a transformation of the superstructure. The result will be a new consciousness.[8] Thus, it is necessary to understand that schools are part of the superstructure, which is shaped by the forces of production—or lack thereof, as is the present situation. Most educational solutions, for example, presume to prepare students for imaginary vocational opportunities. It is not possible to embark on genuine school reform that reflects economic conditions that do not exist. The present educational paradigm is based on economic imperatives appropriate in an era that ended 35 years ago.

The solution-du-jour for stubbornly deficient student skill attainment levels is the No Child Left Behind Act of 2001 (NCLB). At its core, NCLB required schools to initiate a rigorous high stakes testing schedule. The objective of NCLB is to strengthen accountability systems covering all public schools and students. NCLB requires annual testing for all students in Grades 3 through 8. School districts and individual schools must make adequate yearly progress (AYP) toward statewide proficiency goals. Failure to meet those standards will result in corrective action and restructuring measures. These corrective actions can include the dismissal of teachers and principals, as well as the closing of schools. Thus, the testing is understandably called "high stakes."

NCLB represents a reversal in the direction of the current teacher-centered/student-centered continuum. In recent years the student-centered extreme, with its focus on self-esteem issues, character education, diversity and tolerance programs and the elimination of grades and ranking, was beginning to dominate classrooms. NCLB instigated a forceful movement in the opposite direction.

The terms of NCLB prescribed a return to the "tell and test" teacher-centered classroom. Some research suggests that overemphasizing this type of rote achievement leads to a number of problems. These include the loss of a student's intrinsic interest in learning. Focusing on performance in a narrow range of subject matter will obscure the excitement of exploration. A fear of failure will reduce a student's desire to experiment and try things themselves if they are worried about making a mistake.

Testing reduces a child's desire to accept challenges. They will choose not to endure the pressure of more difficult tasks and steer toward easier ones. Thus, the quality of learning is diminished. The long-term goal of acquiring new skills will be discouraged by the need for short-term achievement. Children will explain their performance by test results rather than the degree of effort expended.[9] In a May, 2006 Congressional Committee report it was suggested that NCLB would require significant change in order to be effective.[10]

A 2008 report by a professor of education who served as an education Assistant Secretary during the formulation of NCLB, states that NCLB might actually have been enacted as a way to expose the failure of public education. The objective of NCLB was to have all public school students in Grades 4 through 8 to perform at grade level in reading and math by 2014. The professor noted that this objective was entirely unrealistic since research revealed that all students begin at different levels academically and develop at varying rates. The failure of NCLB would, presumably, have resulted in an effort toward the privatization of education which was the actual intention of the plan.[11]

Offering NCLB as a viable school reform alternative fails to consider important classroom exigencies. An educational policy must contemplate the character and experience of students. In particular, disciplinary problems, absenteeism, and violence issues severely impact time-on-task. Going through the motions of teaching a class without actually having the ability to successfully execute a lesson plan is an exercise in futility. NCLB does not provide guidance or relief from the pathologies endemic to the contemporary student population.

Any effective reform has to embrace macro-environmental concerns existent in the larger economy, as well as micro-environmental classroom contingencies. Classroom discipline and academic relevance are at the center of our educational debacle. These are two extraordinarily complex and challenging problems to overcome. Avoidance will not make them disappear. There has to be an exacting effort to confront and resolve the real educational predicaments. It is pointless to develop remedies to symptoms without actually addressing the essence of the problem.

CHAPTER 3

THE CAUSE

OLD ORDER VERSUS NEW KIDS

The primary demands identified by teachers for improving student performance are a need for more parental involvement; a need for smaller class sizes, and a need for better classroom discipline. Specifying parental involvement and smaller classes as compelling issues is an attempt to obscure teachers' singular concern—discipline. Why do they require more parents or fewer students? It is because of discipline concerns.

Remonstrating about parent involvement and class size is subterfuge invoked by teachers who are always held responsible for discipline problems. Teachers are told in no uncertain terms, "There are no excuses." Teachers, rightly or wrongly, are blamed for all manner of classroom disciplinary problems. It would not be unexpected for teachers to identify other issues over which they presumably have no control.

Classroom discipline problems reduce valuable time-on-task for all learners. A reduction in time-on-task invariably leads to inadequate student achievement since actual instruction is limited and children can't learn what they are not taught. However, teachers are not usually culpable for student misbehavior. Existing curriculum and instructional designs used by teachers fail to account for the dramatically changed nature of the twenty-first century student body. Schools cannot be effective until they

Education Redux: How to Make Schools Relevant to Our Children and Our Future,
pp. 19–43
Copyright © 2010 by Information Age Publishing

become responsive to the *New Kids* that have been produced by major generational changes.

Our education system has failed to adapt to the vital structural transformations in the nature of our economy, culture and children. As Marx described, changes in the forces of production will lead to a concomitant alteration of the superstructure. A new type of economy will yield *New Kids*. The *New Kids* represent an entirely unique definition of a child's formative years.

Childhood is a social construction that reached a more advanced stage of conceptualization in the eighteenth century. During this period, recognition of childhood as a phase with its own distinctive requirements had developed. Nurturing became an important responsibility of both parents and the government. Children, under the control of adults, had to be taught logical thought, self-control and deferred gratification. Still, the innate capacities and curiosities of children were to be treated as a matter of importance.

A process of socialization was operational where children were slowly inducted into adulthood based on the revelation of privileged information that only adults could offer. In the twenty-first century information age, the need for socialization by adults disappeared as children had access to the same media and electronic resources as adults. They were able to acquire the same information.[1] The result is a higher level of independence among children. In the age of media ubiquity, it is pointless to preserve the myth that children are intellectually and psychologically dependent on the adults with whom they have only periodic personal contact.

The engine driving the media saturation, to which everyone is exposed, is corporate advertising. Companies are motivated by a primal need to sell stuff—as much stuff as they can. To serve this mission, media and advertising entities have nurtured the evolution of Americans into insatiable consumers. The mission was accomplished by appealing to peoples' most base and juvenile instincts. The creation of markets and products that universalize adolescence in behavior and tastes is often referred to as infantilism. Adults indulge in puerility and young children are coerced into growing up too quickly, as they are turned into aggressive consumers at the earliest possible age.

The Infantilist Ethos shapes the ideology and behavior of our radical consumerist society much like the Protestant Ethic of hard work and delayed gratification defined the entrepreneurial culture of the productivist early capitalist society. The result is a hyper-consumerism, a homogenation of taste, an ideology of privatization, and labor exploitation. All of these conditions are characterized as a triumph of capitalism.

However, the success of capitalism yields important challenges. As the economy changed from manufacturing goods into manufacturing needs, what individuals do alone at the mall has become more important than what they do in the public square.[2] This behavior contrasts with the notion of the Protestant Ethic. The Protestant Ethic is the psychological foundation that enabled development of capitalist civilization in colonial America.

Influenced by the theology of Calvin, followers accepted the sanctity of business. Labor was not just an economic means, it became a spiritual end. Choosing a profitable occupation was preferred to poverty. It required the virtues of diligence, thrift, sobriety, and delayed gratification—asceticism. The personal satisfaction achieved from producing a good was preferred to the sense of triumph attained from consuming a good.[3]

The Protestant Ethic was an influential dynamic in the development of the Industrial Revolution that took shape in the early nineteenth century. In 1831 a French magistrate, Alexis de Tocqueville, visited the United States in order to observe and report the social and political aspects of the industrializing nation. He portrayed Americans as individuals willing to make sacrifices based on an "enlightened self-interest." Americans believed that serving the best interests of the community best served the interests of the individual. It is prudent to sacrifice for the general welfare in anticipation of benefits that individuals would enjoy resulting from collective action.

However, in the latter part of the nineteenth century as manufacturing techniques advanced and productivity substantially improved, a strategy aimed at increasing profitability in the face of widening competition launched a process of consolidation to achieve economies of scale. Manufacturing companies and facilities were aggregated into giant corporations with huge production operations serving the entire country and international markets. By 1904 about one-third of U.S. manufacturing capabilities were consolidated into 318 companies. These giant companies exercised greater control over the market, as well as supply chains, which were often purchased in attempts at vertical integration—where one company owned each step of the manufacturing process. Ford Motor, for example, could assemble an automobile in Detroit beginning with the Ford-made steel from iron ore that was hauled out of Ford-owned mines in Minnesota.

Productivity gains enabled large corporations to create millions of middle class jobs. Advances in technology permitted fewer workers to produce more goods and, thus, generate added profits for their employers. During this period, employers were more generous in sharing the increased profitability with their workers in terms of offering them higher salaries. This assured employers of a more loyal and dependable workforce that continued to produce needed goods, and it enabled their employees to become middle class consumers of industrial product.

Giant corporations were more efficient but had become uncomfortably powerful. Interlocking Boards of Directors further consolidated power in the hands of fewer corporate executives. As production greatly expanded, new customers became harder to find. The result of industrial overcapacity was a saturation of markets. An oversupply of goods put downward pressure on prices. Thus, large corporations had to engage in constant marketing to create more demand to prevent prices from falling. Mass consumption had to be aggressively cultivated to complement mass production.[4]

The Great Depression of the 1930s was primarily the result of an overinflated economy. The Depression caused production capacity to be substantially reduced. However, after the U.S. entered World War II in late 1941, the military's industrial supply requirements necessitated a rapid increase in industrial production capacity.

The end of the war in 1945 would normally have represented a serious industrial capacity utilization problem. However, between 1946 and 1964 there were close to 80 million American children born. They are referred to as the Baby Boom. The generation prior to the Baby Boom, the Silent or Swing Generation (1933-1945), produced only 29 million children. The generation subsequent to the Boom, Generation X (1965-1977), produced less than 45 million babies, based largely on improved birth control drugs and devices, and the availability of legal abortions. Baby Boomers presently represent about 39% of the adult U.S. population. Generation Xers are currently 22% of the adult population.

Boomers were the product of post-World War II adults who were suffused with an optimism based on an end to the War and the Depression. The period after World War II, during which Boomers were being raised, represented unprecedented prosperity and great expectations. From 1940 to 1960 real income rose by close to 30%. Education also played an important role. With the passage of new mandatory school attendance laws, the number of children age 14-17 remaining in school rose to 73% in 1950 from 50% in 1930.[5]

Boomers represent a unique cohort based on their size alone. With the 1950s proliferation of television ownership, the Boomers were an attractive market for advertisers. By age 16 it was estimated that each Boomer had watched 12,000 to 15,000 hours of television. Because of the cohort size significant consideration was given to the preferences of the Boomers. The attentions of virtually all cultural and social institutions revolved around the Boomers. The result was a culture of self-absorption and, ultimately, a trend characterized by an overarching interest in acquiring wealth and status.

Gen Xers, the group that succeeded the Baby Boomers, were popularly described as slackers. However, prominent Xers include individuals like the founders of Netscape, Dell Computer, Google, Yahoo, eBay, Craigslist, and Kurt Cobain, leader of the early 90s Grunge movement. The slacker moniker derived from the perception that all Xers are responsible only to themselves. The Xer disposition for self-indulgence is an extension of both Boomer values and increased saturation of product promotion. However, a component of the Xer self-indulgent ethos is knowledge acquisition from pop culture trivia to more philosophical insights. Being smart is a quality Xers claim is absent from the Millenial character which admires more superficial traits based on appearance and style.[6]

The Millenials represent an expansion of the abandon that began with the Boomers. Beginning in the mid-1970s and continuing through the 1980s and 1990s America experienced a Baby Boomlet or Echo Boom. The new generation, usually called Millenials, consists of children born to Boomer parents who chose to have babies when they were older. Millenials are increasingly the children of working mothers. In 1960 the rate of labor force participation by women with children under age 18 was 28%. By 1998 the rate was 71%.[7]

In many respects, Boomers' children are cared for like other designer possessions. The daily routines of these Designer Children are carefully planned since a child's success is an important reflection on their parents' status—much like having a nice car or house. Children are an important personal statement. The level of attention given to Millenials, naturally, encourages them to turn inwards and become highly self-absorbed.

A consequence of living in the most consumer-oriented society in the world is that Americans must work longer and save less than any other industrialized country. The consumer orientation begins in childhood. Materialistic and exclusionary messages appear in ads exploiting the anxieties of young people. Anxiety advertising has fashioned children to become autonomous and empowered consumers. They have substantial influence over, not only their own purchases, but also those of their parents. It has been estimated that the size of the "influence market" where children influence parent purchases exceeds $1 trillion annually.

Much of this influence is seen as "guilt money." In the majority of households, both parents have to work long hours to maintain an income sufficient to meet their consumption needs. Parents often compensate for the lack of time spent with their children by spending more money on them. For example, with 4½% of the world population, Americans purchase 45% of all toys produced worldwide.[8]

When today's more affluent parents do find quality time to spend with their children, there is an unnatural tendency to be radically overprotective, both physically and psychologically. Sending kids to school with sanitizing gels to use in school bathrooms, rubberized playground surfaces to eliminate scratches and cell phones to keep constant track of kids' whereabouts are evidence of this trend. Further, psychologically sanitized childhoods where children are protected from an inferior grade in a particular class, antidepressant prescriptions to children ages 6 to 14 having risen by over 300% in the past decade, and a parent calling a teacher to address a concern over their child's difficulty with Gestalt thinking are becoming routine.

The consequence of parental overprotection and over-management are children and young adults unable to sharpen their identities, meet difficult challenges and cope with periodic failure. In the past, children inherited much of their social status from their parents. The reason for hot-house raised children today is that parents gain much of their social standing from the success of their children—like their other possessions. The pressure on affluent kids to succeed has had a serious impact on the rise in self-destructive behaviors on college campuses. These include an increase in drug use, binge drinking, self-mutilation, eating disorders, obsessive pursuit (stalking), date violence, depression and anxiety disorders, and suicide attempts.[9]

The viewpoint of the child has become the basis of authority and action. The process of de-centering the adult view and centering the child's perspective has been referred to as "pediocularity." This is a profound change that transcends parent permissiveness. It privileges the preferences of the child, while obscuring parent choice.[10] Parents, the traditional countervailing influence in controlling inappropriate child behavior, have been neutralized. Broken homes, financial distractions (often caused by overconsumption) and a pervading permissiveness resulting from statutory encumbrances have both undermined and relieved parents of their custodial commitments.

Children's appetites for more of anything are also satiated with food. McDonald's, which often targets kids in their advertising, discovered the economics of selling much more food for a little more money. People wanted to eat more, but would not buy two meals for fear of looking like a glutton. They would, however, buy value meals containing much larger portions. Many meals went from 590 to 1,550 calories.

As the number of working women increased through the 60s and 70s, the proportion of dollars spent on "food away from home" also grew. In 1970, 25% of the food dollar was spent on food away from home. By 1996, 40% of every food dollar was spent on meals away from home. The result is an epidemic of obesity in both children and adults. In 1991 the portion of the U.S. population identified as obese stood at 12%. By 2000 the portion of the population rated obese almost doubled to 20%. The large size clothing segment rose from 7.5% in 1995 to 9.4% in 2000.

In kid's sports the American Youth Soccer Organization grew from 35,000 in 1974 to 500,000 in 1989. The new twist offered by soccer over little league baseball and football was "everybody plays."[11] This policy reduced the need to stay fit and commit to extensive practice and conditioning which encouraged a competitive spirit among participants.

Students' sense of entitlement has precipitated a decline in manners and etiquette, more cheating, and a healthy disrespect for teachers and authority.[12] Cheating has reached critical levels, from copying papers off the Internet to devising test taking schemes involving tapping out answers in a type of Morse code to arranging different colored M&Ms to represent letter options in multiple-choice tests. The stand-bys of writing answers on hat-brims, legs and water bottle labels, and memorizing questions to give to students taking the test later in the day are also common. An Internet service increasing in popularity is www.turnitin.com. The website claims to identify plagiarism by comparing student papers with works posted on the Internet and various other databases.[13] Many universities subscribe to the service.

The notion of self-esteem, a dominant theme, keeps the focus on each child's desires. A narcissistic society gives increasing prominence and encouragement to narcissistic traits without strictures from the past. Cultural devaluation of the past and hostility toward previous experience allows others to define needs for us. With no sense of historical continuity, it is possible to cultivate transcendental self-absorption.[14]

An historical disconnect makes *New Kids* qualitatively different than the children from previous generations. Sex, drugs, and rock and roll (SDR) became a significant component of high school activities in the 1960s. The introduction of SDR into the high school experience was legitimized by being overtly less about self-indulgence than about righteous rebellion. As an expression of protest against the Vietnam War, materialistic acquisition promoted by Madison Avenue, feigned Victorianism and corporate conformity, SDR carried an important message aimed at changing society for the better.

Forty years later, the message of SDR has long been lost, though the profligacy has surely retained its allure. According to a recent study of 9th to 12th grade students in urban and suburban public high schools, 70% had engaged in some type of sexual activity with another person, 66% had consumed some amount of alcohol and 36% had used some type of illegal drug.[15]

TIME Magazine's 2006 Person of the Year Award further galvanized the celebration of self-adulation. The recipient was—You. Americans decided the most important person in their lives was—them.[16] It's all about various forms of the First Person Singular. The World Wide Web community helped to engender this phenomenon. Web 1.0 was organized around pages. These pages were largely created by businesses promoting their products and services. Web 2.0 is organized around people. It consists of wikis, blogs, podcasting, networking tools, YouTube, MySpace, Facebook, and so forth. If it has to do with you, it's worth telling someone. Web 2.0 is about changing the way the world changes. Everyone is acknowledged simply for participating. There are no winners or losers.

The notion of fame has also changed. It is no longer predicated on talent and hard work. Many celebrities are famous for being famous rather than their acting, musical or dancing skills. In surveys among young people, more prefer to be famous than to have increased intelligence, strength or attractiveness.[17] As venerated publications like *TIME* and *Atlantic Monthly* experience circulation declines, celebrity obsessed magazines like *People* and *Us Weekly* are sustaining double-digit growth.

The child celebrity industry consisting of charm schools, pageants, conferences and agents is also growing rapidly. Some of this desire to standout could be a reaction to America's growing uniformity. Cookie cutter national chains and franchises like McDonalds, Starbucks, Gap, Foot Locker, and Wal-Mart have helped to make conformists out of consumers. Pursuing celebrity is also the result of a child's focus on their own importance despite the lack of unique achievements.

Many individuals are striving to become important without cultivating any unique or desirable abilities—to become pseudo celebrities. In addition, the massive expansion of media outlets over the past few decades has fueled the development of the pseudo-event. Pseudo-events possess the following characteristics: They are not spontaneous, but contrived. For example, they are not an earthquake, but an interview. A pseudo-event is created for the purpose of being reported or reproduced. The occurrence is arranged for the benefit of reporters. Its success is measured by how widely it is reported. A pseudo-event's relation to the underlying reality of the situation is ambiguous. It is intended to be a self-fulfilling prophesy. For example, celebrating the 30th anniversary of a particular institution suggests that it is distinguished. This suggestion is what makes it distinguished.[18]

As pressures increase to keep the presses rolling and the television screen always busy, news gathering turned into news making. The interview turned into lengthy television panels, questioning of public figures and rambling conversation programming. However, the proliferation of this activity made it more difficult to create pseudo-events of distinction. Thus, the reporter becomes the conceiver of news by inciting a public figure to make statements that sound like news. These pseudo-events can spawn additional pseudo-events. Pseudo-events can lead to pseudo-qualifications as those in the spotlight are deemed qualified by virtual of being in the spotlight. Pseudo-celebrities and pseudo-events are representative of young people's experiences and their preferences.

In the current revolution that is Web 2.0, these trends represent a flattening of culture where the line between creator and consumer, expert and amateur is becoming increasingly indistinguishable. All manner of inspired endeavor from uninformed political blogs to inept home videos are able to reach a large audience. Participatory principles prevail in this process of democratization. Every posting is considered another version of the truth—another person's version of the facts. The result is a significant decline in product generated by costly mainstream professional sources from newspapers and magazines to Hollywood studios.

Critics decry Web 2.0's delivery of only superficial observation and raucous opinion.[19] However, the frequent mergers and acquisitions of media outlets including studios, record labels, book publishers and others, limit the number of opportunities for new and untested creative efforts. Web 2.0 affords authors, artists and analysts a channel to a vast audience. Although the Web is a facilitator in the proliferation of mindless material, it is not the source of that material. The desire to both produce and consume bizarre entertainment content is a function of our weak educational system. Schools that produce a larger proportion of knowledgeable and thoughtful graduates will assure improved Web 2.0 content.

The new social and economic model represents the postmodern condition. By contrast, the modern industrial bureaucracy was characterized at the beginning of the twentieth century as follows: (1) There are fixed jurisdictional areas ordered by rules—either laws or administrative regulations; (2) required activities within the bureaucracy are distributed as official duties; (3) officials have the authority to issue commands in order to complete their official duties; (4) employees have the qualifications to fulfill their required duties; (5) there is a clearly defined hierarchy and; (6) management presumes expert and thorough training.[20]

The contrast between the modern and postmodern organization is stark. New models of production are based on community collaboration and self-organization rather than hierarchy and control. In Web 2.0, consumers become "prosumers" where they cocreate goods and services instead of just consuming as end-users. Leaders should learn to embrace a new art and science of collaboration.[21] The collaboration is described in terms that include: open source, social networking, crowd sourcing, smart mobs, peering, openness, sharing and acting globally. Mass collaboration occurs on sites like MySpace, YouTube, Linux, and Wikipedia. The low cost infrastructure of the allows thousands of participants in cocreating products. A requirement is the development of social capital. Postmodern media has the potential to enable vast social and economic progress. To be realized, the intellectual level of input must be significantly improved. Proper education has to play a critical role.

As noted, the machine driving changes in technology and social transformations is capitalism. However, capitalism is intrinsically flawed. Capitalism invariably leads to an affluence predicated on a consumer ethic with a hedonistic foundation, which is destructive to the moral disciplines of capitalist production. Capitalism also leads to large financial and bureaucratic structures that contradict the spirit of entrepreneurship, which is the essence of private enterprise.

In order to sustain growth, wealth should be produced in a manner where the good fortune of others multiplies their own. This perspective is not as intuitive as the acquisitive impulse. Growth cannot be measured by additional sales of soap, clothing or cars. Long-term growth is to be measured by investment in new technology. The investment is defined as replacing existing plants, equipment and products with new and better ones. Ultimately, economic conflict is not about government and business, capitalists and workers, or liberals and conservatives. It is based on the past and the future. It is between the existing configuration of industry and the industry that will be its replacement.[22] Schools must prepare children to acquire the necessary long-term perspective that is ultimately in their best interest, even though it may seem to conflict with the need for immediate gratification.

Discipline

The school day represents a finite number of hours. Although the prospect of lengthening both the school day and the school year is standard fodder in school reform conversations, the real issue is not just the number of hours the child is in school or the hours that school is in session, but the number of hours that actual teaching and learning happens. Time spent learning in a classroom is identified as time-on-task.

Disciplinary problems necessarily result in diminished time-on-task. The significance of time-on-task in classrooms as it relates to discipline problems has been studied extensively. Students responsible for disciplinary problems exhibited, (a) low perceived cognitive competence (self-efficacy), (b) low perceived relevance of schoolwork and (c) a belief that norm-breaking behavior elicits peer approval. All three contributed to the incidence of off-task behavior and opposition towards teachers.[23]

First, low perceived cognitive competence or a lack of self-efficacy refers to an individual's level of confidence in their learning capabilities. A high level of self-efficacy is critical to a student's success. Students must have a belief in their ability to succeed. Without that belief, failure is the more likely result. Students with low perceived cognitive competence, or low self-efficacy, tend to compensate for their limitations by minimizing the value of schoolwork and the significance of teachers.[24] Students exhibit this tendency by acting-up in class or just not paying attention to the work.

Many educators respond to students with low self-efficacy by substituting unearned praise for recognition of actual achievement. Offering unearned praise is the basis of the self-esteem movement. Unfortunately, contrived compliments are not likely to improve a child's self-efficacy. The *New Kids* are mindful of this pretense. They always knew who in the class is doing well and who isn't. That's mostly what they talk about.

A number of education professionals have expressed concern over the self-esteem movement is U.S. schools. An overemphasis on self-esteem is disrupting all our notions of intellect, character and community. In order to protect student psyches from the damaging affects of failure, school curricula have been dumbed-down. Dumbing-down deprives children of the opportunity to develop their full potential and, in the process, real self-esteem. The relentless concern with students' feelings is resulting in students who are so inwardly focused that they lack empathy and respect for others. Thus, schools are producing children who are only capable of making decisions based on their own emotions, rather than on logic or consideration of the wider consequences of their actions.[25]

It is important for children to learn about fairness. Fair behavior is instrumental to long-term profit maximization. Fair behavior includes, for example, not reducing wages during periods of excess labor supply and not raising prices when demand is slack. People establish the fairness of actions based on a reference transaction. A reference transaction is a relevant precedent that sets the terms of future exchanges. Customers or employees who suspect they are being treated unfairly are likely to search for alternatives. Thus, firms or individuals that behave unfairly will be punished in the long run.[26] It is important for schools to provide students with appropriate perspective on fair and reasonable behavior.

Second, the perceived low relevance of schoolwork is an escalating problem. For example, one of the primary functions of K-12 education is to provide students who choose to attend college with the appropriate tools needed to complete their schooling. It is presumed that once students obtain a college diploma, they will be rewarded with generous adult prosperity—good job, house, car, and the ability to adequately support a family. However, due to increasing college education costs and declining employment prospects, the guarantees inferred by a college degree have become suspect.

Two-thirds of the students who are graduating colleges have accumulated significant debt from school loans and credit card companies. Some of this debt reaches into the six figures. At the same time, large companies have been outsourcing many professional jobs to developing countries where labor costs are substantially lower than in the United States. As a consequence, previous entry-level low paying jobs in food service, retail and face-to-face customer service offer the only available work. Having only low-wage options and the obligation to service tremendous debt severely diminishes the optimism that should be an important component of a young person's character.[27]

New Kids are not oblivious to this prospect. They have seen a significant rise in a new class of workers, the In-Vestor Class. The In-Vestor Class consists of millions of Americans who must work for poverty level wages in a colored vest or hat, shirt or apron so they match the corporate signage. It is the fastest growing occupational segment. The number of workers in entertainment, recreation, restaurant and hotel service, for example, rose from 1.6 million or 1.4% of the workforce in 1990 to more than 10 million or 8% of the workforce in 2000.

Another reality is that only 27% of Americans over the age of 25 have a 4-year college degree. This means that 73% do not have a degree. Those who did not spend 4 years in college earned 4 years worth of work experience and seniority. Increasingly, as college graduates are competing for the same nonprofessional jobs as nongraduates, they are put at an actual disadvantage for having spent 4 years away at school.

Third, there are peer-related inducements to rule breaking behavior. In particular, at-risk student pathologies make teaching in poverty-stricken urban and rural neighborhoods especially difficult. School is a microcosm of the neighborhood. An account from a teacher in a South Side Chicago Public School describes a world of teenage pregnancy, drugs, alcohol, gang-banging, kids raising themselves and the relentless stress and woe of poverty consuming these children. The omnipresent violence inside and outside the school is a merciless distraction.[28]

Classrooms consist of incessant talking and kids shouting to be heard over the talking. Students are wandering around without permission, touching and bothering each other. Shouting questions and comments like, "This is stupid." Passing gas, throwing things, hitting, fist fights, deviant sexual acts, planting feces around the room and yelling out the window to gang-banger friends are all part of the daily routine.

Students swear like sailors, destroy school property, steal school and each other's property and periodically show up to class with an assortment of weaponry. In many schools there are virtually no remedies for this behavior other than an occasional suspension. Teachers are held responsible for this behavior. They are told, "There are No Excuses." The result is one-third of the teachers quit after 3 years and one-half leave after 5 years. Despite their appalling behavior in school most of these children are God-fearing and attend church on a regular basis.

Another example, Hartford, Connecticut has been identified as America's second poorest city, despite being the capital of one of the richest states. Terms such as "concentrated poverty," "racial isolation" and "social isolation," readily apply to this overwhelmingly Black, Hispanic, and poor city where the once largest employer, the Fuller Brush Company that employed 2,500 workers is now a welfare office.[29]

In one city high school only 5.5% of 10th graders met state goals in reading and 3% of the 10th graders met state goals in math. Kids were usually cared for by a range of relatives and foster care. Less than 50% of birth mothers were care givers and more than 75% of fathers were deemed not significant. Employment for those heads of households who did work consisted of cashiering in large chain stores, hotel maid, doing off-the-book chores or running an informal taxi service if a car was available. All of these jobs paid poverty level wages. The most reliable jobs were prison guard, bus driver, postal worker, or nurse's aide. Guardians who did come to school were often angry because they anticipated that they and their children would be mistreated.

Since the state test given in connection with No Child Left Behind mandates contained no questions on science or social studies, those subjects were rarely taught. The public school system spent more than $4 million on a literacy program called Success for All (SFA) which declared that learning to read early is the key to later success. It is necessary to correct reading problems early through 'interventions' by tutors and through family support.

In 2003 SFA claimed it was being used by 1,500 schools in 48 states. SFA called for cooperative learning—splitting children into teams that discuss, evaluate and answer questions. There are drills on vocabulary, word sound, and deconstructed stories. The program offered minute by minute instruction. When the program failed to improve test scores, the developers were quick to blame a failure of implementation. No discussion about handling severe disciplinary problems and their sources.

The degree to which students are psychologically connected to what is happening in their classrooms is referred to as their level of engagement. Children not committed to school are not good students and are unlikely to become part of the skilled workforce. A 1994 study of 20,000 ethnically diverse high school students revealed that a high proportion of students said they spent most of their time in school "goofing-off" with friends, have cheated on a school test within the last year and 9 out of 10 say they copied someone else's homework within the past year.[30]

The survey found that students spend no more than four hours a week on homework and two-thirds of high school students work during the school year. Of the students that work, about half work more than 15 hours per week, and about 17% work more than 25 hours per week. Less than 25% discuss schoolwork with their friends and only 10% would like to be associated with the "brains," as opposed to the 50% that want to be part of the "partyer" or "druggie" crowd. Only 20% of parents consistently attend school programs. More than 40% of parents never attend.

No Child Left Behind was an attempt specifically to reach these kids. In view of their pathological behavior, the solution was to do more testing and place unsupported mandates on teachers and administrators without any new programming or instructional guidance. Any effective solution must address the *New Kids* realities which they do not.

A 2005 Kaiser Family Foundation Study of *New Kids* revealed that 8- to 18-year-olds spend nearly four hours daily watching television, including videos and prerecorded shows. In addition, time spent on computers and video games outside homework is 2 hours per day. More than 6 hours each day are spent with media. By contrast, children spend less than 1 hour doing homework daily and do 1½ hours of physical activity each day. Total reading time is 43 minutes per day. A typical 8-18-year old lives in a home with an average of 3.5 TVs, 2.1 video game consoles and 1.5 computers.[31]

A culture of individualism induces disciplinary problems. Individualism is reinforced by means of electronic gadgetry like TVs, iPods, Gameboys, PlayStations, Xboxes, cellphones, and other devices controlled by a single user. In addition to advancing individual exploits over team participation, these appliances may deliver content rife with violence and sordid sexuality deluding impressionable young minds. The images serve to corrupt student values and priorities.

Despite being faced with intensifying pathological behaviors, contemporary legal rights and principles play an increasingly important role in the classroom. In this age of litigation, schools are no longer protected domains where teachers rule with impunity. In addition to case law precedents, growing legislation regulates all aspects of classroom activity.[32] Some of the basic principles include:

~ Keeping public schools neutral in religious matters;
~ Teachers and students are entitled to freedom of expression;
~ Teachers may be dismissed if it is determined their private activities impair their teaching effectiveness;
~ Students cannot be denied due process—rules must be reasonable, nonarbitrary and equitable;

~ Bad behavior cannot be punished using academic penalties—grades cannot be reduced to serve disciplinary purposes;

~ Corporal punishment may not be misused;

~ Teachers must keep students safe from unreasonable risk or danger by enforcing rules of safety in school activities;

~ Teachers must avoid derogatory evaluations on permanent records, and

~ Teachers must not photocopy in violation of copyright law.

Though these principles appear reasonable and just, they represent a wall of resistance behind which kids can readily take advantage of school personnel and prevent teachers from accomplishing their missions.

One of the popular solutions recommended to address classroom misbehavior involves the use of psychostimulants. These drugs are prescribed to children diagnosed with Attention-Deficit/Hyperactivity Disorder (ADHD), which was previously known as attention deficit disorder (ADD). ADHD is recognized as a neurobehavioral disorder. It is characterized by persistent inattention and hyperactivity-impulsivity. This behavior often results in substantial functional impairment.

Use of psychiatric drug therapy for behavior disordered children did not begin until the 1960s. From the 1960s to 2000, psychostimulant drug treatment for U.S. school children increased 100-fold. In the 1990s alone, psychostimulant use increased 700%. The most commonly prescribed drug is methylphenidate, which is often referred to as Ritalin. Currently there are 5 to 6 million children receiving ADHD drug treatment using psychostimulant drugs sold under the brand names, Adderall, Concerta, and Metadate.

In addition to children being treated for ADHD, there have been recent substantial increases in the prescription of other psychotropic drugs. These include antidepressants, mood stabilizers and new antipsychotic medications. There is a significant range in the percentage of children diagnosed with ADHD within different states. Southern states, such as Alabama, Louisiana, West Virginia, Kentucky, Tennessee, and Arkansas have a larger incidence of children aged 4-17 having been diagnosed with ADHD.[33]

It is widely believed that these drugs are overprescribed. Consideration must be given to the fact that children misbehave for a variety of reasons other than as result of neurobehavioral disorders. Most bad behavior is attributed to issues related to parenting, family and community environment. Certainly, a particular school situation, which hopefully makes a positive contribution to a child's behavior, can also have a significant negative impact for a variety of reasons. They range from not getting along with a specific teacher to having problems relating to one or more class-mates.

Equality

There is a substantial quantity of popular literature citing disparate funding as the root cause of achievement differences between predominantly White and largely Black schools. The funding differences are highlighted despite considerable evidence that significant social problems are the most likely source of educational inequality. A popular 1991 work offers an entertainingly anecdotal contrast of schools in poor urban areas and affluent suburbs.[34] The descriptions establish that the vast differences in academic performance between schoolchildren in more prosperous neighborhoods and those in low income areas are almost entirely the result of differential funding levels at the respective schools.

At that time, it may have been appropriate to be concerned about a funding disparity. For example, in 1989 the City of Chicago spent $5,500 for each student in the secondary schools. By contrast, in the highest-spending Chicago suburbs there was an investment of between $8,500 and $9,000 in each high school student. In certain areas of the state of Illinois, the amount paid per student in the poorest neighborhood school was as low as $2,000. The amount paid per student in the most affluent Illinois neighborhood was $10,000—a noteworthy difference.

There were substantial differences in academic performance in these schools that, coincidentally, corresponded to funding levels. Without an analysis of the myriad of variables contributing to student performance, a conclusion was reached that the funding levels were the source of the achievement differences. Arriving at this conclusion possibly boosted the author's credentials as an accomplished social reformer. The funding disparity was assuredly an easy target.

In an updated 2005 book, the same author revisited the same schools and the same issues. He suggests that the problems described 14 years earlier persist or have worsened. The differences in academic performances between the wealthier school districts and the poorer districts have actually widened. The data cited in support of this claim appears reliable. However, the author continues to maintain that the problem can only be resolved through increased funding of minority neighborhood schools—closing the funding gap between schools in wealthier neighborhoods and those in less affluent areas.[35]

Interestingly, the author cites updated information on school funding. One table presented indicates the amount spent for each student in an affluent North Shore suburb, Glencoe, IL, is about $10,000. The amount the Chicago Public Schools, which are overwhelmingly poor and minority, spends per student is over $8,000. This is a difference of only 20% compared with the 400% difference revealed in the earlier book. The Chicago Public School system serves approximately 100 times more students than Glencoe.

If the benefits of size are considered, wherein Chicago can realize economies of scale in making purchases and in administration, it may be that there are actually more financial resources available to Chicago students than to Glencoe students. Yet the difference in academic performance between the students in the two school districts has widened over the period of almost a decade and a half. Although the author does not come to this conclusion, it is evident differential funding was not the source of the extensive discrepancies in academic achievement between students in the affluent suburb and those in the inner city schools.

Prior to the 1966 release of the Coleman Report, the definition of educational equality had been measured only in inputs. These inputs were represented by funding levels, teacher qualifications, textbooks, buildings, facilities, and so forth. The Coleman Report was the first to survey outputs. Outputs were determined by student performance in achievement and standardized testing. This change made possible the discovery that financial inputs were, in fact, not the dependent variable in predicting student achievement.

Coleman confirmed that student performance is significantly improved in environments where fellow students come from backgrounds strong in educational motivation and resources. Often, there are relatively small differences in the physical and economic resources of schools in Black and in White communities. However, there are substantial differences in educational resources provided by classmates. These educational resources are afforded by parents in the form of books, educational games, computers, trips to museums and, in general, a strong parental commitment to their child's schooling including regular communication with teachers and administrators.

Other nonpecuniary variables affecting school performance are related to classroom dynamics and parental control. For example, it is important to note that teachers cannot teach beyond the level of the most advanced students in the class. Classrooms consisting of largely "at-risk" students will experience limitations in the level of instruction a teacher can impart.

An additional problem is in the existing teacher/student relationship. The manner in which schools exercise authority over children is referred to as *in loco parentis*. The notion of *in loco parentis* suggests that, under circumstances where parents are exercising limited authority over children's behavior, schools are bound to similar limitations. By contrast, more authority inheres in teachers where parents attach considerable importance to their children's schooling.[36] One of the most important indicators of a child's likely success in school is their attendance in a school populated by classmates where there is significant concern for education fostered by the parents of all students. Peer pressure exerts a considerable degree of influence over all students, for better or for worse.

Another indicator of expected school performance is the intelligence quotient (IQ) of the child. Measuring an individual's IQ is a general way to express a person's intellectual performance relative to a given population. This process was developed in the early 1900s. The U.S. Army began using IQ tests to classify and assign recruits during World War I. Ranking the worthiness of individuals strictly on the basis of an IQ test can be both unfair and damaging. For example, the passage of the Immigration Restriction Act of 1924 by Congress was bolstered by psychometric "experts" claiming immigrants had below average intelligence and their entry to the U.S. should be limited.

During the 1930s there was widespread use of IQ tests developed by David Wechsler and improved versions of the Stanford-Binet Test. In the 1960s and 1970s a few behavioral scientists began to suggest that IQ was a hereditary trait and certain groups were more likely than others to inherit below average intelligence. This position led to considerable controversy because of the high proportion of Blacks with low test results. As a result major school systems throughout the country limited or banned group-administered standardized tests.[37]

In response to the questionable utilization or abandonment of IQ ranking for individuals, a theory of multiple intelligences was introduced. This theory suggested that people had different types of talent that would enable them to excel in a variety of areas. The range of talent included, linguistic, musical, logical-mathematical, spatial, bodily-kinesthetic and two forms of personal intelligence—intrapersonal and interpersonal. Thus, someone having difficulty on linguistic or logical-mathematical tests should receive some consolation for having musical, athletic or interpersonal skills.

Although possession of nonacademic skills may have some future benefit in pursuing a career, they are not substitute for important reading and math abilities. Multiple intelligence theory served as a diversion from a strict focus on academic success. It did not serve the purpose of promoting equality through equal education.

Nineteenth century reformers were committed to the belief that education was the solution to both individual failures and larger social problems encountered in the pursuit of equal opportunity. With this in mind, the linkage between the federal government and local schools began immediately after the Civil War. Its goal was to transform 4 million ex-slaves into literate citizens. The federal government provided free public school for adults and children in the former Confederacy. For the first time, public schools connected race, citizenship, and equality.

However, this experiment in social democracy lasted only a decade. By the beginning of the twentieth century, schools were primarily serving the purpose of preparing young people for the industrial workforce and Americanizing new immigrants.[38] Current public policy which has a central goal aimed at closing the racial gap in American education is the No Child Left Behind Act of 2001 (NCLB). When students leave schools without a high school level education, their futures are in jeopardy.

Regardless of the efforts expended under NCLB, there are a number of risk factors affecting Black students that limits their academic performance. These include, low birth weight, single-parent households and birth to a very young mother. It has also been noted that Black children watch an extraordinary amount of television—almost triple the number of hours White children watch TV. Black households have a relatively small number of books and Black children also appear less ready to conform to behavioral demands. There is a concern among Black children who believe ineradicable racism in American society will prevent educational success from ever paying off. However, census bureau studies indicate that Black college graduates will earn close to $1 million more during their working lives than those who dropped out of high school.

Despite this evidence, there is an oppositional culture that is hostile to educational achievement. The perception that academic achievement will not lead to a good job, means that resisting schools becomes an act of racial rebellion. There is a connection between racial identity and school performance. If students consider Blackness as being associated with playing basketball and listening to rap music, as opposed to studying geometry and chemistry, schools will have a difficult time changing achievement outcomes.

The National Assessment of Educational Progress (NAEP) created by Congress in 1969 tests representative samples nationally of school kids in 4th, 8th and 12th grades. These test results consistently show that Blacks in the 12th grade are at least 5 years behind Whites and Asians. Hispanics do not do much better. Black students graduating high school have skills equivalent to White 7th or 8th grade students. There are a number of reasons for this discrepancy. One is that Whites are more than 60% of the nation's school children while Blacks and Latinos combined are less than one-third. Consequently, curricular material is more likely to be disposed toward the experiences of White children.[39]

Other reasons for the disparity in academic performance between Whites and minorities are increased risk factors. These risk factors begin in the prenatal stage. Poor women are less likely to experience sufficient weight gain because of the lack of a nutritious diet. If poor women smoke, they are likely to continue to do so through their pregnancies. The result is that babies born to poor women are at a higher risk of being born premature and at a low birth weight. Low birth weight babies are twice as likely to experience developmental delay or congenital defects. They are also at greater risk for a variety of long-term disabilities. These infants are more likely to demonstrate "abuse provoking" behaviors, such as prolonged crying.

Early childbearing is also associated with adverse developmental outcomes. Among poor children, 47% had mothers who gave birth before the age of 20. Among nonpoor children, only 17% of the mothers had given birth before they were 20 years old. There is a strong association between economic deprivation and child maltreatment. All of these factors combine to negatively impact a poor child's performance in school.[40]

Concerns about oppositional culture have been raised in recent discussions among members of the Black community. In 2004 at an NAACP celebration of the 50th anniversary of the *Brown v. Board of Education of Topeka* Supreme Court decision prohibiting the separation of public facilities for Blacks and Whites, entertainer Bill Cosby spoke of the culture of failure in the Black community. Evidence cited included, an extraordinarily high school dropout rate, the highest percentage of any American racial group in prisons, "No Snitch" campaigns and tolerance of criminal behavior, violent and misogynous rap songs, kids wearing their clothes backwards with "pants down around the crack and dresses all the way up to the crack," people not speaking intelligible English, drug and alcohol abuse, thuggery, wanton violence, especially towards women, and women with eight children, each child having a different father.

Federal data revealed in 2004 that Black Americans, who were 13% of the population, accounted for 37% of violent crimes, 54% of arrests for robbery and 51% of murders. The nation's prison population is 44% Black and 33% of all Black men between the ages of 20 and 29 on any given day are either in jail, on probation or on parole. Much of the criminal activity is related to drug abuse.

Rap music's core message is to nurture a sense that Black men are embattled aliens in their own land. Images glorifying guns, jewelry, sex, and big cars promulgate detrimental behavior. In 2002, 68% of Black children were born to unwed mothers and 35% of Black women who had a child out of wedlock lived in poverty. These self-defeating habits have created a large segment of uneducated Black people that are increasingly disconnected with mainstream society.[41]

According to the Bureau of Labor Statistics, the 2007 unemployment rate for Whites age 16 or older was slightly above 4%. The 2007 unemployment rate for Blacks age 16 or older averaged about 8.4%, or more than twice the White unemployment rate. High unemployment in the

Black community is an important cause in the propagation of a range of counterproductive mores which are evident among the feckless youth. For example, many unemployed young men substitute taking pride in achieving exploitative sexual encounters for the self-respect usually attained through the accomplishments of occupational success.

In the Black community, the perception among a number of teens, girls in particular, is that a pregnancy will not interfere with the prospect of a lucrative career since they do not expect that option is readily available. The result is a self-fulfilling prophesy where teenage pregnancies impede academic progress which reduces employment opportunities.[42] Offering plans such as NCLB, which focuses on testing children in a narrow range of subject matter, without addressing the larger social problems is certain to have no positive outcomes.

Unfortunately, Black leadership, consisting of local Baptist preachers, is inclined to concentrate their oratory on the injustices to which Blacks are subjected. These preachers insist that responsibility for eradicating the prolific violence, drug-dealing, larceny, joblessness, out-of-wedlock births, and general misbehavior in the Black community must be borne by Whites. The preachers speak more of entitlement than personal responsibility. This creates a Catch-22 since the White community is increasingly disposed to a strategy of distancing itself from the Black community due to the increasing intensity of the bad behavior. The solutions must be found within the Black community. The solution is effective education, which is currently unavailable in local public schools.

Destructive social mores are not limited to the inner city Black populations in Northern states. Students in Southern states are also immersed in a culture that assures they consistently perform below the national average. In 2005 the national NAEP math score was 278. Alabama, Arkansas, Louisiana, Mississippi, Tennessee. and West Virginia had an average score of 267. The 2005 national reading score was 260. These six Southern states averaged 255. Midwestern states score above the national average.[43]

Lower test scores, as well as lower wages in the South are a response to the power of a racist ideology. The social structure of the antebellum South was predicated on the authority of a power elite—the large plantation owners who were White. Not only were Blacks enslaved, but poor Whites worked under abhorrent conditions with inadequate compensation. After the Civil War Blacks continued to be relegated to second class citizenship working as landless sharecroppers at subsistence income levels. Poor Whites received a similar meager income for their labor, but they additionally received a psychological wage. The elite Whites, to protect themselves from dispossession after the War, got poor Whites to "settle for being White."

An ideology of White supremacy was promoted by playing on fears of Black reprisals for slavery and promulgating the prospect that Black men would begin raping White women as retaliation for a history of White men raping Black women. The psychological wage, "At least I'm White," served to subjugate poor Whites.[44] It would follow that Southern White children would be less inclined to embrace the need for an education if they believed their Whiteness was a sufficient achievement.

The racism that is presumed to be part of the Southern way of life is not confined to the South. There are many all-White communities in Northern states. They are often called Sundown Towns since they require all Blacks to leave town after dark. Adjacent communities, Anna/Jonesboro in Union county Illinois are 100% White according to a recent census. Anna became all White in 1909 after expelling its entire Black population. Town residents refer to the name, Anna, as an anagram which says, "Ain't No N---ers Allowed." A nearby town, Vienna, Illinois similarly removed its Black residents in 1954. White people in Vienna burned down all the Black resident's homes. Vienna remains all-White.[45]

The standardized exam given to all 11th graders in Illinois is called the Prairie State Achievement Exam (PSAE). The state has an average score for each school based on the scores in reading, writing and math. According to the Illinois State Board of Education, the average PSAE score for Vienna High School in 2003 was 45.8%. This is almost 20% lower than the average score for all Illinois high schools. Anna-Jonesboro High School scores were also below the state average. In addition to the psychological wage, there is also a psychological test score, "At least I'm White."

The culture of the South, in terms of education, income, and occupations, is prominently on display in Arkansas. A look at that state offers some perspective on the Southern social and economic condition. Originally part of the Louisiana Purchase from France in 1803, Arkansas became the 25th state in the Union in 1836. Arkansas was a slave state and fought with the Confederacy in the Civil War. Presently, agricultural employment in the United States is between 1% and 2%. Arkansas agricultural employment is closer to 6%. The leading crop in Arkansas is rice. About one-third of all rice produced in the U.S. comes from Arkansas.

The leading farm product is the chicken broiler. Chicken broilers are chickens 5 to 12 weeks old. Arkansas leads the nation in chicken broiler production. Food processing is the largest industry in the state. Tyson Foods, based in Springdale, AR, is the world's largest producer of chickens, pork, and beef. With $25 billion in annual sales, Tyson's 120,000 employees and 7,000 poultry growers produce more than 40 million head of chicken each week.

Another leading industry is transportation. Based in Lowell, AR, J. B. Hunt is one of the largest trucking companies in North America with annual sales of $2.4 billion. Hunt employs a total of 15,700 individuals of which 11,600 are drivers.

Arkansas, with a total population of 2.7 million people, is also home to the largest corporation in the world. Bentonville-based Wal-Mart employs 1.5 million people. Its annual sales exceed $300 billion. Wal-Mart has about 3,000 discount department stores throughout the United States. Its low prices are achieved through almost exclusive purchases of imported products from China, and paying poverty level wages to its employees. Wal-Mart has also been the subject of several lawsuits for forcing employees to work through unpaid breaks, making employees work off-the-clock, discriminating against women employees and a failure to pay appropriate overtime wages. Annual employee turnover has been estimated at 40%. This means Wal-Mart must hire over one-half million new employees each year.

In 1947 Congress passed the Taft-Hartley Act over the veto of President Truman. Taft-Hartley allowed states to outlaw the closed union shop. In 1947 Arkansas was one of the first Southern states to adopt this provision, as well as other antiunion provisions. None of these publicly traded corporations mentioned above are unionized. The median household income for the United States is $42,000. Median household income in Arkansas is $32,000 or about 24% less.

In September 1957, the City of Little Rock planned to desegregate its schools in compliance with the 1954 Supreme Court decision. However, then Governor Orval Faubus ordered the state's National Guard to surround the school and prevent entry to any Black students. The situation ended three weeks later when President Eisenhower sent 1,000 members of the 101st Airborne Division of the Army to assure entry of the Black students. Nationally, 27% of those over 25 hold a bachelor's degree or higher. In Arkansas the number is 17%. Traditionally, Arkansas has finished 49th in national education surveys. The usual Arkansas response is, "Thank God for Mississippi."

About one-half of the Arkansas population lives in rural areas (2,500 people or less). With vanishing well-paid manufacturing jobs and attendant management and engineering positions, the United States is experiencing the complete disappearance of the middle class. More and more, as real income drops and good jobs become more scarce, individuals will be reduced to satisfying only their basic needs—from cheap food to fashion items to electronics. Chicken pluckers, truck drivers, mud farmers, and cashiers may be the jobs of the future. A glimpse of the attendant lifestyle can be seen in Arkansas.

At 44 million people or 14.4% of the U.S. population, Hispanics and Latinos are the nation's largest minority group. Of this population, more than 28 million or almost 10% of the entire U.S. population are of Mexican descent. According to recent Census Bureau data, 54% of Mexican households contain children under the age of 18 versus only 31% of the households in the general U.S. population. Of the total U.S. population over the age of 25, 27% has a bachelor's degree or higher. Among U.S. Mexicans only 8% hold a bachelor's or higher degree and 41% speak English less than "very well." Per capita income for U.S. Mexicans is about half of the national average per capita income.[46]

The reasons given for the unusually poor demonstration of academic prowess among Mexicans include, a belief that Mexican American parents do not value education or that they do not put a sufficient emphasis on education, and that oppressive and inequitable schools reduce educational opportunities through lowered expectations and a differentiated curriculum. Language barriers, poverty, juvenile delinquency and other self-destructive behaviors, as well as the poor academic performance of Mexican Americans put their student population "at risk." Defining student populations as "at risk" would engender a self-fulfilling prophesy wherein schools would tend to become indifferent to student achievement.[47]

The issue of relevance is also a factor in the quest of a higher education. Many Mexicans and their children are in the U.S. illegally. It is difficult to make long term decisions about pursuing an education and career with the prospect of being arrested and deported at any time. Also, illegal Mexican students who may excel academically cannot obtain financial assistance for college costs.

Aside from a sizeable legal Hispanic population, there are an estimated 12 million illegal Mexican immigrants. The period beginning 1990 to 2000 has been the largest era of immigration in U.S. history. Just as turn of the twentieth century Russian Jewish and Italian immigrants came to fill the garment factories of that time, Hispanic and Asian migrants now occupy the positions as cutters and sewing machine operators. Unlike their predecessors, recent Mexican immigrants entered the United States illegally. Apparel manufacturing is among the world's largest industries. It is also a highly fragmented industry with many small businesses and, consequently, lends itself to pervasive worker exploitation. Workers are paid by the piece, and there is a considerable amount of outwork, which is work subcontracted to individuals making garment parts, like cuffs, collars, or pockets. Much of this work is done in homes. These arrangements lend themselves to labor abuses, such as paying less than the minimum wage and cheating workers on their hours and piece counts.

This contrasts with agribusiness, another common source of immigrant jobs which requires difficult manual labor. Agribusiness may be somewhat less exploitative since it is typically consolidated under the ownership of large corporations due to the high level of capital intensity. Labor law violations would tend to be more visible and, thus one assumes, more likely to be remedied. Restaurants are also recognized a "multiple labor law violators." Because of the illegal status of Mexican workers, it is difficult to complain to authorities about the conditions.[48]

Most illegal Mexican immigrants come from poor rural communities where local schools do not extend past the sixth grade. Schools with advanced grade levels often require travel, the cost of which is not subsidized. Since many Mexicans live on subsistence level agricultural activities, they are unable to afford transportation to schools with grades beyond grade six and, consequently, do not further their education. The perspective on limiting education is brought to America.

CHAPTER 4

FUTILE RESPONSES

Many seemingly logical solutions for constructive educational reform have been proffered. Proposals include new buildings, vouchers, charter schools, religious schools, school uniforms, single sex schools, preschool programs, No Child Left Behind, teacher merit pay, diversity education, after-school programs, summer programs, longer school hours and years, tutoring, vocational programs, boot camps, parent training, and so forth. A recent proposal for Chicago Public Schools included rewarding high school students in cash for getting good grades. Up to 5,000 freshmen at 20 schools will be offered $50 for an A, $35 for a B and $20 for a C.[1]

All of these superficial treatments address symptoms without acknowledging the core impediments to student achievement. Even more importantly, these options fail to be responsive to the unique assets *New Kids* possess.

The most vital issue in classroom dynamics is time-on-task. Students cannot learn without sufficient instructional time. The primary cause for the lack of quality instructional time is disciplinary distractions. To address the low yields of classroom time-on-task attributable to disciplinary challenges, three established instructional approaches are typically employed. They are operant conditioning, standard operating procedures and subterfuge.

Operant conditioning represents time-honored schemes to encourage good behavior and discourage bad behavior through a system of rewards and punishment. The methodologies used in operant conditioning or

Education Redux: How to Make Schools Relevant to Our Children and Our Future, pp. 45–64
Copyright © 2010 by Information Age Publishing

shaping or classical conditioning were developed in St. Petersburg, Russia in the late nineteenth century by a physician experimenting with a dog.

Standard operating procedure is a reversion to rudimentary management principles originally developed for improving efficiency in industrial production during the Second World War. Engaging accepted common business practices seems to resonate with and, ultimately, placate the usual critics. These management principles were developed in the 1940s.

The last option is subterfuge which consists of denials that an intractable discipline problem exists. Inane political posturing replaces legitimate instructional efforts in academic subject matter. A contrived preoccupation with school hegemony serves to divert attention from the need for students to acquire measurable academic skills.

Operant Conditioning

The basic elements of operant conditioning or shaping are described as positive reinforcement, negative reinforcement, rewards and punishment. Positive reinforcement is the strengthening of behavior by giving rewards. Negative reinforcement increases desired behavior by removing an aversive stimulus. For example, a child cleans his or her room to stop their parent from nagging them about it. Punishment, such as scolding or withholding a desired good like dessert or allowance, is also likely to reduce undesirable behavior.

Conditioned responses based on rewards and punishments have been developed to control classroom behavior. Conditioned responses have been elicited both through individualized teacher/student interaction and through broader campaigns, such as boot camp for those guilty of chronic misbehavior and various types of token programs where students are offered coupons or vouchers that can be exchanged for prizes of some sort.

Conditioning was introduced in 1890s Russia by Ivan Pavlov who began a series of experiments related to the feeding of his dog.[2] Pavlov noted that the dog began salivating when food was placed in front of it. He referred to the elicitation of the dog's salivation at the sight of food as an unconditioned response. Pavlov then began ringing a bell whenever he brought the dog food. After a period of time the dog would begin to salivate whenever it heard a ringing bell. Pavlov referred to this phenomenon as a conditioned response since the dog began salivating without food present. Continued delivery of food after ringing the bell was done to reinforce the conditioned response. Failing to bring food after ringing the bell over a period of time would lead to an extinction of the salivating. The process has been identified as classical conditioning.

In the U.S. around 1950 another psychologist, B. F. Skinner, began a series of experiments based on the principles of operant conditioning. Skinner built a box that contained a lever which was attached to a food source outside the box. A rat or pigeon was placed in the box. After a period of time the animal discovered that whenever it pushed the lever, food would be delivered to it. Using conditioned responses, Skinner did a number of experiments with the animals in the box. According to Skinner, the most important aspect of conditioning is reinforcement. Skinner suggested that students are able to be taught under an arrangement he termed contingencies of reinforcement.

Although children learn without teaching in their natural environments, in a classroom teachers arrange special contingencies. These contingencies expedite learning. Teachers execute instructional plans that are expected to foster a student's knowledge acquisition. There are three types of behaviors that distinguish an educated person from an uneducated person. The first type, which is predicated on time, is wisdom. From infancy a child will acquire knowledge of his or her environment simply by responding to it. Children learn by doing through the process of trial and error.

Second, individuals learn through acquisition of specific information by means of a formal education. A teacher plays an active as a transmitter of knowledge. Students are able to absorb this knowledge after subdividing it into meanings, concepts, facts and propositions. Third, a child learns through cognate construction. In this stage, the teacher edifies or builds on the learner's prior knowledge. Throughout the process, a child learns most effectively through reinforcement and shaping.

Skinner describes machines that assist in the process of reinforcing learning. In the 1920s Sidney Pressey developed an apparatus for automatic testing. The device consisted of four buttons that corresponded to correct answers on a multiple-choice test. If a student gave the correct answer, the machine would move on. If the answer was incorrect, the student would continue to make choices until they answered correctly. Using the machine for instructional purposes, a student could proceed at their own pace.

As early as 1954 there were hand cranked teaching machines available where numbers and letters would slide into view to reinforce arithmetic and spelling knowledge. Teaching machines assist in arranging the contingencies of reinforcement. Without the use of individualized teaching apparatus, teachers tend to rely on aversive controls in their classrooms. Aversive controls consist of ridicule, scolding, sarcasm, criticism, detention, extra homework, withdrawal of privileges, and so forth. Unfortunately, aversive controls invariably lead to student resentment, which interferes with or precludes learning.[3]

In Tom Wolfe's *The Right Stuff*, the story of America's Mercury Seven Astronauts, he describes the training of the seven jet pilots selected to take the first manned flights into outer space in 1961. Although these individuals were highly skilled in flying experimental jet aircraft, the first space flights would be largely automated. The rocket ships and capsules would be controlled by computers onboard and on the ground.

To ensure the safety of the astronauts, the first flight was taken by a specially trained chimpanzee, No. 61 or Ham. The chimp was taught to throw switches when corresponding lights lit up. The trainers used operant conditioning by attaching an electrified pad to the monkey's foot and giving it a shock whenever it failed to respond properly to its prompts. The human astronauts went through similar training, but without the electrical shocks. The first space flight with the chimpanzee went flawlessly. The monkey correctly performed all of the given tasks.

The second flight was essentially the same as the first except that a human was substituted for the monkey. During the second flight the astronaut forgot to turn off a manual switch when setting the equipment on automatic. The result was some wasted rocket fuel which would have created a significant problem on a longer flight. The third flight, which was about the same as the first two, also used a human. Upon splashdown at the end of the flight, the astronaut hit a switch at the wrong time triggering the hatch to open prematurely. The result was the astronaut ended up in the ocean and almost drowned while the capsule filled with water and could not be retrieved prior to sinking.[4]

Conditioning is the most common practice for controlling classroom behavior. Across cultures, disciplinary techniques vary. A study comparing methods used in China, Israel and Australia, found that Chinese teachers were the most inclusive and supportive of students.[5] Chinese teachers are also less aggressive and punitive than Israeli and Australian teachers. Classroom discipline follows two forms. The first is coercive, consisting of yelling, sarcasm, and group punishment. The second is relationship based, involving discussion, hints, and recognition.

Prudent classroom behavior is crucial since it prepares students to be responsible citizens and it enables teachers to complete their lesson plans without distraction, thus increasing time-on-task. Researchers have suggested that relationship-based discipline appears to be the more effective of the two approaches. These policies were not in common practice in the U.S. schools Skinner studied.

Using material rewards to promote behavior modification is entirely consistent with society's acquisitive orientation. The wisdom of getting something for doing something seems immutable. It represents a logical system for raising children, teaching students, and managing employees. There is an equity principle which specifies that individuals should be rewarded or punished based on their behavior. This principle is founded on the standard of fairness.

However, it is vital to consider the prospect that giving people what they want or need on a contingent basis will result in unintended negative consequences. For example, the more rewards are used, the more they will be expected. Since learning is intrinsically valuable, it is important that it occurs absent material rewards. Motivating people with carrots and sticks, is demeaning and dehumanizing. It suggests that people are being manipulated by external motivations in the form of incentives. However, individuals do not just react to their environment, they act on it. People are intrinsically motivated.[6]

Rewards also create resentment. In order for one person to control another, there must be unequal status. Rewarding emphasizes rewarder's superior power. Rewards also punish since people who do not receive rewards consider that a punishment. Rewards undermine an inherent curiosity and the desire to learn. Several prominent experiments with children revealed that reward-driven children under perform those learning for its own sake. Making students learn through a system of rewards will cause them to be lost as learners. Learning is discovery, which is a natural inclination. As noted by Skinner, rewards are the primary technique used in classroom reinforcement.

The 1992 book, *The Learning Gap*, describes some of the differences between U.S. and Asian (Japanese, Chinese and Taiwanese) schools.[7] The book suggests that there are a number of alternatives that can be used to condition children other than offering simple rewards and punishments. One of the observations is that Americans are more willing than Asians to attribute children's academic success and failure to their innate abilities. Asians assert the importance of environmental factors and the children's own efforts in determining their academic performance. As a result, there is no tracking in Asian schools, and teachers are more patient in working with students having difficulties handling their lessons. Teachers are not dismissive of students they believe do not have the intellectual competence to learn.

Asians spend more time in school. American children spend 50% of their year in school while Asians spend two-thirds of their year in school. Consequently, the Asian kids perceive the school as central to their lives. They spend more time on homework and 97% of school children have a separate desk for schoolwork at home. Only 63% of American school children have a separate desk for schoolwork in their homes.

Asian children own an average of 114 books. American children own an average 67 books. All Asian children carry a small notebook between home and school. The notebook is to show both parents and teachers the work the student is doing both at home and at school. In Asia, daily newspapers commonly publish special pages with articles written for children of different ages.

Americans place a high value on the notion of potential to achieve, rather than the achievement itself. Mental testing is the linchpin of the U.S. meritocracy. Meritocracy's overseers brand those who perform poorly on standardized tests as deficient or incapable. Yet, SAT tests, which are required by most colleges and universities, explain just 16% of the variation in actual college freshman grades. The best predictor of performance is the student's high school grades.

Standardized test scores tend to be highly correlated with socioeconomic class. Standardized tests reward passive, superficial learning, drive instruction in undesirable directions, and disrupt meaningful educational reform. There is a widespread tendency to teach to the test. Assaults on affirmative action in the late 1990s stressed the use of testing to establish "merit" over issues like race and gender.[8]

Asian classrooms have 35 to 50 students. They are taught to organize their time and materials efficiently so minutes are not wasted during transitions between classes and subject matter. There is a new classroom leader chosen each day that is partially responsible for class discipline. Students are also responsible for cleaning the school.

Kids mostly work in groups. Students are grouped to maximize academic diversity. Asian children are less competitive and know how to handle themselves in groups by imposing discipline on each other. There are fewer discipline problems since students tend to perform better. An improved sense of self-efficacy makes it less likely that a student will misbehave.

Each class is followed by a 10-15 minute recess. This gives the children more time to socialize. Only 30% of their time is spent at desks. The remainder of the time, children are working in groups. There is less recess time in U.S. schools. Students spend 50% of the time at their desks. Asian teachers have group building techniques. They create projects that require more than one person to accomplish. Large classes can be effectively managed if teachers are not stressed and classroom discipline is not a problem.

There is more interdependence in Asian schools. In the United States and its schools, a culture of individualism is pervasive. The culture of individualism places more emphasis on the innate abilities of each student. This focus on inherent capacity has insidious implications. Those with higher capabilities are less motivated to work hard. Students who believe they have low ability doubt they will succeed and will not make the necessary effort. Asian students are taught that an investment of time will assure academic success.

IQ tests are administered both in the United States and in Asia. However, the results are given considerably more weight in the United States. The results have a more restricted use in Asia since they put far more emphasis on effort. Grades have greater import in Asia. They are often posted and compared. In the U.S. grades are kept private. This leads many parents to believe their children are doing better than they are. U.S. teachers try to avoid failure by giving easier tasks to students having difficulties.

Assigning sizeable significance to IQ tests results in widespread tracking. Tracking stigmatizes kids early and it is unlikely they will perform well in the future. All Asian kids attend the same classes with faster learners helping the slower learners. There are no special education classes in Asia. There are only special schools for children with specific disabilities—blind, deaf or severely handicapped. Being a good student is most important in the mind of the Asian parent. It is not the most important issue in the mind of U.S. parents. Most U.S. parents have a high level of satisfaction with their child's academic performance. Therefore, children see no reason to improve.

Though tracking does not exist in Asia, there are differing perspectives on its usefulness in the U.S. Those opposed to tracking insist that it subverts equality. Students in the lower tracks have less access to high-status knowledge and fewer opportunities to engage in stimulating learning activities.[9] Tracking replicates inequality along the lines of social class and race. Students in lower tracks are not valued as much as students in higher tracks. Those tracked in lower level classes have lower self-esteem.

Academics who favor tracking suggest that students learn better when grouped with those who are academically similar. Slower students have a more positive attitude when not placed with those more capable. It is easier for teachers to accommodate students in homogeneous groups. Further, the brightest students will be held back and not perform to their full potential if they are in a mixed class that does not challenge them.

Tracking can play an important role in classroom discipline. It is easier to prepare an effective lesson plan if the plan accommodates a larger number of students in a classroom. A classroom full of students with a wide academic performance range would make a single plan difficult to implement—smarter students will be bored by simple material and slower learners will be unable to keep up. There is no simple answer in the tracking polemic.

The current perspective on educational attainment can be summarized in the need to set "high but achievable standards." The fundamental problem with this approach is, in a word, variance happens. The abilities of students are far ranging. Consider the folly of the position that all children can run and basing standards on time trials. There are obviously many children, for one reason or another, that are ambulatory and cannot even walk. Is it reasonable to hold back children with considerable athletic prowess to set an "achievable standard" for all? Many children would have to spend time not running at all.

Education reform more focused on standards is likely to increase the disparities between the cognitive haves and have-nots.[10] The most fair and effective solution would revolve around the ability of a school to maintain some combination of group work for all to benefit, with better students helping those requiring more attention. In addition, an academic agenda would include a format for students to work individually in order to sustain a pace of learning with which they are comfortable.

Standard Operating Procedure

A widely recognized and circulated category of curriculum and instructional methods are analogous to the standard operating procedures associated with formal management doctrine. Since World War II and the arrival of the Baby Boom generation, methodology applied to educational planning was designed employing principles established for business, industry and the military. These educational methods are consistent with the standard operating procedures that were developed in conjunction with the World War II warfare supply effort. The need for production efficiencies during wartime led to many innovations in manufacturing procedures. The principles that were ultimately adopted had broad acceptance. The level of approval made it unnecessary to demonstrate their effectiveness in a school environment.

In 1933 Ralph W. Tyler was director of research for the evaluation staff of the Eight-Year Study (1933-1941). During this study Tyler began to develop his approach to education research. He believed that scientific method could result in the establishment of successful teaching and learning techniques. Tyler suggested that it was possible to determine educational success or failure by evaluating student behaviors.

Tyler's influence on educational policy was particularly significant since he was president of the National Academy of Education. Tyler also contributed to the innovative structure and underlying policy that was established in the Elementary and Secondary Education Act (ESEA) passed in 1965. ESEA included the Title I provision that offered financial assistance to schools with at least 40% low income students based on U.S. census data.

All of this led to the curriculum development model of the late 1940s based on a business model. Setting behavioral objectives would become the basis of determining the level of educational accomplishment. The objectives would govern curriculum and instructional strategies. The guiding principles of curriculum were described in four concepts.[11]

1. Stating objectives to guide students through selected learning experiences.
2. Selecting learning experiences likely to be useful in attaining the objectives.
3. Organizing learning experiences for effective instruction.
4. Evaluating the effectiveness of learning experiences.

It sounds simple enough. According to this theory, learning occurs through the active behavior of the student. Students learn what they do, not what the teacher does. Students in the same class can have different experiences. However, a successful curriculum would produce specific desired results.

This 1940s theory of curriculum and instruction continues as the guiding principle in twenty-first century schools. Using Tyler's basic principles, the role of the curricularist and teacher shifted to assuming the role of a scientist. Tyler's methods required the need for a hypothesis in the development of any curriculum. The hypotheses were then tested using observation and scientific methods. If anticipated student behaviors were not in evidence, adjustments to the plans were made.

The introduction of statistical analysis into physics was an important early twentieth century discovery. It was useful in explaining systems of enormous complexity, as well as a system consisting of a single particle in a field of force. Statistics created a probabilistic universe. Physics would no longer claim knowledge of what will always happen, but what will happen with overwhelming probability.

Because of a need to dramatically improve logistical efficiencies for both military and domestic production applications during the Second World War, statistical analysis began to be applied on an almost universal basis. At the end of World War II the term "cybernetics" was created.[12] It refers to the process of communication and control. The transmission of information serves to integrate many parts of a complex system. Negative feedback precipitates modifications resulting in homeostasis, which is the mechanism that resists entropy and chaos. Routines become self-sustaining through a process of feedback and response.

Tyler's curriculum model was consistent with the perspectives of the postwar era. Scientific method was applied to virtually all manner of daily activity from the factory floor to distribution channels to service institutions and schools.

Another prominent proponent of the application of statistical analysis to engineering processes was the statistician, W. Edwards Deming. During the Second World War, Deming assisted the defense department in its effort to enhance the quality of war materials. His advice was to constantly improve every process for planning, production, and service. This was accomplished by doing statistical analysis on defect rates for each component. The utilization of statistical analysis to address World War II productivity requirements and quality control was a development promoted by critics of bad corporate management which, up to that point, had been pervasive. Companies were exhorted to constantly improve quality, productivity in order to advance their competitive position.

Increased levels of quality and productivity would occur simultaneously by properly engineering the product, production line, and supplier chain. Promoting employee involvement through quality circles and using statistical analysis to achieve zero defects would eliminate the somewhat arbitrary numerical production quotas and work standards that had been in use. Quotas, it was argued, represent an unnecessary ceiling for those able to produce more, and frustrate those who produce less. Teamwork should be employed to solve problems.[13]

Using statistical apparatus to facilitate effective administrative practices led to the establishment of management as a discipline and field of study. In business there is an important relationship between an individual worker and their organization, and between an individual and their work. The character of our society is determined and patterned by the structural organization of Big Business.[14]

The integrated industrial unit, as a social reality, is the most important event since the beginning of the twentieth century. The structure of business, the substance of which is based on the use of machinery, and profitability based on free market prices, led to social engineering. The corporation was shaped as a social institution to achieve its purpose, which was to produce goods with a maximum economic return. The institution is an instrument for the organization of human efforts to that end.

School policy throughout the latter part of the twentieth century and through the implementation of NCLB has been shaped by the perspectives of big business. As the preferences and organizational imperatives of big business changed from production in the twentieth century to marketing in the twenty-first century, the relationships between workers and management changed. Similarly, the relationship between students and schools would inevitably undergo a transition.

Another business management approach to education was described in the early 1960s by Robert Gagné. Gagné developed a theory identifying different levels of learning. The importance of these classifications is that each one requires different types of instruction. The five major categories of learning are: verbal information, intellectual skills, cognitive strategies, motor skills and attitudes. Different conditions are necessary for each type of learning.

In addition, the theory outlines nine instructional events and their corresponding cognitive processes. These are: (1) gaining attention (reception); (2) informing learners of the objective (expectancy); (3) stimulating recall of prior learning (retrieval); (4) presenting the stimulus (selective perception); (5) providing learning guidance (semantic encoding); (6) eliciting performance (responding); (7) providing feedback (reinforcement); (8) assessing performance (retrieval); and (9) enhancing retention and transfer (generalization). In developing any type of instructional material, Gagné's theories of learning are widely implemented. The instructional events and the cognitive processes to which they correspond also represent an adherence to traditional management principles.

In addition to NCLB with its accountability obsession, the focus on business perspectives has led to the expansion of vocational education. With concerns about global competitiveness and widening income disparity, workforce preparation has become a vital topic. Community colleges are the traditional source for vocational education in areas like hairdressing, auto/motorcycle mechanics, cooking, truck driving and healthcare.

However, with more students opting out of learning conventional school subjects, vocational training is being pushed down to the high school level. Acquiring technical knowledge and skills is crucial to evading membership in the ranks of the working poor. Schools offering occupational training must be responsive to ever-changing workforce needs. The most useful set of skills will always be in basic reading, math and writing. These competencies will enable an individual to adapt to evolving labor market demands. In addition, by starting children in vocational training at a younger age, they are being precluded from advancement to college programs. Cultural literacy or knowledge in a broad range of subjects is also sacrificed.

Cultural literacy is knowledge of the major domains of human activity from sports to science.[15] Current teaching strategies suggest that reading skill is a general purpose procedure that can be applied to all texts. This perspective is flawed. Reading and critical thinking are not content independent. Reading programs that are fragmented and based on inconsequential material cannot provide the general knowledge students need to gain proficiency in reading. Children must be trained to be culturally literate. Cultural literacy is the only basis of opportunity for disadvantaged children to surmount the social determinism that condemns them to the same educational and social condition as their progenitors. Cultural literacy will break the cycle of poverty by enabling effective communication with strangers.

The approach presently undertaken in schools is not consistent with a curriculum that would support cultural literacy. NCLB, the predominant standard in education, is defined by conventional business canon. Its emphasis on teacher and school accountability is an attempt to ameliorate children's educational performance using strategies associated with business conduct.

The resulting "teach-to-the-test" does not promote the accrual of wide ranging knowledge. One of the consequences is that fourth grade U.S. students score 9th in reading among 35 countries—in the top 26%. By 10th grade, American students score 15th among 27 countries—the top 56%. Among White students, 59% cannot read at a proficient level. Eighty-five percent of Hispanic students cannot read at a proficient level and 88% of Blacks cannot read at a proficient level.[16] As students progress through school, their relative reading abilities decline as their ability to fully appreciate and absorb content deteriorates.

As second half of the twentieth century proceeded, a shift in the type of work in which most people were engaged changed from industrial or goods production to postindustrial or service and information production. This shift spawned new challenges to education. The definition of industrialization should consist of a wide view of economic processing systems. These systems are engaged in the continuous extraction, reorganization, and distribution of environmental inputs to final consumption. All of these processes require significant amounts of information to reach completion.

The development of the needed controls amounts to a "Control Revolution." One of the first analysts to identify the most important control technology of the industrial age was Max Weber in describing bureaucracy beginning in the late nineteenth century. The pervasiveness of bureaucracy represented critical new machinery for controlling the unrestrained energy of the Industrial Revolution. After World War II, concepts of control shifted to information-processing, communication and control technologies exemplified by the computer. This lead to the emergence of the information society. The information society emerged in response to the nineteenth century crisis of control.[17]

A pure business or business management approach is consistent with the principles of accountability endemic to NCLB. The three most common explanations for the failure of schools are incompetent teachers, students that can't learn, and inadequate funding.

However in management theory the owners of a failing business don't blame their employees, customers, or budgets. Owners hold their management people responsible. Similarly, the difference between successful and failed schools is this approach taken to school management. This approach is consistent with most information age/corporate re-engineering perspectives. The seven keys to successful school management are identified as:

1. Every principal is an entrepreneur, as opposed to a bureaucrat. This enables formerly rule bound principals in old-fashioned top-down school districts to deal effectively with nonroutine situations. Providing localized empowerment gives administrators more of a stake in their school performance levels.

2. Every school controls its own budget, as opposed to central office control. School-site budgeting facilitates school-based management. Principals are more knowledgeable in prioritizing funds for their own institutions.

3. Everyone is accountable for student performance and for budgets. This includes administrators, teachers and parents. Each one is responsible for spending money wisely.

4. Everyone delegates authority to those below. Teachers in particular should be given extensive autonomy. Horizontal networking among peers must be cultivated. Teachers should share information and experiences about their students.

5. There is a burning focus on student achievement. There has to be a belief that every student can and must learn if the school is doing its job correctly. A focus on student achievement may produce different activities at each school depending on the circumstances.

6. Every school is a community of learners. School staff, students, and the community need an unequivocal commitment to the academic objectives of each school.

7. Families have real choices among a variety of unique schools. If schools cannot attract a sufficient number of students, they will close. The proven power of competition within a public school system will assure the availability of excellent school options.[18]

This formula represents an extension of popular corporate re-engineering literature of the 1990s. It does not account for dramatic changes in the student body and the need to address an economy that has transitioned out of the information age. It is a highly localized perspective on school management that adds support to a fragmentation resulting in the 15,000 separate school districts in the United States. The result is a duplication of efforts and a lack of resources needed for research and development in curriculum and instruction that addresses the needs and abilities of the contemporary student population.

There is a new historical epoch that has succeeded postindustrial society or the information age, which was acknowledged back in the 1960s. It is the "knowledge age." In the knowledge age, knowledge is the steel of the new economy. It is the essential commodity underpinning all economic activity. The knowledge age will not just be filled with information. It will embrace intelligence and comprehension. Moving through the twenty-first century it is necessary for nations to replace their educational and training institutions with high-tech learning systems that prepare students for the new age. It is not sufficient to simply reform existing schools.[19]

- There are a number of ways in which learning in the knowledge age must change significantly:
- Learning is now a transhuman process where interacting with computers and networking apparatus has replaced learning as just a human process.
- Learning now permeates all aspects of social activity—work, entertainment and home life. Learning is no longer confined to the box of a school classroom.
- Learning was a linear process between a teacher and a student. Learning is now interactive where everyone is both a learner and a teacher.
- Learning was primarily a task of childhood. It is now a lifelong pursuit.

The new connectedness to knowledge and learning has been referenced as hyperlearning. The speed at which we are able to develop our hyperlearning capabilities will determine the success of our educational system.

An increasingly "smart" environment, such as cars, houses, appliances, and toys, requires an exceptional level of comfort with communication infrastructures and hypermedia tools. The expertise is in the network. Students are required to interact with the network, both in terms of accessing its outputs and making it adapt to the learner's inputs. In the hyperlearning world, learning and expertise are everywhere. People become engaged in learning at any time and at any place. Attempting to confine it to a specific time and place—school—is increasingly problematic. The standard operating procedure model is based on a physical plant that is no longer relevant.

Using varying forms of operant conditioning, attempting to focus on an agenda that is inconsistent with purely academic prerogatives and emphasizing testing without reformulating the teaching process will assure a continued lack of student achievement. An educational program that will result in improved student performance has to be based on the prerogatives of a new era of knowledge rather than the logistical demands of the post-World War II industrial era.

Aside from the fact that school curricula have failed to acknowledge the relevance of knowledge age learning imperatives, these curricula have also failed to respond to significant changes in manufacturing management policies that have been expanded over the past 23 years.

These principles are described in Toyota's Production System (TPS) which is based on the concept of continuous improvement. Continuous improvement extends beyond actual improvements suggested by individuals. It is about continuous learning and embracing change. The focus is on high-value-added "flow" that would change according to customer demand and continue to run efficiently. An environment is created that nurtures both individual responsibility and team building among all participants in the production process, product development system and supplier relationship management.[20]

TPS has 14 key principles that are divided into the four "P"s. The first "P" is Philosophy. All management decisions are based on long-term thinking despite any negative impact that may have to short-term financial objectives. The second "P" is Process. Keep workload even, eliminate waste and avoid overproduction. Use visual controls to maintain quality and stop production when quality is compromised. The third "P" is People and Partners. Respect and challenge your people and teams, and help your suppliers. The fourth "P" is Problem-Solving. Thoroughly investigate all problems, solve by consensus and implement solutions rapidly.

Lean production is the goal of TPS. The lean production process is a "pull" system that starts with customer demand and replenishes at short intervals only what the next operation removes. In effect, the next process is the "customer." Lean production is accomplished by developing a culture where all participants are compelled to continuously improve. Goals are achieved by designing manufacturing practice to include established production cells, problem-solving groups of workers, and incentives for solving problems and a learning resource center for employees.

All waste must be removed from the system. Waste includes producing items for which there are no orders only to create excess inventory, waiting due to unnecessary line downtime, unnecessary moving of materials or employee motion, producing defective parts, and losing opportunities by not engaging employees and their ideas.

The Toyota Production System or process of continuous improvement is the state-of-the-art method used in manufacturing all of today's products from shoes to automobiles. The system represents a considerable leap from the simple feedback procedures developed during the Second

World War. The continuous improvement approach has a distinct application to classroom activity. To be effective, however, administrators, teachers and students have to fully "buy-in" to the continuous improvement process. This means it is necessary to reconsider prior education ideology.

A curriculum based on the rudimentary premises applied to manufacturing of the 1940s needs of the to be updated. Although competent students cannot be stamped out like car fenders, having the resources and intent to continuously improve on a student's knowledge acquisition process is as important as finding better ways to process goods. The historical standard operating procedures should be abandoned in schools just as they have been discarded in contemporary production processes. To the extent that educational authorities are anxious to duplicate manufacturing processes, they should, at least, duplicate current operations.

Subterfuge

Given the need to confront a broad array of forces encouraging troublesome behavior, customary techniques have not proven effective. As a result, subterfuge or diversionary activity has become a preferred strategy. Subterfuge refers to a preoccupation with the issues involving diversity, tolerance and self-esteem. This sleight of hand strictly panders to popular political considerations rather than addressing real instructional needs. Diversity and tolerance are important topics that have a place in a school curriculum. Yet, they do not represent a curriculum that would substitute for the presentation of subject matter necessary to augment student performance in fundamental academic skills.

The self-esteem movement has led to the lowering of standards to prevent students from feeling bad about themselves. Grammar schools do not give grades and some high schools have considered eliminating grades. Lack of grading conceals a child's ability to achieve from both teachers and parents. Information about their children's performance is often limited to a couple of parent-teacher conferences each year. The resulting lack of feedback on their children's school performance has led many parents to feel extraneous to the school-child relationship.

There are others who claim that observations on the decline of American student achievement and statements that today's students no longer have the skills to compete globally are inaccurate. Assertions of worsening student performance are based on reduced national test scores, such as those on the SAT. The problem with the conclusion that lower test scores indicate a failure of our schools is that it does not consider the changed nature of the test-takers. The majority of early postwar year's test-takers were upper-class Ivy League-bound students. In more recent years, the majority of test-takers are from more diverse socioeconomic groups. Critics insist there is a culture bias the test, rather than scholastic ability that is solely responsible for the lower scores.[21]

Making excuses or spinning test results is a popular form of subterfuge. The NAEP tests, which confirm poor student performance, are and have been given to all students at designated grade levels.

An interest in student preferences began in the early part of the twentieth century. John Dewey provided foundational work that reflected the tenets of the Progressive political movement. Dewey was instrumental in conceiving a student-based approach for educational purposes. Prior to his work, instruction was accomplished primarily by rote memory. In the classroom, teacher commands prevailed. Dewey suggested that a more effective teaching method would include the experiences and preferences of the learner.[22]

Thus, a curriculum continuum or dialectic was established between teacher-centered and student-centered prerogatives. A traditionally conceived curriculum would be predisposed toward teacher demands. A progressive agenda would emphasize student predilections.

Dewey's analysis was revolutionary in much the same way Karl Marx's economic assessments were pioneering when introduced a few decades before. Marx described the relationship between capital and labor. Both Marx and Dewey manifestly framed the relationship between superiors and subordinates—in the workplace and in the classroom. The interests of each of the opposing parties, the thesis and antithesis, would best be served by achieving a synthesis or middle ground where everyone receives fair consideration. The theory being that, if one party was accorded a significant advantage over the other, prospects for both parties would be diminished.

John Dewey began his university teaching career in 1884. He joined the faculty of The University of Chicago a decade later. His background in philosophy and psychology lead to the development of his perspectives on Progressive education. Progressive education contrasted with traditional education, in that, it emphasized experience, experiment, and purposeful learning.

Traditional learning relied on cultural heritage for content. Progressive education focused on the learners' impulse, interest and the current problems of a changing society. Dewey emphasized, however, that neither traditional nor progressive education represented a complete educational solution. There must be a combination of the two. Education represents a scientific method for studying the world and acquiring the cumulative knowledge of meanings and values. Scientific study enlarges experience. However, it is only educative when it rests on continuity of significant knowledge. Thus, there must be continuity and interaction between the learner and what is learned.

Appreciating the critical nature of student predispositions, another educator in the early part of the twentieth century, Lev Vygotsky, defined the Zone of Proximal Development (ZPD). An ardent Marxist born in Russia in 1896, Vygotsky sought to reformulate psychology according to Marxist methodology. In 1922 he was committed to making the new socialist state successful. His focus was on education, remediation, and illiteracy among the hundreds of ethnic groups that formed the new nation. He wanted all to participate in the new society.[23]

The ZPD is a Marxist tool-and-result psychological method. It asserts that learner accomplishment will be enhanced through collaboration and support, as opposed to students working alone. Researchers have introduced the term "scaffolding" to describe the process by which an expert assists a learner in executing a task beyond the learner's capability. Scaffolding, like ZPD, is a construct where control of a task is transferred from expert to novice. Learning methodologies emphasize that teaching occurs when assistance is offered at points in the ZPD at which performance requires assistance. ZPD is a student-centered teaching device. A student-centered program is often referred to as constructivist.

As an outcome of transcendent concerns with student discipline, curriculum design has moved decidedly toward the student-centered or constructivist extreme. This movement is bolstered through concepts like multiple intelligence theory. Rather than concentrating on exacting academic performance standards, multiple intelligence theory suggests schools should confer merit on students for distinctive motor skills or interpersonal aptitude.[24]

Another leading diversion from intellectual achievement standards is critical pedagogy. Critical pedagogy is concerned with the political economy of schooling—the construction of student subjectivity.[25] Critical pedagogy asserts education serves to reproduce the technocratic and corporate ideologies that characterize dominant societies. Schools create individuals whose social function is to sustain and legitimate the interests of the state. Teachers are the "clerks of the empire." Schools are the "company store" providing students with the technical expertise to fit into corporate hierarchy. Critical pedagogists perceive schools as ideological arenas where sorting mechanisms empower certain groups, based on race, class and gender, over other groups.[26] They believe it is important to confront the structures of oppression and the myths legitimating injustices towards disadvantaged students.

The tradition of critical pedagogy represents an approach to schooling that is committed to the imperatives of empowering students and transforming the larger social order in the interests of justice and equality.

Critical pedagogists complain that students are viewed as receptacles that memorize narrative mechanically. Teaching becomes an act of depositing or banking information to insure students remain oppressed.

With their attention on vast conspiracy theories, the critical pedagogists suggest there is an oppressive hidden curriculum. The issue of a hidden curriculum was addressed by the de-schooling movement, which was a product of the social fervor of the 1960s. The need to dis-establish schools was consistent with the rebellion against a technological and social structure that was responsible for propagating ethnic and gender inequities. The schools' subliminal agenda served to reinforce values inconsistent with those promoting a more Progressive social order.

The mere existence of an institution that all children were required by law to attend suggests an undue imposition on individual freedom. Schools inculcate children with the notion of age discrimination since adults are not required to attend a school. Schools introduce teachers as moralists who indoctrinate children with societal norms. Schools instill in children that organizations directed by scientific knowledge are efficient and benevolent, and that increased production and consumption will lead to a better life.[27]

Another perspective of the 1960s was offered in the methods of *Summerhill*. Summerhill was a school founded in Suffolk, England in 1921.[28] All Summerhill students are reared in happiness. They are happy and any unhappiness they may have brought is to be cured. All crimes and hatred can be reduced to unhappiness. Making a student sit at a desk will produce docile uncreative children who will have only money as a standard of success. It is necessary to make the school fit the child, rather than having the child fit the school. The child is innately wise and realistic.

Therefore, Summerhill renounced all discipline, direction, and suggestion. Lessons are optional. Though students have the option of attending classes, they all end up in classes at some point. Exams are given in each class, though students have a choice of taking them or not. Usually, only those interested in attending college opt to take the exams. Children are able to find their own level. Instructional methods are not critical since those students who choose to take a particular subject are likely to learn it no matter how it is taught. Thus, all the kids are happy. Rules are made by a school parliament. Children are wise and accept social rules. These are the lessons of Summerhill.

Character education, another subterfuge, articulates the importance of moral values, ethics and citizenship. It ties academic curriculum and evaluation to the development of good character. Character issues are addressed in schools. However, they are not directly related to academics. Rather, moral edification was imbedded in activities like gym, art, home economics, and through many extracurricular classes and organizations, besides in the home and through religious affiliations. A concentration on character education can be a distraction from the purveyance of academic skills.

Immersion in student-centered trivia serves to diminish the impact of the actual instructional process by diverting attention from academic performance. It is through academic performance that social biases can be confidently overcome. Well-educated students and adults are less likely to encounter the cost of societal prejudice.

Critical thought is the antidote to corporate and governmental brainwashing. The ability to think critically is predicated on having strong academic skills. A preoccupation with the political and social implications with the role of school in society diverts attention from developing innovative instructional tools. Although Dewey cogently framed the relationship between teacher and student, he offered no prescriptions for implementing his concepts. It is up to teachers and administrators to determine effective student-centered instructional techniques.

The endorsement of multiple intelligences, critical pedagogy and character education in the school curriculum was challenged in 1987 by Allan Bloom.[29] Bloom maintained that producing independent thinkers is the objective of a democratic education. However, the central problem in education and in society is cultural relativism in the guise of tolerance where all conceptions of political and social standards are equally valid.

Students should be concerned with the permanent problems of mankind. These would be better addressed through an old Great Books conviction rather than a devotion to the emergent. Bloom describes the youth rebellion of the 1960s as the beginning of the cultural relativism movement. This movement has led to a dilution of academic standards.

As expressed by Dewey, attention to student preferences and experience is a vital component to education. Teaching in a command environment where students are required only to absorb information delivered by a given instructor will, for a variety of reasons, limit the child's interest in learning. However, student-centered learning is a guidepost to finding innovative means to engage a child. Student-centered learning is not a political agenda that serves to sidetrack the need for academic competence. It represents an important instructional perspective that considers the predisposition of the learner in a teaching environment.

CHAPTER 5

RELEVANCE

As noted, the issue of relevance is central in trying to manage classroom disciplinary problems. Students innately grasp the relationship between their attendance in school and the importance of developing skills needed to succeed in adulthood. All students make the connection between school and future success. However, the issue of relevance is particularly important in working with at-risk students. If the likelihood for success becomes significantly diminished, interest in class will wane proportionately.

Economic prospects are largely dependent on national trends. The nature of the U.S. economy, with respect to the number and types of jobs it creates, as well as the nature of its participation in global economic developments affect classroom behavior. Unfortunately, no instructional methods or curriculum guidelines acknowledge this elemental reality. Schools are administered as if they exist in a vacuum.

The cohort of recent high school and college graduates ages 18 to 29 represent a group of 43 million people often referred to as Millennials, GenY or the echo Baby Boom. These YouTube viewing, disaffected, Internet connected Americans are having a significant effect on the current political landscape. They are motivated by a world view informed by epic economic uncertainty. Weaned on a devotion to self-esteem and entitlement, they are confronted in adulthood by the reality of having to pay off a massive college loan debt, a crumbling economy, poor job prospects,

Education Redux: How to Make Schools Relevant to Our Children and Our Future,
pp. 65–104
Copyright © 2010 by Information Age Publishing

deflated salaries and benefits, unattainable housing, Social Security insolvency, terrorism, war, and health care and environmental crises.

Inflation adjusted earnings for college graduates, for example, have fallen 8.5% since 2000. A 2008 survey of Millennial voters indicated that 80% considered the economy "very important" versus only 61% naming the environment as a major issue. The result has been a significantly higher level of participation in election politics. Political candidates at all levels and from all perspectives are responding by calling for massive and fundamental change.[1] Although the specifics of anticipated changes can be elusive, the need to embrace change is unmistakable.

In June, 2008 17 girls, none of whom were older than 16, at Gloucester High School in a Massachusetts fishing town were expecting babies. This was a fourfold increase in the number of pregnancies from the previous year. The principal of the school responded that the unusually high number of pregnancies was the result of a pact between the girls to get pregnant and raise their babies together. One of the fathers was a 24-year old homeless person. The school superintendent lamented that, "Families are broken.... Many of our young people are growing up directionless."

Nationally, teen pregnancies rose in 2006 for the first time in 15 years. With regard to the publicized pregnancies, other students at Gloucester High were quoted as saying, "They were excited to have someone to love them unconditionally," and "No one's offered them a better option."[2] The perspective of the 17 pregnant teenagers is analogous to that of individuals who are contemplating suicide. By assuming the burden of raising a child at their young ages, the girls are deliberately limiting their opportunities for having a lucrative career.

In 1897 French sociologist Emile Durkheim described three different types of suicide. There is egoistic suicide which results from an individual being detached from societal norms. The second type of suicide is altruistic where individuals are so influenced by social demands they lose perspective of the importance of their individuality. Last, there is anomic suicide. Anomie refers to a situation where social and economic institutions no longer serve the needs of the individual. Individual anomie is the result of disturbances in the collective order. A feeling of anomie is driving the behavior of the 17 pregnant girls, as well as the self-defeating behavior of many young people.[3]

The effect of the national economy on school discipline is evident in the example of Japan. School policy in post-World War II Japan was driven by a national mission to accelerate renewal. Rapid attainment was accomplished through standardized curriculum, rote learning, and fierce competition for grades. Though the pressure was intense, diligence and high achievement assured a student's adult financial success. Getting a job with a large Japanese company meant lifetime employment with attractive wages and benefits.

Through this model Japan rose out of the ashes of World War II to become the second largest economy in the world behind only the United States. By the 1980s, the postcollege job market in Japan had constricted and students began to show signs of stress. There was a discernible increase in violent incidents and suicides in the elementary and middle schools. With the collapse of the Japanese economy in the 1990s, which further compromised children's future, student motivations and test scores dropped substantially.

In 2002 educational officials sought to enhance student autonomy by reducing the content of the core curriculum and offering many classes as electives. The result of students' newfound independence and diminished adult income expectations has been the complete collapse of classroom discipline.[4]

Like Japan, the U.S. has experienced a similarly dramatic economic transformation. Since 2000 America has lost more than 3 million manufacturing jobs.[5] Many of these job losses were a consequence of productivity gains achieved through technological innovation. However, the vast majority of the jobs disappeared after having been exported to low wage Asian countries, most notably China. Service sector employment also declined as customer service, back office operations and software production were outsourced to India and aerospace and electronics engineering moved to Russia where wages and benefits are a fraction of U.S. levels.

The Internet has increased the ease of moving service economy jobs offshore. It is expected that positions doing legal work, accounting, health care and others will continue to leave the United States. As the educational systems in these Asian countries improve and their populations become more competent, the service job outflow from America will accelerate.

Substantially reduced wages and benefits paid to production employees is the primary reason American corporations send jobs out of the country. The U.S. tax code also provides an incentive to send jobs offshore. The issue is the manner by which profits from foreign subsidiaries of American corporations are treated.

There is a 35% corporate tax on profits earned in the United States. However, American corporations are permitted to defer paying taxes on foreign subsidiary profits until those profits are returned to the United States. Often, that does not occur for years. For example, GE has $62 billion in "undistributed earnings" sitting offshore, Pfizer has $60 billion and ExxonMobil has $56 billion. The delayed payment policy means that the U.S. takes in less in corporate taxes, as a portion of economic output, than almost every other major economy. The tax code encourages American companies to set-up offshore enterprises.[6]

The historical process by which U.S. manufacturing jobs appeared, moved and disappeared can be appreciated in a description of the evolution of a Paterson, New Jersey firm, Universal Manufacturing Company. During the Revolutionary War, General George Washington and Colonel Alexander Hamilton encamped at what would become Paterson, NJ. Hamilton surveyed the Great Falls of the Passaic River and recognized the vast industrial potential of the area using the falls as a source of energy.

His vision was realized in the nineteenth and twentieth centuries, as the city became a major manufacturing center. One Paterson firm, Universal Manufacturing Company, was started in 1941 by a local entrepreneur. Universal manufactured ballasts for the lighting industry. The ballasts were used in fluorescent light fixtures which were frequently installed in office buildings such as those in nearby New York City. The Teamsters organized Universal in 1950 after advising its management that union electricians would not be installing their non-union made product. By the early 1960s, Universal had grown to 1,200 employees.[7]

Looking for expansion opportunities in 1961, Universal management was approached by officials from the State of Mississippi. The governor, Ross Barnett, was offering them a package of incentives, including protection from union organizers. Governor Barnett gained worldwide notoriety in 1962 when he stood at the schoolhouse door attempting to prevent James Meredith from becoming the first Black student at the University of Mississippi in Jackson.

Factory production had expanded rapidly throughout the American South with the passage of the Taft-Hartley Act in 1947. Taft-Hartley was passed over the veto of President Truman. The Act permitted states to pass right-to-work laws that outlawed the closed union shop. Right-to-work laws made it extremely difficult for unions to organize Southern manufacturing facilities. Many southern states passed right-to-work laws in order to attract manufacturers eager to pay lower wages and benefits, and to avoid the demands of organized labor with respect to working conditions. During the 1950s and 1960s many corporations moved their manufacturing facilities from Eastern and Midwestern states to the South for access to workers at a reduced cost.

In 1963 Universal opened their new plant about 35 miles outside Jackson, Mississippi. Within days of the opening, the IBEW (International Brotherhood of Electrical Workers union) made it clear to Universal that its members would not be installing ballasts without a union label. The IBEW soon organized the plant despite substantial interference from local authorities.

In 1986 Universal was sold to an electrical components conglomerate, MagneTek. MagneTek closed the Paterson plant in 1989 and management was negotiating a move to Mexico into a maquiladora. A maquiladora or maquila refers to factories in Mexican towns along the United States-Mexico border. The maquiladora imports materials and equipment on a duty-free and tariff-free basis for assembly or manufacturing. The factory then re-exports the assembled products—usually back to the originating country. Wages and benefits are substantially less in Mexico than the U.S. hourly rates in Mexico were less than $1. Universal's move to Mexico was completed in 1991.

In 1998 the Mississippi plant closed, apparently without any significant consequences imposed by the unions. The success of organized labor in the first half of the twentieth century was predicated on the moral imperatives articulated by its great leaders. They did not just assume responsibility for their dues paying members, but shouldered the burden of all working people, the environment, the economy and other significant political issues of the day. They promoted a Progressive agenda that was considerate of the needs and rights of all working people. However, by the late 1990s union influence in the manufacturing sector was rapidly disappearing.

The changes Universal underwent can be compared to the concept of scientific revolution. In science, paradigms are created to serve as a foundation for describing phenomena. These paradigms provide models, which include law, theory, application, and instrumentation. From these models, coherent traditions of research emerge. Research occurring within the context of the paradigms is called normal science. Normal science is firmly based on the achievements that a scientific community acknowledges as a foundation for further practice.

As researchers encounter anomalies, wherein nature violates the paradigm-induced expectations that govern normal science, there may be a continuation in the exploration in the area of the anomaly. The extended exploration may lead to a crisis in the initial paradigm and the emergence of a new scientific theory. This process is defined as a scientific revolution. The new theory, then, becomes the paradigm, which is the basis for new experimentation.[8]

The process continually repeats itself. A demand for more and lower priced products continues to push manufacturing to locations with the lowest labor costs. Shifting jobs to new locations necessarily changes the occupational paradigms in the locales where manufacturing has been abandoned. Education and curriculum are integral to the process of normal science or changes in occupational paradigms.

The level of technological development and the type of economy that technology spawns are the criteria around which an educational curriculum must be constructed. Students have to be schooled to address specific types of vocations when they become adults. As technological and vocational paradigms change, educational institutions must reflect those changes.

The theory of scientific revolutions also provides an important perspective when examining of the three phases of technological development. Each phase is archetypal, in that, it represents a model upon which all elements in society formulate their structure and vision.

The three phases are preindustrial, industrial, and postindustrial. The labor force in preindustrial societies is primarily engaged in extractive industries—mining, fishing, forestry, and agriculture. Work consists of a contest against Nature. It is the utilization of raw muscle power practiced in inherited ways and conditioned by a dependence on the elements, such as the seasons, the nature of soil and the amount of water. Daily rhythms are shaped by these elements. Productivity is low and the economy is subject to weather and international commodity price fluctuations.[9]

Industrialization developed out of the need to produce nonextractive goods more efficiently. Industrial societies are goods producing communities. The labor force operates in a contest against fabricated nature. The environment is technical and rationalized. It is predominated by machines. Rhythms are mechanically paced, methodical and evenly spaced. Energy and machines transform the nature of work. Skills are reduced to simple maneuvers. The artisan is replaced by the engineer and semiskilled worker. There is an elaborate hierarchy and bureaucracy. Organizational designs are closely related to the gradations found on the factory floor.

The industrial form of production that had emerged in the nineteenth century replaced the artisan as the primary producer of goods. Products made by artisans represented the work of an individual or the collaboration of a small number of people. Goods produced by industry were created through the coordinated activities of a large number of individuals assigned to specific tasks—the division of labor. Production changed qualitatively from a simple mode to advanced complexity. Discipline, the tyranny of the clock, constraints of supervisors, mechanical rhythms, and the differentiation of tasks associated with industrial production and the division of labor became embedded in other spheres—political, social, economic, and so forth.

The highly complex interdependence of labor led to an organic solidarity. Organic solidarity contrasts with a mechanical solidarity where relationships are less dependent on the work of others. Mechanical solidarity is based on common background, heritage and type of work. The shared interests of agricultural communities would be an example of mechanical solidarity.[10] Organic solidarity is about working toward a common cause.

Finally, postindustrial society is predicated on the production of services. Work is based on a relationship between persons. Information and communication replaces muscle power and energy. The central person is a professional who has attained skills through education and training. Society is communal where the community transcends the individual. Cooperation and participation are the primary elements of work. Knowledge and the ability to make connections is the primary tool of postindustrial society.

Personal behavior is largely determined by these developmental phases. During the late 1950s, as America was entering its service economy phase, the dictates of consumption were replacing the imperatives of production. The sensitivities of the populace were shifting from being inner-directed to other-directed. Inner-directed children internalized goals imbedded by the families. Other-directed individuals are more responsive to the expectations and preferences of others. Peer groups replaced adult authority.

This shift was influenced by both precipitous prosperity and by the growth of mass media advertising, particularly television. Inner-directed society had replaced tradition-directed. Tradition-directed members of society had a highly conforming social character based on their tendency to follow tradition.[11] Tradition-directed, inner-directed and other-directed behaviors closely track the evolution from extractive to industrial to postindustrial production.

Trends in education are strongly influenced by the dynamic described in these three phases of industrial development—extraction, industrial, and postindustrial. America's extraction or preindustrial stage proceeded from the Colonial period beginning in 1642 until 1776 and into the National Period, which ran from 1776 to the middle of the nineteenth century. During this era the majority of American workers were engaged in activities, including agriculture, mining, and forestry.

As noted, daily rhythms were largely shaped by Nature and natural wealth. Schooling was not a necessary prerequisite for employment since most work was on the family farm and needed skills were learned from parents. One important concern was that children could read and understand the principles of religion and the laws of the Commonwealth. In 1647 the Puritan colony of Massachusetts required every town of at least 50 families to appoint a reading and writing teacher to assure that citizens would have knowledge of the scriptures. This was known as the Old Deluder Satan Act since the main objective of the old deluder, Satan, was to prevent familiarity with the Bible.[12]

The Puritans' commitment to education was based on making certain that colonial America did not foster the growth of an illiterate group of citizens that became a permanent underclass evocative of those in Europe. These early Puritan laws were the foundation of the American public school movement. Values taught in Puritan schools included, respect for authority, delaying gratification, neatness, punctuality, honesty, competition, respect for the rights and property of others, patriotism, personal responsibility, and obeying rules and regulations.

Unlike the mostly Puritan New England Colonies, the Middle Colonies, which were Delaware, New Jersey, New York, and Pennsylvania, were more religiously and ethnically diverse. Missionary societies and various religious and ethnic groups established their own schools. The purpose of these institutions was to educate their own children in reading, writing, and religious teachings.

Though colonists in New England and the Middle Colonies were attempting a break from England's culture and tradition, the Southern colonies did not wish to abrogate English custom. On the contrary, Southerners chose to replicate British institutions by remaining loyal to the Anglican Church and perpetuating the values of the landed gentry. Plantation owners focused on enjoying refined activities, such as music, literature, dancing, and horse breeding. Those lacking the appropriate birthright were expected to be satisfied with their inferior stature. Religious institutions and the limited schooling available to those not favored by birth rigorously upheld rigid social class distinctions.

Latin Grammar schools, first established in Boston, were set-up for upper class children. Their role was to support the religious and social institutions of the era. In 1751, the academy was developed to provide education at the secondary level. The academy was based on the ideas of Benjamin Franklin to address the needs of those students not attending college. Franklin wanted to offer a practical curriculum consisting of grammar, classics and composition. It also introduced many practical skills, including carpentry, printing, cabinet-making, farming, and book-keeping.[13]

The National Period, beginning in 1776, sought to connect education to the notions of popular government and political freedom. President James Madison and Thomas Jefferson were ardent supporters of expanding educational facilities. The Northwest Ordinances of the late 1780s reserved sections in each township for public schools. Secular forces emerging at the turn of the nineteenth century were sufficiently assertive that religious influence in public education began to weaken.

Through the Colonial and National Periods an individual's reliance on Nature and personal strength inspired a belief in powers greater than man's. Religious training was an important requirement assisting those working the land that had to overcome the vicissitudes of weather and other natural obstacles. The inception of the early 1800s secular movement was consistent with changes marking the beginning of the Industrial Age. Work was becoming more rationalized.

Dr. Benjamin Rush of Pennsylvania was an integral part of this new movement. He was a champion of the study of science over the traditional Latin and Greek classics. Rush promoted free colleges and universities since they would produce graduates able to generate wealth in each community. William McGuffey was the author of America's most popular textbooks between 1836 and 1920. His *Readers* had a moral tone promoting patriotism and a faith in American institutions. Rush, McGuffey, and others during the mid-nineteenth century represented the beginning of a transition from the preindustrial to the industrial period. Science and order was starting to replace religious and traditional teachings related to a faith in Nature that was evident in Colonial schools.

Another change taking place was based on teaching methods introduced by the Swiss educator, Johann Pestalozzi. In his 1801 book, Pestalozzi wanted to establish a "psychological method of instruction." He placed an emphasis on spontaneity and self-activity. Children should arrive at their own answers rather than be given ready-made answers. Though his experience is rooted in preindustrial times, he recognized the "inner dignity of each individual for the young as truly as for the adult."

Pestalozzi's perspective is consistent with the political views of, then, President Thomas Jefferson.[14] Jefferson, author of the Declaration of Independence, believed that an educated citizenry was critical to the well being of a republic. Pestalozzi and Jefferson were part of an evolution in sociopolitical perspectives. They represented an early change from a teacher-centered to a student-centered focus.

As events precedent to the industrial revolution began rapidly unfolding in the latter part of the nineteenth century a movement toward universal education emerged. The National Education Association organized three committees between 1893 and 1895. The Committee of Fifteen was set to deal with elementary education. They reduced elementary grades from 10 to 8. The elementary curriculum lessened the focus on the classics in favor of reading, writing, grammar, spelling, arithmetic, science and history. The elementary curriculum was diversified and enriched.

The Committee of Ten described subjects central to the high school curriculum. These included the classics, as well as an emphasis on advanced math and science. The Committee on College Entrance Requirements identified the course work necessary for college admission. This Committee sought to strengthen the college preparatory aspect of the high school curriculum.

The three Committees were clearly laying out a total curriculum designed to address the new demands to be made of students entering the workplace in industrialized America. By 1900 industrial workers outnumbered those engaged in agriculture. Students had to be prepared, not only for work in large factories but also needed a foundation for facing the demands of living in cities where the plants were located. The essential structure of schools and their curriculum was designed by the three committees beginning more than 110 years ago. The same structure is used in schools today.

To continue the sequence of school development, in 1916 educator Abraham Flexner, who was instrumental in reforming American medical education, proposed a Modern School for secondary education. The Modern School rejected Latin and Greek studies in favor of a curriculum consisting of science, industry, civics and aesthetics. According to Flexner, subject offerings should be based primarily on their utility. Education should serve a real purpose rather than rely strictly on traditional assignments. Flexner understood the type of education needed in times of rapidly changing technologies.

Another educator of that period, Edward L. Thorndike in the early 1920s did extensive psychological experimentation that resulted in his Law of Effect. Thorndike's work related to tracking stimulus-response effects. He concluded that habits were strengthened or weakened based on the nature and frequency of stimulus-response pairings. Thorndike was an early developer of the behaviorist approach to instruction. Thus, beginning with the late nineteenth century committees through early twentieth century theorists like Dewey, Flexner, and Thorndike, curriculum and instruction concepts, as well as the egg crate school design took the shape and form that persists today, more than 100 years later.

Vig Time

Bell is best known for explicating the three phases of technological change—extraction, industrial, and postindustrial or information. Each of these phases matured and yielded to subsequent developmental stages. To correctly evaluate Bell's description of technological progress, it is appropriate to consider the three phases he described, not on a linear or progressive dimension, but as a cyclical arrangement As the postindustrial period has aged and become increasingly outsourced to emerging countries, like India and China, the technological development process is going full circle. The tremendous wealth created through the value-added industrial and information periods is now being extracted.

During the preindustrial era, extraction was portrayed as a contest between man and Nature. The era that has succeeded the postindustrial era is one of wealth extraction. The era of wealth extraction can be characterized as a match between man and the vicissitudes of risk. Though the practice of arbitrage seeks to minimize risk since the buyers generally thinks they have a locked-in seller and sale price prior to making an acquisition, there is still no absolute guarantee the purchased asset can be resold at a profit.

The uncertainty contrasts with industrial era production policy where goods are produced based on prearranged purchase orders, where creditworthy buyers become contractually obligated to buy a specified amount of product at an agreed price. Since the same level of rational exchange does not exist in the present era of extraction, religious fervor is more pervasive. Religious involvement is apparently able to address the uncertainties imposed by Nature and by risk-taking.

According to the Federal Reserve Consumer Balance Sheet, the total U.S. household net worth is in the neighborhood of $56 trillion.[15] With those assets we now have entered into the era of wealth extraction. However, that wealth is no longer just in the ground. Much of it is now a liquid asset—cash or marketable securities. The age of wealth extraction is evidenced in a review of America's largest industries. The U.S. imports virtually all of its consumer goods, like clothing, shoes, toys, housewares, and electronics. The United States is also a large importer of services, such as software, engineering, accounting and bookkeeping, and call center services. Its largest exports are scrap metal, scrap paper, cardboard and plastic, farm and excavating machinery, and investment capital.

The most profitable U.S. corporations in 2007 were oil companies selling imported oil and banks. Much like oil companies, scrap recyclers and farms, banks are in the wealth extraction business. Their constant trading and manipulative activity in currencies, stocks, bonds, options, derivatives, hedge funds, and real estate is a means of drawing out cash in the form of fees, commissions and speculative investment without introducing any value-added component.

Financial derivatives are securities and financial instruments that are not fundamental securities, such as stocks and bonds. Derivatives depend on the value of fundamental securities but offer traders and investors an opportunity to create markets around a variety of contracts. One type of contract is an option. There are two sorts of options—call options and put options. A call option gives its owner a right to purchase an underlying security at a specific price for a specified period of time. A put option gives its owner the right to sell an underlying security at a specific price for a specified period of time. Swaps are another type of derivative. A swap is an agreement to exchange cash flows over a period of time. For example, in an interest rate swap one party will agree to pay a fixed rate of interest on a security over a period of time while the second party pays a floating rate over that same period.[16]

Thus, derivatives, such as options and swaps offer traders and investors instruments allowing them to bet on future movements, up or down, of stocks and interest rates. The attraction to trading derivatives is that they are less expensive to purchase than acquiring the fundamental securities. The largest options exchange is the Chicago Board Options Exchange (CBOE). The CBOE was established in Chicago in 1973.

All of these financial instruments are the tools of a wealth extractive economy. The creation of implements of this nature is consistent with the invention of machines and machine tooling used during the industrial revolution. The INTERNET bubble of the late 1990s and the real estate bubble of the early 2000s are evidence of a wealth extractive economy. Trillions of dollars worth of individual investment funds were sucked out of savings and put into general circulation.

In addition to private wealth extractive activity, there is a growing market in the sale of government owned wealth including essential infrastructure, such as roads, bridges, and parking facilities. Recent sales include Chicago's downtown parking system to Morgan Stanley and Virginia's Pocahontas Highway and the Indiana Toll Road to global financial firms.[17]

The purpose of these sales is to raise needed cash on a short term basis for states and municipalities. Increased Medicaid spending and pension funding obligations coupled with the unpopular prospect of raising taxes when families are already struggling make these sales an attractive option. Corporate players prominent in the wealth extraction business are eager trading partners.

Explosive growth in gambling represents another wealth extraction activity. In 1976 American legally bet $17.3 billion. In 1996 $586.5 billion was bet.[18] This includes riverboat casinos, land-based casinos, horse and dog racing, off-track betting, poker championships, lotteries, and church bingo games. In 1984 the three major forms of gambling, casinos, lotteries and pari-mutuel betting, took in $15 billion in revenues. By 1995 these three forms of gambling generated more than $55 billion in revenues. Gambling had become the largest component of the U.S. entertainment industry. By 1993 every state but Utah and Hawaii permitted some form of legal gambling. As recently as the 1988, casino gambling was legal in only two states—Nevada and New Jersey.

In a recent survey of 2,630 representative U.S. residents at least 18 years old, it was determined that 82% gambled in the past year. This compares with a 63% participation rate in a 1998 survey. The lottery was the most common form of gambling with 66% of respondents having played in the previous year. Next most common were raffles, office pools, and charitable gambling at 48%; casino gambling at 27% and horse/dog racing at 2%.

Gambling rates declined with age, though frequency among those who gambled showed small increases with age. The frequency of gambling decreases with increasing socioeconomic status. The rate of pathological or problem gambling for those in the top socioeconomic quintile was 1.6%. However, the rate for problem gambling for those in the bottom quintile was 5.3%.[19]

Lotteries are the fastest growing source of state revenues. The first legal lottery in the twentieth century was created by New Hampshire in 1964. A fundamental problem with state lotteries is that they invent an exaggerated impression of the chance of winning.[20] As one observer remarked, "Your chances of winning are virtually the same, whether you purchase a ticket or not."

State sponsored betting now encompasses sports betting, introduced in Oregon, and video slot machines in South Dakota. Opponents insist lotteries promote an ethic of easy money over the value of hard work. They also suggest that legal gambling leads to illegal gambling, crime and corruption. As a tax, lotteries appeal disproportionately to the poor and uninformed.

States sold lotteries as painless substitutes for taxes. The money raised would be used for important causes, like education. However, reporters investigating state lotteries discovered that they neither lowered taxes for their residents, nor improved funding for education.[21] Further, by producing a large number of compulsive gamblers, lotteries created a burden of almost $11 billion a year for states and their residents.

Lotteries are not efficient methods for producing public funds. In 1995 state lotteries generated revenues of $32 billion. After paying administrative costs and prize money of $21 billion, states netted only $11 billion. Further, states that specifically earmark lottery funds for education will reduce the amount of money paid for education from general revenue funds. The result is the proportion of state spending dedicated to education has not changed despite available lottery revenues.

Government sponsored gambling enterprises represent a limited number of opportunities to create new jobs and public revenues. The fairly rapid proliferation of gambling occurred as a result of an "if-we-don't-our-neighbor-will" mentality among legislators. It is the legislators and the gambling industry itself that advocate for gambling. There are no public advocacy groups for gambling legalization. While gambling is promoted by appealing to economic revitalization and new jobs, gambling promoters are not wont to acknowledge the hidden costs.

Gambling's hidden costs include, the diversion of investment capital from potential value-added businesses, draining consumer capital from existing businesses, and the public and private costs incurred to deal with the growing number of individuals afflicted with gambling problems, who can lose their jobs and get involved in criminal activity to pay off debts. Gambling takes the most from those least able to afford it, damages existing economies and can be highly addictive.

To maximize the return on gambling, governments apply professional marketing techniques, develop sophisticated new games, hire "theming" consultants to create dream worlds and use demographers to profile segments of potential players.[22]

In an 1831 Supreme Court Case, *Cherokee Nation v. Georgia*, a principle was established that an Indian tribe is a "distinct political society ... capable of managing its own affairs and governing itself." They have the "power to make substantive law in internal matters" As a consequence of this settled law, in a 1987 Supreme Court Case, *California v. Cabazon Band of Mission Indians*, the court held that California could not apply its regulatory statutes to gambling on the reservation unless it prohibited gambling throughout the state. Since California actually promotes gambling in the state through its state lottery, tribes could operate games on their reservations without state regulation.[23]

The decision led Congress in 1988 to pass the Indian Gaming Regulatory Act (IGRA). The IGRA permitted casino gambling on Indian reservations. It even allowed tribes without preexisting reservations to buy land and establish new reservations. From 1988 to 1997, tribal gambling revenues rose from $212 million to $6.7 billion. By 1998 there were 260 Indian gambling facilities operating in 31 states.

Some tribes reported that gambling revenues have been used to improve infrastructure, build better housing and schools, and provide health care services. Gambling has also provided employment for thousands of tribal members. However, rates of poverty and unemployment among Native Americans remain the highest of any U.S. ethnic group. Poor health, alcoholism, incarceration, and suicide rates are also among the highest. Income level, education and home ownership rates are at the low end. Single car accidents are the number one cause of death on reservations.

Indian casinos negatively impact surrounding communities by creating significant increases in traffic on local roads, deteriorating highway infrastructure and imposing higher costs for police and emergency services. These problems have led to adjacent property devaluations and more crime.

In 1997 Americans spent $220 billion on entertainment. Audio, video, and computer equipment accounted for $81 billion, publications $52 billion and $48 billion went to gambling. Only $6 billion was spent on movie tickets. The social costs of gambling include pathological gambling, crime, bankruptcies, family disruptions, divorce, domestic violence, child abuse, and suicide.

Large financial institutions are able to create wealth extracting, non-value-added profits through a process called arbitrage. Arbitrage is defined in the dictionary as the simultaneous purchase and sale of the same or equivalent security, commodity contract, insurance or foreign exchange on the same or different markets in order to profit from price discrepancies.

The currency markets offer a good example of how arbitrage actually works. A currency trader who chooses to purchase Japanese yen with U.S. dollars at the going exchange rate, should not be able to realize a profit by purchasing euros with the dollars and, then, buying the yen with the euros. The relationships between various currencies in the market must remain efficient so third party transactions do not yield profits. However, anytime the relative value between two currencies changes, an arbitrage opportunity is created. Traders can realize small profits by trading through third currencies until prices in the entire market adjust to the initial change. Since the margins are small, there are billions of these transactions each day. To make this activity profitable, traders must deal in very large volumes.

One company engaged in this type of arbitrage activity is Long-Term Capital Management (LCM). LCM specialized in making convergence trades. Convergence trades were arbitrage actions based on fixed income assets, such as Japanese, European or U.S. government bonds. As the bonds became mis-priced relative to each other, arbitrage opportunities were exploited. To create enough trade volume to make these small margin trades attractive, LCM had borrowed $125 billion.

In 1998 the Russians devalued their currency, the ruble. This unanticipated action placed LCM's borrowed capital in serious jeopardy. The failure of LCM would have been so significant that the entire American banking system would have been severely impacted. As a result, the Federal Reserve Bank had to orchestrate a $3.5 billion bailout. Most banks and investment firms generate considerable profits from financial arbitrage transactions. In addition to currency, there are financial instruments called derivatives. Investment firms and companies like Enron specialized in trading these artificial and little understood by nonprofessional investors contrivances.

Forbes Magazine lists the top five global companies as Citigroup, General Electric, American International Group, Bank of America, and HSBC Group. These are all financial institutions. Though GE does some manufacturing, it has been selling off its manufacturing assets, such as household appliances which it had been producing for about 100 years. The only actual manufacturing company in the top 10 is Toyota.

Financial institutions do not create wealth. They do not transform oil to raw plastic or raw plastic to consumer products. Their profits are generated through financial manipulation and the extraction of vigorish—defined as a charge taken by a gambling house or bookie against bets placed. Vigorish, or the Vig, comprises charges analogous to interest, fees, commissions and good will. The business of extracting the Vig is the primary financial driver of our economy.

The ascendancy of finance is the source of the subprime mortgage debacle that is resulting in one of the largest plunges in home values. Financial institutions that were re-packaging traditional home mortgages as mortgage-backed securities and collateralized debt obligations were realizing enormous profits from selling these loan packages into commercial markets.

Since the number of low risk home loan borrowers was limited, lenders sought high risk borrowers (Ninjas-No Income, No Job or Assets) in order to expand their markets and profitability. Growing credit and consumer debt led the financial services sector in 2006 to represent 21% of the gross domestic product (GDP). The manufacturing sector was reduced to 12% of GDP in 2006. As recently as the mid-1970's, these percentages were reversed.[24]

Maximizing the Vig is a priority for all major corporations. Wal-Mart, for example, does approximately $30 billion in sales each month. They receive payments from their customers immediately through cash, check, or credit card sales. Wal-Mart does not pay their suppliers for 30 to 60 days. This process provides Wal-Mart with a constant float of $50 to $60 billion from which they can earn a return. If they earn only 4%, the annual cash flow is more than $2 billion in Vig. That amount represents about 20% of their net profits.

The drive for banks to increase Vig is evident in their efforts to expand credit card use. Users typically pay about a 20% annual interest rate on their balances. In addition, the credit card companies collect a 2% to 4% fee from the retailers for each transaction. Thus, banks are motivated to actively pursue sales of various types of debt to unsuspecting consumers. These include car loans, boat loans, vacation loans, Refis, credit cards, overdraft protection, and credit insurance to name a few. Although a percentage of consumers fail to repay these loans, the high interest rates charged to people who do pay more than offsets the losses.

Some of the primary marketing targets are college students. Most teenage college students are too willing to accept the easy credit. This is the beginning of the disconnect between the amount of money a person earns and the amount they are able to spend based on the ready availability of credit. When consumers take out their plastic credit card, they tend not to make the connection between the card and the spending of real, hard-earned money. Several years ago credit card company First the U.S. paid the University of Tennessee $19 million for information on their students and alumni in order to offer them credit cards.

The credit card companies, engaging in this type of predatory lending, often sue the parents when students are unable to repay their debts. Though the parents have no legal liability, they will often pay the debts to protect the future credit of their children.[25] Credit card companies are aware of this likelihood.

The recent rise in gas prices, though affecting the entire economy, has a direct impact on gasoline purchases. To adapt to the higher cost, consumers simply buy their gas with expanded credit card use. When gasoline prices are high, drivers use credit cards for 85% of their purchases. When prices were lower, credit card use for gasoline purchases was in the 55% range.

In addition to offering risky mortgages and credit card debt, lenders anxious to get a return on their money are writing high-risk auto loans. The current average car loan term is 5 years, 4 months (64 months). Further, 45% of all auto loans are longer than 6 years (72 months). A number of carmakers are offering 7 year financing (84 months) and there are credit unions making 8 year (96 months) auto loans available.

The result is the average car owner now owes $4,200 more than their vehicle is worth at the time it is sold. These balances are often rolled into the loans for new cars. The term of the new loan is extended to reduce the monthly payment, but the owner's equity in their auto is further reduced. Credit provider Standard & Poor's found that delinquencies among borrowers with the best credit ratings have increased 20% over the past year.[26]

Political leaders have chosen not to respond to the seriousness of our economic maladies. Since 2000 median income for working families has fallen by 5.4%, adjusted for inflation. Health insurance costs have increasingly been shifted from employers to workers and pension benefits have deteriorated. Home ownership for young people age 25 to 34 has gone from 53% in 1980 to 45% at present.

Between 1979 and 2000, married working couples experienced an increase of several hundred hours in the number of hours worked each year. The financial turbulence faced by the majority of American families has failed to arouse fervent public debate. We have maintained a national trade policy that has caused our manufacturing capabilities and the millions of jobs it supported to evaporate. Further, these trade policies have created a permanent, yet unsustainable, trade imbalance which is propped up in the short term by the assumption of an unconscionable degree of debt. The debt obligations or bonds are increasingly being purchased by foreign nations, most notably Asian central banks. The result is a reduction in the value of the U.S. dollar.

At the same time, the concentration of wealth among a small elite has lead to enormous liquidity. This means that a limited number of individuals and corporate entities possess very large amounts of cash. These players are obligated to invest the cash in a manner that will produce a maximum return.

To facilitate the financial speculation that is an inevitable outcome of the need to take full advantage of available vigorish, government controls have been eviscerated. Greed and individual self-interest have been actively advanced. A concern among elites for the welfare of the collectivity, like that evident during the Progressive Era, has largely disappeared. The primary result from the demise of managed capitalism has been monumental busts from dot.com to Enron to subprime.[27]

In September, 2008 Lehman Brothers, one of Wall Street's major investment banks, filed for bankruptcy—the largest bankruptcy filing in U.S. history. Merrill Lynch, another Wall Street institution, to avoid collapse was purchased by Bank of America. AIG, one of the country's largest insurers, is on the brink. All of this activity is in addition to the $200 billion in taxpayer funds that were recently used to rescue mortgage lenders Fannie Mae and Freddie Mac. The cause of the failures were the trillions of dollars of bad loans made by all of these institutions.[28]

By October, 2008 Congress gave final approval to a $700 billion bailout for the country's entire financial system—the largest government intervention in history. The rescue plan, passed over a period of less than two weeks, was considered vital to maintain stability in the markets and prevent economic collapse. The Treasury funds would be used to purchase troubled debt from financial institutions. The purpose is to assure the ability of banks and investment firms to make credit available and prevent normal economic activity from coming to a standstill.[29]

Despite the daily news stories of working people losing their jobs and homes, and being unable to pay for gasoline or food, the wealthy operate in what appears to be another dimension. A concierge business called Quintessentially exists to satisfy the whims of the very rich. Some of their activities include flying a celebrity's favorite teabags from London to Los Angeles, arranging trips to the North Pole and Amazon, renting out the Egyptian pyramids for a private party, and providing a bushel of Patagonian blueberries and albino peacocks for a party on a yacht in the French Riviera.[30]

Every 2 years *Business Week* magazine publishes the results of its survey ranking the top U.S. graduate business schools. In 2006 the top four schools in rank order were, The University of Chicago, University of

Pennsylvania (Wharton), Northwestern University (Kellogg), and Harvard University.[31]

Harvard, a consistently highly ranked business school, is known for producing the Harvard Business School (HBS) Case Study. The case study method of instruction was first developed by HBS in 1921.[32] The idea behind the case study is to create class discussion around real problems in business administration. HBS case studies are used in business schools around the world. Harvard produces approximately 350 new case studies each year. The number of cases sold annually is 6 million. In the course of a 2-year MBA program, students may study 500 cases.

The subject matter covered by HBS cases includes accounting, competitive strategy, government, entrepreneurship, finance, general management, human resources, information systems, marketing, negotiations, operations, organizational behavior and leadership, services and social enterprise and ethics. The case method presents graduate students with the types of decisions and dilemmas managers regularly encounter.

A case details a real problem facing a real person doing a real job. The case method classroom is based on active participation of students in solving problems under the guidance of a faculty member, rather than having students simply absorb data and theories. Every student also acts as a teacher. Students learn by comparing and contrasting each other's opinions and perspectives.

Harvard Case Study literature boasts of the effectiveness of their curriculum in preparing successful corporate and political leaders. Ballooning trade and budget deficits, a home loan credit crunch, the loss of virtually all U.S. manufacturing jobs, increasing unemployment and underemployment, unaffordable gasoline and food prices, and the widening gap between the richest 1% and everyone else might lead one to suspect the value of the Harvard curriculum. An analysis of subsequent decision making activity would suggest that there must be a more suitable curriculum.

It would appear that the HBS Case Studies might be corresponding to the stories of the Wise Men of Chelm. Chelm is a fabled village of pious Jews in Poland whose residents had a unique approach to solving problems.[33] For example, after a snowfall everyone in the village marveled at the beauty of the white trees, white rooftops, and white streets. The children in the school did not want to leave because their footsteps would reduce the beauty of the snow cover. The principal of the school solved the problem by having two men carry each child out of the building across the snow.

One another occasion, the residents of the village became concerned that a nearby mountain was blocking much of the sunlight that would otherwise shine on them. After consideration by the town's wise men, it was decided that they needed to push the mountain out of the way. A group of the village's largest men went to the base of the mountain and prepared to start pushing. Since it was going to be a warm day, they decided to take off their jackets and shirts and leave them in a pile nearby.

After they began pushing, a thief came and stole the pile of clothing. Towards the end of the day, one of the workers went to look for the clothing and discovered it was gone. He concluded that they had pushed the mountain so far that it would be difficult to find the original location of the pile. After reporting these events to the village people, the men were universally hailed as heroes for moving the mountain a great distance.

A road on a high mountain was at the edge of a steep precipice. Though people attempted to exercise caution navigating the road, many ended up falling over the edge and being seriously injured. The wise men considered the problem and decided the appropriate solution was to build a hospital at the bottom of the mountain. So when people fell, the doctors would be right there.

One evening a Chelmite was searching an area around a streetlight. A neighbor came by and asked what he was doing. The first man said that he lost his wristwatch and was trying to find it. The neighbor said he would help and asked where the watch was dropped. In response, the first man pointed to an area some distance away. The neighbor asked why he was looking here if the watch was lost over there. The first man replied, "Because here it is light, over there I cannot see."

A look at some of the choices made by our professionally trained leaders would suggest that many of them were disciples of The Wise Men of Chelm. The decision to send all U.S. manufacturing to China because labor rates are low, even though it means Americans will not have the jobs enabling them to buy the goods shows the wisdom of the Chelmites. Thinking the economy was booming based on consumer spending, even though consumer funds were obtained from banks providing unsustainable mortgages, vehicle loans, and credit card lines.

State governments have been expanding gambling venues as a chief source of revenues to maintain critical services. However, these gambling venues have a disproportionately negative impact on those least likely to afford the financial losses. A commitment by U.S. automakers to building large gas guzzling vehicles because, "that's what people want," even though they are losing billions of dollars and foreign automakers providing smaller fuel efficient vehicles are making record profits. The Wise Men of Chelm continue their dominance of major decision-making activity. The rhetoric of immediate gratification stifles the need to find truly effective answers.

Elvis Economy

Everyday folk have also become ardent wealth extractors. Aside from those speculating on a small time level in stocks and real estate, the giant online auction website eBay has become a secondary or primary source of income. eBay claims more than 168 million registered users. There are 2 billion items listed annually on their website. Many of these items include cars and consumer products with important uses.

In addition, there are large numbers of individual buyers and sellers involved in trading baseball cards, old toys, and dishes, *Star Trek* memorabilia and, of course, Elvis paraphernalia. These items essentially have no utility or intrinsic value. However, the anticipation of enhanced worth over time leads traders to pay ever-higher prices for the Elvis swag and other trinkets.

The market is driven solely on the basis of what has been described as irrational exuberance. Irrational exuberance is a commitment of faith. One believes that whatever the price an item is worth today, someone will be willing to pay more for it tomorrow. The initial values were derived from individuals trying to get rid of Elvis souvenirs laying around in their basements, attics and garages. Micro-arbitrageurs stay busy scouring yard and estate sales in search of below market priced items.

By purchasing these objects at discounted prices and reselling them on eBay at the market rates, they are able to help the Elvis doll and sundry bauble market remain efficient and liquid. Perfect competition is based on perfect information. Since the knowledge of Elvis trifle values are limited to a number of e-Bay traders, the average homeowner wanting to clean out their basement, attic or garage is unaware of the full value of their unwanted stuff. This allows the yard sale pickers to swoop in and do their flea market arbitrage.

Just as Elvis dominates in the small business capital markets, his career legacy is emergent in the employment market. From 1990 to 2004 the percentage of individuals working in manufacturing has slipped by one-third from 18% to 12%. Jobs in finance, insurance and real estate have remained at about 7%. Similarly, construction employment has stayed at about 7% of all employed. However, employment in arts, entertainment, recreation and food service has gone from 1.4% of the total employed in 1990 to 8.5% of the total in 2004—a six fold increase. Elvis lives.

From reselling used Elvis dolls to entertainment and fast food, the Elvis Economy is based solely on faux-wealth generation. Without any value-added component, large and small traders prey on the extraction of the nation's vested wealth, whether in bank accounts, investment funds, or basements and garages. Innovation is now predicated on developing novel banking artifices and finding new tools to out-slicker the eBay bidding process. People are living in Graceland America—watching big screen TV, pushing their remotes, and becoming obese eating "greezy" burgers and fried foods.

The Elvis Economy that flourishes in many middle class communities shares many characteristics with the underground economy found in poor urban neighborhoods. The underground economy is often described using the terms, informal, parallel, alternative, illegal, and black market.

A Southside Chicago neighborhood populated by poor Black people reveals an economy based on off-the-books exchanges of services and the use of a principal local currency—food stamps. Food stamps may be discounted by small local grocery stores by 25% for prohibited purchases of alcohol and cigarettes. They may offer discounts of 50% to exchange the stamps for cash. These transactions are illicit and, thereby, concealed from the state. They are, however, necessary to provide for the needs of local residents. The interactions follow conventional patterns even though they are, essentially, short term efforts to make a buck.

Usual occupations in the underground include gypsy cab drivers, psychics, house burglars, car thieves, drug dealers, house painters, pastors, prostitutes, musicians, gun traders, pimping, auto mechanics, gang affiliated extortionists, janitors, cleaners, domestic help, waiters, entertainers, shoe shiners, tailors, and general laborers. Other types of entrepreneurial activity consist of taking boarders, selling foodstuffs, homemade clothing, counseling services, counterfeit social security cards, hairstyling, manicures, pirated music, costume jewelry, paintings, how-to manuals, and kitchen supplies.

Sales take place on the street, in parks, and at bus and train stops. Customers include police and city workers, both looking for a bargain and wanting to maintain positive community relations. Other customers are security personnel, factory employees, staff at local schools, delivery people (UPS, Postal Service), construction workers and local health care workers.

Although some of these activities, in and of themselves are not illegal, the failure to report income, obtain appropriate licensing or insurance coverage amounts to hustling since these people are compelled to operate under the radar. Hustling engenders considerable insecurity, crime and exploitative behavior. These vocations produce limited amounts of cash and significant amounts of uncertainty.[34] The nature of this activity is consistent with the spirit of the Elvis Economy.

From 1995-1999 the S&P 500 Index increased an average of almost 25% each year. The Dow Jones Industrial Average more than tripled from 3,600 in 1994 to 11,800 in 2000. During this same period, the U.S. gross domestic product increased less than 40% and corporate profits rose by less than 60%. Historically, stock market booms more closely tracked corporate earnings growth.[35] It is evident the rise in the stock market was completely disconnected from economic realities.

On January 15, 2000 the stock market began its dramatic slide. The Dow dropped from 11,800 to 7,300 on October 9, 2002. This represented a 38% loss of value in the market, which was estimated to equal 7 to 8 trillion dollars of investor cash.

The impetus behind the unprecedented rise in stock values has been described as irrational exuberance. Irrational exuberance is wishful thinking that obfuscates reality. Investors continue to support high prices based on enthusiasm rather than actual underlying stock value. Investors are drawn into the market through envy of the success of others and through a gambler's excitement. It's a way of getting something for nothing.

After the stock market crash, investor funds moved into the real estate market. Over the past several years, real estate values have reflected a similar irrational exuberance. High prices were being paid in the belief that prices would inevitably go higher yet. The increases in home prices since 1997 are much higher than increases in homeowner's incomes. In some areas of the U.S., beginning in 1985 until 2002, the median price of a home rose from 4.9 years per capita income to 7.7 years per capita income. This has made mortgage payments unsustainable for many homeowners. The real estate bubble was also supported by easily obtainable financing.

Lenders were anxious to offer higher interest loans to individuals with marginal credit. These were called subprime loans. The theory was that due to rising home prices, a foreclosure would probably not result in a loss to the lender since the house could be sold at an appreciated price sufficient for the lender to recover its loan and the related costs. Further, many existing homeowners began using the rising equity in their homes as collateral in order to refinance larger first mortgages, take a second mortgage or obtain other types of equity loans. People were using their homes as ATM machines.

Consumers spending these borrowed funds, which amounts to hundreds of billions of dollars that many will be unable to pay back, have been fueling the U.S. economy. In essence, the economy is running on fumes—borrowed money that cannot be repaid. This is another Inconvenient Truth. The borrowed funds represent wealth extraction.

With the bursting of the real estate bubble, it appears the next target of investor wealth is the commodities markets. Oil, wheat, corn, soybeans, steel, and other actively traded commodities have experienced historical price escalation in recent months. The higher prices are based on investor speculation related to probable increases in the global demand for these relatively finite products.

The price of a barrel of oil, for example, had more than doubled in 1 year between the middle of 2007 to the middle of 2008. From 2002 to 2008, the price of a barrel of oil increased from $20 to $140. Speculation in oil futures through investment funds that track the price of oil and other raw materials has risen in the past 5 years from $13 billion to $260 billion.[36]

Like other speculative activity, high prices will induce existing and potential producers to create more supply and, at the same time, encourage reduced consumption. The eventual result will be falling commodity price levels which will cause speculators to exit these markets. Prices will then fall and many investors will see their personal equity plummet, as with earlier investment bubbles.

On October 24, 1929 the New York Stock Market crashed. Between September 3, 1929 and November 13, 1929 the market lost more than half its value going from 452 to 224. Many historians have conjectured about the nature of the financial and political schemes that led to the collapse. Easy credit, buying in the margins, and the lack of adequate oversight and controls all contributed. However, it was ultimately the result of feverish and unrealistic optimism—irrational exuberance or getting something for nothing.

Within months jobs were eliminated across the country, prices on all goods and services collapsed, banks closed and mortgages were foreclosed. As the value of securities dissipated, investment and consumer spending evaporated and suicide rates increased. Across the country in 1925 the number of suicides per 100,000 of population was 12.1. By 1932 the number of suicides had risen to 17.4 per 100,000, an increase of 44%. The 1932 suicide rate in New York City was 21.3 per 100,000.[37] Suicide rates are an indicator of the severity of some underlying problem.

To obscure the Inconvenient Truth about the current uncertain financial conditions, politicians, academics, economists, and analysts continue to use established terms to describe our economic footing. However, in the Elvis Economy the descriptive terms used no longer apply. Traditional measures of the economy, such as consumer price index, unemployment rate, and productivity, do not correlate to their original meanings. The underlying structure of the economy is changing, and new metrics are needed to determine the performance of the economy in creating jobs, wages, and wealth.

As every school child knows, all pricing is based on the principle of supply and demand. It is the invisible hand of the marketplace. When supply outstrips demand, prices go down. When demand surpasses supply, prices go up. In the industrial-based or value-added economy, competitive enterprises operated according to this fundamental premise.

Rising prices were usually an indication that demand and the economy were strong.

This is not the situation today. The persistent merger and acquisition activity among large corporations in the commodity and financial sectors has eliminated the conventional competitive forces that create traditionally defined market conditions. Oil, chemical, and steel companies, as well as banks and investment banking firms have consolidated to a point where a handful of giant companies control the basic material and capital access needed in the production of all the items we use. The production companies maintain no excess capacity and are quick to use their market positions to raise prices and profit margins regardless of market conditions. Thus, inflation can occur completely outside the imperatives of the free market.

The current high oil prices have provided an ever-decreasing number of huge oil companies with windfall profits. When this occurred in the 70's, consumers were outraged and Congress passed a Windfall Profits Tax. In the Elvis Economy economists are calling the ill-gotten profitability and consequent liquidity (large companies sitting on a pile of cash) a positive factor in the economy.

Employment is the hallmark of any economy. Individuals must have the opportunity to get a job and make a living. Historically, a reduction in unemployment rates was a positive factor in the economy since it meant that more people were employed. This is not the situation today. Economists refer to a Natural Rate of Unemployment between 4 and 5%. This is based on frictional unemployment, or people changing jobs for whatever reason. Though they are experiencing temporarily unemployment, they are busy looking for new jobs.

In today's economy there are a rapidly growing number of structurally unemployed. These are people who have lost their jobs to cheap foreign labor and cannot find other employment because they have limited skill sets or employers consider them too old—over 40. Many have given up looking for work and are, therefore, not counted as unemployed. As the number of unemployed-not-looking-for-work rises, the reported unemployment rates go down. People unemployed-not-looking-for-work has been estimated at 6 to 8% of the workforce. Individuals working as little as two hours per week, even though they are seeking full-time employment, are also not considered unemployed. These "temp" workers, who represent the fastest growing segment of the labor force, have been estimated as high as 18% of the workforce.

Finally, there are the underemployed—people working 40 hours per week and earning less than a living wage. They comprise an estimated 22% of the workforce. Adding up all of these numbers, one discovers that close to 50% of the entire U.S. labor force is unemployed, unemployed-not-looking-for-work, or underemployed. Talking about an unemployment rate of 5 or 6% is highly misleading since it does not properly reflect the realities of the job market.

Productivity is another buzzword to which economists and politicians often refer. Economist and social theorist Karl Marx developed the concept of productivity more than 150 years ago. He understood that it is the basic nature of capital to invest in machines to reduce the cost of human labor. Purchasing machine tools, computers, and robots makes people more productive. A machine enables workers to produce more goods using less labor.

Throughout industrial history, the increasing level of capital investment, and the improved productivity that resulted, was a positive economic indicator. Capital investment produced important scientific and technological progress necessary for continued prosperity. The benefits of increased productivity and the consequent reduction in production costs enabled employers to pass along a portion of the ensuing profits to their employees. This resulted in a higher standard of living for everyone. Therefore increased productivity, or higher output per employee, was good for employers, workers and economic prosperity.

This is not the situation today. A significant amount of the current productivity gains achieved over the past few years are the result of lower labor costs. However, these labor cost reductions are not the result of capital investments in new machinery. They are the result of shipping well-paying U.S. jobs to China and other developing countries where workers earn only a few cents an hour. American production capacity is being rapidly abandoned. The imported goods are far cheaper, so American companies can sell more with fewer workers, therefore productivity is higher.

The problem is that there is no investment in the future and Americans are forced to work for less and endure a lower standard of living in order to compete with low wage Chinese workers. This process has been referred to as a race to the bottom. In addition, the U.S. is running more than a $300+ billion annual trade deficit with China. As a result, China is holding one and one-half trillion dollars of American debt that has to be repaid at some point.

Inadequate planning and self-deception are leading to a severe deterioration of the government's financial wellbeing. The rapidly aging population of the U.S. will include double the number of current retirees and only 15% more workers to support them by the year 2030. Instead of having 16 workers to cover each beneficiary, there will be only two. In 1950, the number of males over the age of 65 still in the labor force was at 46%. The number of males over 65 in the labor force today is closer to 17%. The female rates were 10% of those over 65 in the labor force in 1950 and 9% today.

Higher taxes, reduced health care and retirement benefits, and less spending on important needs like education and defense will be inevitable. There will be an increased likelihood of tax evasion, high inflation, political instability, high crime rates and insolvent financial markets. The American economy will be moving toward Third World status. Much of the problem lies with the 77 million aging Baby Boomers born between 1946 and 1964. The Boomers paltry rate of procreation, a retirement that will last as long as the length of a lifetime in the not too distant past and a low savings rate coupled with a propensity to consume will represent a significant challenge to the long term solvency of the economy.[38]

Growing economic insecurity is an issue that may be a less significant part of the public discourse than matters, such as unemployment and expanding income inequality. But economic insecurity has a tremendous psychological impact on individuals. Economic insecurity is a product of the trials families endure in the burgeoning "ownership society."

The impetus supporting the development of the "ownership society" is a transfer of risk from the collective to the individual. The philosophical underpinning behind this movement is a trend away from personal entitlement to a commitment to personal responsibility. Specifically, ballooning obligations for health care coverage and retirement planning formerly assumed by employers and government agencies are being converted to individual responsibilities. Social Security privatization, Medicare Reform, Health Savings Accounts, and other tax incentive programs have been proposed to have individuals deal with economic risks on their own.

As both manufacturing and middle management jobs are rapidly being shed, workers are required to accept progressively lower rates of pay and make the attendant lifestyle changes. Economic insecurity rises with this level of employment volatility. The movement towards the "ownership society" is perpetuated by an ideology of mistrust of the government and politicians. In addition, a drive by businesses to increase profitability is pressing for relief from the cost of employee benefits.[39]

The enduring political polemic is between liberal or entitlement preferences versus the conservative or personal responsibility perspective. As with any dialectic, the resolution is positioned somewhere in between the extremes. Nineteenth century craft production yielded to the efficiencies of mass production. Huge capital investments in plants and equipment enabled unskilled workers right off the farm to produce vast amounts of increasingly higher quality goods at progressively lower prices. The evolution of mass production, in terms of the increased level of capital investment and technological improvements, inevitably led to a situation of overproduction.

Overproduction was the cause of economic depression which translated into mass unemployment, business closures, and bank failures. An oversupply led to lower prices which made companies unprofitable. Many companies went out of business. This created a shortage of product that eventually started pushing prices higher. Flattening the unsettling boom to bust and back business cycles could only be accomplished through government intervention. Mechanisms to exercise control over money supply and interest rates, as well as the creation of a welfare state providing a safety net for unemployed workers were initiated beginning in the early 1930s during the Great Depression.[40] Thus, markets operated independently, but required some government regulation to make the business cycle highs and lows less extreme and potentially less harmful to wage earners.

Since the early 1970s the United States has moved in a decidedly conservative direction. The effect of the altered political landscape has been a widening of the income gap, as wealth becomes concentrated at the top. The richest 1% of the population saw their income more than double between 1979 and 2003. During the same period, household income for the bottom quintile rose by only 1%. CEO salaries were 27 times the average worker pay in 1973. By 2005 CEO salaries were 262 times the average worker's.

Job growth is highest in arts, entertainment, recreation, and food services.[41] Many of the positions available in these categories are nonunion, low wage and often temporary. The restaurant industry is the nation's largest employer with more than 3.5 million fast food workers, who are minimum wage earners. In the late 1990s the minimum wage was worth 27% less than in the 1970s. Annual employee turnover in the fast food industry is 300-400%.[42] The average employee lasts 3 to 4 months. Foodservice equipment is developed to be intuitive so that it is easier to do something right than wrong. The goal in the industry is "zero training," as opposed to paying a living wage and lengthening employment longevity.

Another consequence of conservative political proclivities is a concentration of various industries into national and international enterprises. Retail sales have become concentrated among large global store chains. They have doubled their market share since 1996 to 30% of the amount Americans spend annually.

Wal-Mart alone accounts for more than 1 out of every 10 dollars spent on food, clothing, toys, and hardware. Its 1.5 million employees are notoriously paid poverty level wages with no health care benefits. Further, in counties where Wal-Mart stores open, overall employment actually drops.[43] Big-Box retailers, unlike local stores, do not contract for services in the communities in which their stores are located. Accounting, legal services and advertising firms are hired at the national level.

Decent labor rates are maintained through government and union intervention.[44] With union membership and influence waning and the government prioritizing business interests over those of workers, prospects for secure, well-paying jobs are continually being reduced. These realities and the financial difficulties they cause in many students' homes eclipse flimsy psychological strategies that may be employed to deal with classroom disciplinary problems.

One of the reasons for the decline in union membership is management's increasing ability to restrain union organizing activities. Employer-friendly labor laws and probusiness federal regulatory boards have been the source of policy changes that have resulted in only minor punishments to employers that obstruct organizing drives by improperly intimidating or coercing workers. Workers have failed to effectively resist management influences. The reason is that much unionizing activity occurs in workplaces, such as retail, food, and low-level health care where annual worker turnover is high. Wal-Mart annual worker turnover is 50% and McDonald's is as high as 400%. Workers are often unwilling to risk the negative consequences of participating in a union organizing campaign if they do not believe they will be employed long enough to enjoy the benefits of their efforts. This is a Catch-22, in that, it is the low wages paid by those industries that largely contribute to the high employee turnover.

Workers in industries where jobs are readily exportable are unlikely to support union activity if they are led to believe that their factory or backroom operation may close down domestic operations if union efforts are successful.[45] In industrial scenarios where wages are better and employee turnover is minimal, efforts by companies to fight unionization are based on a threat to close plants and move jobs offshore.

Aside from low wage food industry employees and traditional manufacturing workers, another substantial group of workers is described as the Creative Class. More than 30% of the U.S. workforce or 38 million workers are members of the Creative Class. Creative professionals engage in occupations that include scientists, artists, engineers, designers, writers, musicians, and creative people in business, education, health care, and law. Members are purveyors of creativity, which is a basic source of economic growth. Creativity inheres to individuals not companies. In a creativity-driven economy both corporate entities and geography become collateral considerations.

The human and social capital acquired by individuals is compelling. Targeting an individual's creativity diminishes the importance of dress codes, lifestyles, schedules, and typical hierarchical management imperatives. Virtual enterprises based on online interaction are the new workplaces. In order to fully and successfully participate in Creative Class ventures, it is necessary to develop both a store of useful knowledge and information, as well as the ability to innovate and synthesize. The creative ethos is a significant departure from the conformist ethos of the past.[46]

Despite the large and growing number of workers in the Creative Class, their ranks like those of their blue collar predecessors are also subject to transfer offshore. A recent Princeton University study suggests 22% to 29% of all U.S. jobs are offshorable within the next 10 to 20 years. Consumer demand for more and less expensive goods continues to drive jobs to developing countries where labor costs are low. With the U.S. manufacturing sector having lost millions of jobs to offshoring in the past 2 decades, the remaining jobs are primarily in the service sector.

Service sector jobs can be divided into two categories. The distinguishing factor between the two categories is the ability to deliver the service electronically over long distances. Personally-delivered jobs range from janitors, waiters, taxi drivers and day care workers to surgeons and top management positions. Impersonally-delivered jobs include call center operators, insurance claims adjusters, and data entry clerks to accountants, scientists, and software producers.

Advancements in information and communications technology (ICT) facilitate the offshoring of impersonally-delivered jobs. The American workforce consists of over 140 million jobs. As the workforce in China and in India become more advanced, the number of creative U.S. jobs that could potentially be offshored to those countries might reach at least 30 million.[47]

A realistic assessment of the economy is crucial to any evaluation of the educational system. The purpose of education is to prepare children to assume adult responsibilities. Those responsibilities include the prospect of work and becoming a good citizen. Types of work and definitions of citizenship are determined by the all-encompassing economic imperatives. Further, in order to engage children in their lessons, the connection between school and real world expediency must be clear and unequivocal.

Children, through their exposure to the media and adults generally, develop a personal agenda at increasingly earlier stages. If school is not in accord with students' priorities it will not be successful in influencing their behavior. For example, in destitute towns from New Jersey to Mississippi, gambling was introduced on the premise that the tax revenues would be used to fund education initiatives for the benefit of young people. But from the students' perspective, how much education are they going to think they need if the available work is likely to be in a gambling casino? In the past, students anticipating work in a manufacturing related occupation would more likely be inclined to embrace a particular skill set offered in school if they thought it would be useful to them as an adult.

These skill sets would range from engineering and management to mechanical and shop proficiency.

The breach in U.S. post-war economic prosperity occurred in 1973. Economists have established 1973 as the beginning of the decline of the American standard of living for several reasons. The most prominent was that it was the beginning of the present long term decline in real wages. Real Wages are defined as wages currently paid that are adjusted for inflation. Since 1973, with the exception of a brief period in the late 90s during the stock market bubble, real wages paid to American workers have been dropping. This means workers are earning less than they made more than 3½ decades ago.

Real wages have traditionally tracked advances in productivity. As technological progress and capital investment enabled workers to produce more and, thereby, generate increased profits for their employers, labor usually received some portion of the benefits. As the result of improvements in productivity, real wages from 1950 to 1973 increased by almost 50%.

Despite continued productivity gains, between 1974 and 1994 real wages declined by 20%. Unlike the past, U.S. workers were not the beneficiaries of the efficiencies they achieved. Profits were retained by corporate ownership. The failure to share newly created profits with workers has resulted in a higher concentration of wealth at the top. Presently the wealth controlled by the top 1% of U.S. households is 38%. The wealth possessed by the bottom 80% of U.S. households is 17%.

Unions were the principal mechanisms to assure labor their equitable portion of corporate profitability. Through the 50s and 60s union membership reached 33% of the workforce. Currently, it is about 7% of nongovernmental employees. Trade liberalization agreements beginning with the General Agreement on Tariffs and Trade (GATT) in 1947 through additional import concessions during the Kennedy administration led to a significant reduction in U.S. manufacturing.

In addition to the reversal of wage growth in 1973, there were a number of domestic and international shocks occurring that year. These included the opening of the Watergate trials. Several of President Nixon's aides were indicted for breaking into Democratic Party headquarters. A number of these individuals were imprisoned and the President was forced to resign the following year.

In 1973 the U.S. Supreme Court ruled that an individual's right to privacy is broad enough to encompass a woman's decision to terminate her pregnancy. The *Roe v. Wade* judgment legalized abortions. A substantial and vocal opposition movement initiated by several religious organizations responded to this event. A passionate debate continues over the issue of abortion rights. The abortion issue has become a part of U.S.

political debate with one party demanding candidates supporting a woman's right to choose and the other requiring candidates to support the rescission of abortion rights. The political spotlighting of abortion rights has helped to deflect attention from declining income distribution equity.

In January 1973 Nixon halted all offensive action in Vietnam. In November, Congress passed the War Powers Act preventing any further military action. The North later overran South Vietnam. America lost the war. In October 1973 the Arab-Israeli conflict began. For America's support of Israel, the oil producing Arab nations restricted petroleum exports. The result was a gasoline shortage, a tripling of the cost of a gallon of gas and long lines at fuel pumps. Today's high oil prices can be traced to the events in the Middle East in 1973 when Arab oil producing companies began to impose their priorities on world markets. Increased oil revenues fortified their influence.

With the passage of the General Agreement on Tariffs and Trade (GATT) and the Kennedy Round of 1962 which slashed tariffs and reduced import restrictions, David Rockefeller, president of Chase Manhattan Bank and his brother David, Governor of New York, actively promoted a major office development in Downtown Manhattan.

The purpose of the project was to establish New York as a leader in the newly expanded free trade arena. The project would enhance the image of New York, as well as greatly improve property values in the area. After many years of planning and execution, their vision was realized. On a rainy Wednesday, April 4, 1973 in front of a crowd of 4,000 people they attended the formal opening and dedication of the World Trade Center.

Replacing American manufacturing with the Elvis Economy is not a sustainable initiative. As U.S. invested wealth continues to be extracted and dissipated, it will be necessary to implement a long term, constructive economic plan. A strategy of this nature will not be adequately defined by sound bites or overly simplified, sugar-coated political declarations. A realistic approach that confronts the need for foundational change is the only way to go.

Communist China

Virtually all of U.S. manufacturing has been relocated to one country—China. The willingness of the Chinese government to aggressively support the expansion of its manufacturing capabilities and keep its workers' wages obscenely low has guaranteed the transition from U.S. based production to importation from China. The result is millions of lost American jobs and an annual trade deficit in the hundreds of billions of dollars.

In 1997 the U.S. trade deficit with China was $50 billion. By 2007 the annual trade deficit with China, ballooned to $256 billion[48]—a 600% increase in a short 10 years. The total 2007 U.S. trade deficit was $712 billion. In 2001 the total U.S. trade deficit was $365 billion, or about one-half the current amount.

Since 1997, approximately 6 million manufacturing jobs were lost in the U.S. In addition to blue collar workforce losses, supervisors, managers and engineers were displaced. China now holds more than $1.7 trillion in U.S. debt that must be repaid at some point. Despite Americans' eagerness to turn over millions of jobs, as well as their entire industrial and technological base to Chinese companies and the Chinese people, most know little about that country.

At 3.7 million square miles China's area is virtually identical to that of the United States. The population of the United States. is 300 million. The population of China is estimated at 1.5 billion. The official count is somewhat less because people who violate China's One Child law hide excess children. The purpose of the One Child law, which was instituted in the late 1970s, is to control the birth rate. The official position is that, "There are too many Chinese." To enforce the One Child Law, sanctions range from forced abortions to reduced benefits to families having more than one child. This includes withholding schooling.

Forced abortions can take place into the eighth month of pregnancy. Fetuses are killed by injections into the uterus. If the fetus is still alive when removed from the uterus, it is drowned in a bucket of water. The injections and drownings are conducted by government-employed nurses, who also act to uncover the illegal pregnancies. As a result, during the census count many children are hidden to avoid facing the unseemly consequences.[49]

Since there is no pension system in China, rural Chinese have a preference for boys. Sons are expected to work in order to provide income for their parents in old age. Daughters are expected to marry and care for their children. Because families are only permitted one child, in some rural provinces there are 140 boys born for every 100 girls. Nationwide the official gender ratio is 118 boys born for every 100 girls. This contrasts with a worldwide gender ratio where the number is 105 boys born per 100 girls.

The Chinese gender imbalance is the result of expectant mothers using ultrasound and other technologies which enable Chinese women to abort female fetuses. Where medical screening devices are not available, female infanticide is not uncommon. The unbalanced proportion of female births is causing a dearth of marriageable women. In order to rectify the gender imbalance, the Chinese government is now attempting to offer financial incentives totaling $15 monthly in pension benefits for families not to abort their female fetuses.[50] The government estimates that China will need an additional 30 million brides by 2020. A covert solution to the marriageable women shortage is the importation of North Korean refugee women by middlemen who sell them to local Chinese peasants.

China's Great Wall, which was started in 200 B.C., symbolized its desire to resist Western influences including religion. Only 5% of the population identifies with any religion—Christian, Buddhist, or Muslim. The remaining 95% are officially atheist. China's religious and cultural persecution of Tibet's Buddhist population forced its leader, the Dalai Lama, and 100,000 of his followers to flee to India, despite Tibet's status as an autonomous region of China.

In 1999 China outlawed the Falun Gong sect, a popular religious movement combining Buddhism and Taoism. The ancient Chinese Confucian philosophy and Taoism were focused on order, duties and finding one's place both in society and in the universe. The lack of a monotheistic faith and the absence of a divine truth have resulted in a state of moral relativity among the Chinese people. China's unwieldy size and totalitarian Communist rule has led to a dependence on rapacious officials to maintain order and collect governmental remunerations. A deficient moral compass and unchecked authority has created governance typified by corruption that requires graft for all basic services to be extracted from those least able to afford the payoffs.

The horror that can result from official corruption was prominently displayed in the aftermath of the devastating May, 2008 Chinese earthquake. Thousands of young students were killed after close to 7,000 classrooms collapsed. Many of the parents of children who died alleged that corrupt officials allowed substandard construction of the government buildings in exchange for payoffs. Inadequate use of steel rebar in concrete pillars, a lack of emergency exists and deficient foundations assured the conditions that lead to the children's deaths. In a number of situations the buildings around the schools were left undamaged by the quake.[51]

It is estimated that the May, 2008 Chinese earthquake will claim close to 100,000 lives and leave millions of Chinese citizens homeless. Though the occurrence of earthquakes, which are massive natural catastrophes, are generally viewed as being outside the influence of mankind, unrestrained industrialization may have played a part in this disaster.

In November, 2007 an unusual amount of seismic activity was recorded in the area around the Three Gorges Dam after a nearby landslide killed over 30 people. Construction of the Three Gorges Dam began in 1994 and is expected to be completed in 2009. It is the largest hydropower project in the world creating a reservoir that is 386,000 square miles. The water in the reservoir is over 500 feet deep in an area that was previously dry rock. The weight of this massive amount of water is creating a downward pressure that is triggering a collapse of the Earth's crust and, thereby, drawing in the surrounding mountains.[52]

In response to the horrible and unnecessary deaths of 10,000 school children, many of the grieving parents demanded accountability for the poorly constructed buildings after thousands of classrooms collapsed in the earthquake. However, Chinese government officials chose to create a façade of accord rather than pursue accusations of corruption or negligence. Government officials bought the parents' silence with payments of $8,800 in cash and a pension for each parent in the amount of $5,600. To receive these payouts, parents were obligated to sign contracts affirming their future silence. Parents refusing to sign the contracts have been detained by the police.[53]

In September, 2008 official corruption resulted in a scandal that was responsible for the deaths of 4 children and the sickening of more than 50,000 others. Baby milk formulas and milk products produced by some of the country's largest dairy makers were contaminated by an industrial chemical, melamine, which is used to make plastics and fertilizer. The infant dairy products were spiked with the melamine to artificially inflate the protein counts of water-diluted milk. Consumer complaints about the tainted milk were covered up for months until the Olympics were over.[54]

It is estimated that more than 200 million Chinese workers are exposed to dangerous working conditions. In 2005 there were more than 600,000 cases of pneumoconiosis—debilitating lung diseases. Most were related to workers in the coal mining industry. More than two-thirds of China's energy is provided by coal. In 2006 close to 5,000 workers died in coal mines. China's jewelry and gemstone industry is also responsible for thousands of cases of silicosis caused by inhaling dust created in processing precious stones. More than 5,000 deaths annually in China are attributed to silicosis. There are many "cancer villages" across China. These are towns populated by widows of husbands working in the same toxic industries.[55]

The same barbarous lack of respect for human life is also evident in their treatment of animals, as evidenced by the Chinese tradition of the "Monkey Feast."

Do you know what people in China eat when they have the money? my mother began. They buy into a monkey feast. The eaters sit around a thick wood table with a hole in the middle. Boys bring in the monkey at the end of a pole. Its neck is in a collar at the end of the pole, and it is screaming. Its hands are tied behind it. They clamp the monkey into the table; the whole table fits like another collar around its neck. Using a surgeon's saw, the cooks cut a clean line in a circle at the top of its head. To loosen the bone, they tap it with a tiny hammer and wedge here and there with a silver pick. Then an old woman reaches out her hand to the monkey's face and up to its scalp, where she tufts some hairs and lifts of the lid of the skull. The eaters spoon out the brains.[56]

An ardent nationalism, a fanatical resentment of Japan and an attachment to Taiwan have served as substitutes for religious ideals embraced by the Chinese people. Taiwan had been part of China until 1895 when the Japanese colonized the island. The colonization lasted until 1945. In 1949, after a Communist victory in the Chinese civil war, the defeated Guomindang withdrew to Taiwan. The Chinese believe that the century of humiliation will end when Taiwan is reunified with mainland China.[57]

Chinese nationalism was put on display during the events preceding the 2008 Olympics to be held in China's capital, Beijing. Peaceful protests by Tibetan monks loyal to the Dali Lama seeking Tibetan independence were crushed by the Chinese military which killed a number of the protesting monks. Shortly after these incidents, an Olympic tradition of carrying the Olympic torch through a number of European countries and the U.S. resulted in massive protests directed at Chinese crimes in Tibet and China's broader human rights record.

In response to the worldwide protests, the Chinese government proclaimed that the actions were fomented by an anti-China Western press. China views the 2008 Olympics as symbolic of the rise to its rightful place at the center of world affairs. Disruptions in the world torch relay created a nationalistic rage in China that resulted in counter-protests around the country and among expatriate Chinese around the world, both on the Internet and on the street. This rage is directed at the West which the Chinese believe is attempting to deny China its destiny as a world leader.[58] It is this level of nationalism that has been responsible for both twentieth century world wars.

After more than a decade of civil war, on October 1, 1949 Mao Zedong declared victory for his Soviet-supported Communist regime. In 1950 Mao sent troops into North Korea to assist in the capture of South Korea. The United States defended South Korea against this invasion. The conflict lasted until 1953 at a cost of 54,000 American dead and 103,000 Americans wounded. From 1954 until 1973, the United States was engaged in a war in Vietnam. Communist-led North Vietnam invaded the South with the support of Chinese armaments and technical assistance. The conflict in Vietnam resulted in more than 50,000 American casualties.

In an effort to appease China, President Nixon visited the country in 1972. President Carter announced diplomatic relations in 1979. By November 2001, China was admitted to the World Trade Organization as a full trading partner. As long as China continues to produce inexpensive product for American consumers, there is little political appeal in confronting the past.

Despite its huge investment in industry, 50% of Chinese workers or 750,000,000 people are still engaged in agriculture. These subsistence level farmers produce primarily for their own needs. Many of these peasants have left the countryside to join the 22% of the labor force in industry.

A factory job offers living quarters and a temporary-residence permit migrants need to stay out of jail. Some workers are paid as little as $24 a month and charged $16 a month for food and lodging in a crowded dorm. The minimum wage is set at only $45 per month, yet it is often violated by employers. Workers are frequently physically abused and/or fined for infractions like taking too long in the bathroom, walking too fast or talking back to managers. Paying less then minimum wage and failing to pay overtime after 44 hours per week are some of the abuses which American retailers and consumers allegedly disapprove.

It has also recently been discovered that thousands of Chinese children have been sold as slave laborers in factories producing toys, textiles and electronics for store like Wal-Mart. A number of these children were sold by their parents. Many of the children were auctioned based on body-type. Others were tricked or kidnapped by employment agencies and forced to work 300 hours a month for little money.[59]

To avoid the possibility of having their maltreatment of workers exposed as a result of inspections from U.S. companies, there is a large and visible consultant industry in China based on deceiving the inspectors. Managers at the shady companies are instructed on how to create fake but authentic-looking records and told to remove any workers with grievances from the factory on the day of the audit.

For the past several years companies like Wal-Mart and Nike have insisted that inspections of Chinese factories making their product are acting humanely based on regular on-site assessments. However, during this period Chinese factory managers have become expert at misleading auditors.[60]

China maintains a rigid social class system through a process of registration and identification called *hukou*. *Hukou* determines where you are able to receive services, such as health care and education. *Hukou* cannot be moved from the city one's family comes from. The *hukou* system contains people by preventing them from traveling or changing jobs. It is inherited and defines issues of finance, citizenship, and identity for all Chinese. Though it is possible to get temporary residence permits in different areas, it is virtually impossible to changes one's *hukou*.[61]

Even for those individuals able to improve their position and save some money, the prospect of starting their own business is nonexistent. China is ruled through political authoritarianism. There is no independent judiciary or contract law. All rules are established at the whim of the government. Those inclined to protest these conditions are subject to arrest and imprisonment. In 1989 as students occupied Beijing's Tiananmen Square calling for reforms, hundreds were shot dead by government troops and tanks. Since the end of World War II in 1945, the United States has maintained a significant military presence on the Pacific island of Okinawa which is part of Japan. Twenty thousand Marines are stationed there. Their primary function is to keep an eye on China's expansionist policies in the region, particularly regarding Taiwan.

Our current annual trade deficit with China is in excess of $256 billion. This means they have $256+ billion of our money to spend on their military, technology and infrastructure. We have a bunch of stuff that could have been made in the United States. The blind faith our political leaders have in globalization is deceptive. The 3 million+ U.S. manufacturing jobs lost since 2000 were not a result of globalization. They disappeared because of *Chinaization*. Since entry to World Trade Organization the Chinese economy has been growing at warp speed. Annual growth has been estimated 11%. This contrasts with U.S. growth, which from 1982 to 2002 GDP growth averaged around 3%. Currently it is below 1%.[62]

China's growth has been accomplished at the expense of the United States, Germany, Japan, and all other Western industrialized democratic nations. Last year the economies of both Japan and Germany, the world's second and third largest, contracted. Workers' wage rates in those countries are at or above U.S. wage rates. Both countries' economies are heavily dependent on manufacturing for export. Yet imports were growing faster than exports because of an influx of Chinese goods. U.S. growth has been propped up by its huge defense expenditures—half trillion-dollar annual budget, deficits not withstanding.

The U.S. has seen real wages drop steadily for the past 30 years. German workers, who traditionally earn more than U.S. workers, have recently had to increase their workweek by five hours with no increase in pay. How has China accomplished this remarkable expansion? In a word—steal. They have stolen human capital and intellectual capital. Using hundreds of millions of peasants from the countryside, the Chinese government makes use of incredibly cheap labor, paying literally pennies per hour. Factory workers live like dogs on these wages. Their movements are limited by the government, and they have no hope of improving their conditions.

The second component necessary to create industrial expansion is intellectual capital obtained through deliberate research and product development. Research and development requires a large and long-term financial investment in both training manpower and supporting people doing the work. China has circumvented this investment. It has done so by encouraging counterfeiting. Not only have Chinese companies pirated billions of dollars worth of software and CDs, but also they have produced many fake products from pharmaceuticals to motorcycles. They steal, not only proprietary technologies, but also produce fake branded products, like auto parts and fashion apparel. Tens of billions of dollars in investment in both product research and advertising to create brands are simply stolen.

Suing the Chinese companies in Chinese courtrooms is an exercise in futility. The illegal products are not produced in somebody's basement or garage. They are made in large visible plants. There is no question this activity is promoted by the Chinese government. Their failure to close these operations is clear evidence of their complicity.

At present there are more than 600,000 foreign students attending American universities. These students contribute over $14 billion to the U.S. economy. They come from countries around the world with a large number coming from India and China. The foreign students are extremely important to colleges since they do not require grants, scholarships, and in-state tuition discounts offered to local students. The foreigners pay full tuition, fees, and housing costs.

In recent years China has invested heavily in its research institutions. By offering discounted costs to students in developing countries, China is becoming a destination for many foreign students. Its foreign enrollments have risen from 45,000 in 1999 to 141,000 in 2005.[63] A substantial reduction in revenues paid by foreign students will have a severe negative impact on many university budgets. These losses will have to be made-up by passing through price increases or reducing services.

As the industrial power of China's totalitarian Communist government strengthens, it is clear it intends to use that power politically. It has recently passed a law enabling the use of force to intervene in Taiwan's independence. Taiwan has a democratically elected government. Its democracy and independence was established almost 60 years ago. It is also an ally of the United States. The new law was plainly established as a rebuke to U.S. military power. Recently, China has also confronted Japan, another close U.S. ally, over a disputed neighboring island that is thought to contain oil reserves. The decision of U.S. citizens to transfer their wealth to China must be based on a thorough understanding of the Chinese political establishment which represents a clear economic and military threat to America.

There are economists who claim that America is benefiting from the trade relationship with China. Although there is a significant transfer of U.S. wealth which is creating a tremendous trade deficit, Americans are able to enjoy inexpensive Chinese-made products that they might not otherwise be able to afford.

In 1626 Peter Minuit, the director of New Netherland, was actively engaged in colonizing the area which is now New York City. To defend itself against Spanish rule, Minuit sought to expand its land holdings in order to produce agricultural products for European markets. Manhattan Island was the property of the Lenape Indians. In May or June of 1626 Minuit purchased Manhattan Island from the Lenapes for $24 worth of trinkets. In August of 1626 Minuit bought Staten Island for an unknown amount of trinkets. These trinkets consisted of cloth, kettles, axes, hoes, drilling awls, Jew's Harps and other wares.[64] By continuing to run up trillions of dollars in debt to China the United States is similarly selling out for cloth and trinkets.

CHAPTER 6

SOLUTION

The e-OneRoom Schoolhouse

The only legitimate solution to the evanescence of American wealth and stature is the restoration of its manufacturing base. There has to be an industrial renaissance in America. However, the new industrial age will look very different from the industrial age that began two centuries ago. It will be a kinder and gentler industrial age where the prospect for well-paying jobs is no longer weighed against reduced health and safety considerations and increased environmental harm.

Launching the new age of industrialization cannot be accomplished by government decree. It will be an incremental process begun with a powerful entrepreneurial spirit. At the moment ideological and technically trained industrial entrepreneurs are few and far between. It is, therefore, necessary to specifically cultivate a new generation prepared for the intellectual challenges a re-industrialization presents. The preparation will occur in the e-OneRoom Schoolhouse.

The e-OneRoom Schoolhouse is designed to facilitate individual learning in a classroom environment that is increasingly sullied by distraction. Dogged disciplinary obstacles substantially reduce critical hours of instruction and time-on-task. These problems additionally impede the progress of otherwise engaged students. The present educational institution archetype has ceased to be effective. The egg-crate model replaced

Education Redux: How to Make Schools Relevant to Our Children and Our Future,
pp. 105–128

the one-room schoolhouse more than a century ago. The prevailing design of one classroom/one teacher/one lesson plan and multiple students had its purpose in the modernist order. Modernism's division of labor reinforced structure and conformity.

However, postmodern imperatives demand significant changes to reflect the exigencies of the new landscape. Postmodernism highlights individual choices and initiatives. Relativity has replaced universally accepted behaviors and attitudes. The egg-crate scheme fails to acknowledge this elemental transformation.

Modernism expresses the impact of historical industrialization, science and technology on social structures. In modernism, many residual zones of the nature of old persist. There is still a referent. However, in postmodernism, the modernization is complete and nature is gone.[1] Postmodernism is not a unified movement or system of thought and ideas. It is complex and multiform and resistant to a reductive explication. Postmodernism is simply something "after" modernity.

Educational theory and practice are founded on modernism's discourse and implicit assumptions. Included are enlightenment ideals of critical reason, rationality, and self-direction. Postmodernist notions of de-centered subject constructed by language, desire, and the unconscious contradict modernism's structure.

It is challenging to relate postmodernism to education. Education is involved with the production, organization, and dissemination of knowledge. Postmodernism challenges existing concepts, structures and hierarchies of knowledge.[2] In postmodernism the consumer of information is also the creator of that information. The ability to actively engage that which is culturally produced and transmitted makes the receiver the "producer." Despite the interactivity, it is still necessary to establish a foundation for finding certainty. Knowledge and learning are rooted in modernist discourse. However, the manner in which knowledge is conveyed must acknowledge postmodern perspectives.

Postmodern perspectives are reified in the new media. While teachers struggle to attain basic skills in the new media, the Millenials or Net Generation children or *New Kids* are perfectly comfortable with digital technology. *New Kids*, or the 81 million children born between 1977 and 1997, which some call the Baby Boom Echo, are the first cohort to grow up surrounded by computers, the Internet, cell phones, Nintendos, iPods, and so forth. The *New Kids* are more confident with technological innovation than their parents and teachers. They are able to use digital media to impose culture on the older generation.

Users of the older broadcast media were viewers—there was no interaction. The new media is interactive. Learners develop quicker when they control media rather than being passive observers. Students interacting with media create nonhierarchical work habits. These translate into important workforce skills since the work of the future will not be characterized by the bureaucratic-hierarchical paradigm of the industrial era.[3]

It is necessary for students to acquire the ability to perform at higher order levels of the cognitive domain. The levels were described by a group of educational psychologists.[4] They identified six levels from simple recall at the lowest level to evaluation at the highest level. Popularly known as Bloom's Taxonomy, the first level begins with knowledge, which includes those behaviors that emphasize the remembering by recognition or recall of material. The second level is comprehension. When students receive a communication, they understand its literal message. The third level is application. As an example, application is the ability to apply scientific principles to new situations. The fourth level is analysis. Analysis consists of the breakdown of material into its constituent parts and understanding the relationship between the parts.

The fifth level is synthesis. Synthesis is the ability to assemble the parts to form a whole. The elements can be combined to form a structure not previously evident. Finally, the top level is evaluation. Evaluation is defined as the ability to make judgments using criteria for appraising the accuracy and effectiveness of information.

Much of the testing done in schools requires students to think at the lowest possible level—the recall of information. Effective schooling should enable a child to advance through higher levels of intellectual behavior to become effective learners. Developing critical thinking skills is not just important to the ability to progress through institutions of higher education, but higher order thinking is crucial to the learning process in all grades.

Any solution to boost the educational achievement level of U.S. students has to include progress in both individual academic performance and the expansion of useful and necessary social skills. The importance of the social facet can be described as a need to develop social capital. There are three types of capital—physical, human, and social. Physical capital is identified as tangible wealth, such as cash, real property or personal property. The accumulation of physical capital is the objective which is easiest to understand and is the goal of most individuals.

The second type of capital is human capital. Human capital refers to property of individuals, such as education or specific training and work experience. Human capital is an asset possessed by an individual that is necessary to create a new venture or starting a new job. Social capital is the third type of capital. It is the connection among individuals—social networks and the norms of reciprocity. The old adage, "It's not what you know, but who you know," is an off-handed reference to the importance of social capital.

There has been a significant decline in social capital which is evidenced by diminished civic engagement. For example, activities like voter participation are down by 25% in the last 40 years. Membership in community organizations has decreased substantially. Groups like the Elks, Kiwanis, Lions, and Moose have seen membership decline by 45% to 70% from their highs. These organizations contributed significantly to the welfare of all of their members, as well as providing vital services to their respective communities.

Among workers, union membership in nongovernmental industries has dropped by more than 75% over a 50-year period beginning in the early 1950s. Just as expanded physical and human capital investment improve productivity, a greater investment in social capital benefits both private and public enterprise. The loss of membership in community groups has been the result of a re-orientation from group to individual preferences. Individual preferences are fulfilled through expanded utilization of cable television and iPods, not social involvement.[5] Internet social networking sites like MySpace and Facebook are oriented toward the articulation of individual exploits and preferences rather than facilitating any meaningful group endeavors.

The lack of civic engagement, limited social networking, a general disregard for the broader concerns of the community and the inability to relate individual needs to the complementary and reciprocal needs of others is, in large measure, the single most devastating phenomenon faced by contemporary society.

Reasons for the erosion of social capital and concomitant reduction in community involvement include time pressures due to employment requirements, women in the workforce, residential mobility, suburban sprawl and commuting, disruption of marriages and loosening of family bonds and, the introduction of new media from television to the Internet. Civic disengagement is closely related to the pervasive and addictive nature of television watching. Generational change and lost traditions of civic involvement are also a major contributor to lower rates of community participation.

Levels of social capital have a direct effect on educational attainment. Studies indicate that schools exhibiting a communal and relational trust have a substantial advantage in their ability to provide their students with the best educational opportunities. Academic achievement is closely related to the strength of a network that includes the school, parents and community engagement. Involvement in nonvirtual peer social networks and extracurricular activities are powerful predictors of college success.

A dialectic may be constructed with collectivist or community preferences at one extreme and individual prerogative as the antithesis. The analysis can represent the distinction between *Gemeinschaft* and

Gesellschaft. These notions have become essential concepts in the study of the social sciences. They were defined by Ferdinand Tönnies in 1887.

Gemeinschaft refers to the archetypes of social relationships, such as kinship, friendship and neighborhood. These relationships are conditioned by a natural or integral will which is rooted in temperament and character, as well as an instinctive affinity that creates community bonds. The highly personal nature of relationships is a characteristic of preindustrial societies. *Gesellschaft* refers to individual behavior shaped by rationalism, which has a more individualistic nature. The introduction of machines and a division of labor engenders new sets of social norms. Relationships are based on formal contracts and legal considerations.[6]

The analysis described by Tönnies is similar to the notion of organic and mechanical solidarity explained by Durkheim. The discussions of solidarity or communal interaction are analogous to the concept of market channel suboptimization. Market channel systems, which correlate to solving physical distribution and pricing problems, establish relationships between suppliers, retailers and their customers.

Market channel systems are consistent with the concept of the invisible hand. The invisible hand is an Adam Smith creation describing the process of free trade where consumers and producers make independent buying and selling decisions based on their personal best interests. As the theory goes, the market will settle on distribution and pricing arrangements that are beneficial to each individual participant and, consequently, beneficial to the community as a whole. A systems approach recognizes that an individual firm's objectives can only be achieved by acknowledging the mutual interdependence of each of the participants in a given series of transactions or along a market channel.

The goal of a physical distribution system is to maximize customer service while carefully controlling the costs of transporting goods from the point of manufacture to the final customer. To reach this objective, it is necessary to avoid suboptimization. Suboptimization is a situation where one of the actors in the distribution chain attempts to improve their profitability by reducing their costs at the expense of another actor in the chain. For example, a manufacturer demanding that a retailer maintain larger than advisable inventories so that the manufacturer can reduce their inventory levels may result in cost savings for the manufacturer, but it occurs at a cost to the retailer. If the manufacturer controlled its production schedules adequately, it would not have excess inventory and the manufacturer would not find it necessary to suboptimize the system.[7]

The concept of suboptimization represents a merger between organic and mechanical solidarity, as well as between *gemeinschaft* and *gesellschaft*. It serves to rationalize personal relationships by illustrating the self-serving benefits of acting as a community.

A new approach to education would include a curriculum to foster the growth of social competencies, as well as academic performance. The two have an integral relationship. The e-OneRoom Schoolhouse paradigm, as a replacement for the egg-crate school design now in place, can serve both purposes—effective individualized instruction and social development. The egg crate school set-up has led to failures in both student academic performance and in students' ability to attain social capital.

The traditional one-room schoolhouse included students from the entire K-12 range. Naturally, it was required for them to work on an individual basis since they were at varying ages and levels of competence. Each student had a text and workbook matched to his or her capabilities, not necessarily their age. In this set-up both the teacher and other students who had a more expert knowledge of particular subject matter assisted others in the instructional process.

Teachers made certain each learner was making suitable progress. The fundamental nature of this student interaction, with older helping younger and more competent assisting less competent, provided important training in social skills. In addition, specific exercises requiring participation by all students contributed to the development of social capital. The traditional one-room arrangement has to be combined with state-of-the-art electronic, graphic and curriculum capabilities in the e-OneRoom Schoolhouse.

Teachers

It is not possible to engage in a discussion about classroom dynamics without identifying the role of teachers. Teachers, to varying degrees, are the classroom generals. Their level of competence in the subject matter presented and the ability to control student behavior lays the foundation for likely student achievement. The current political initiative, No Child Left Behind, places almost the entire burden for increasing student performance at the feet of teachers. Although this is not a realistic solution, it is important to carefully examine how teachers can be more effective.

There are several reasons people are attracted to a career in teaching. These include the Interpersonal Theme, which calls for steady contact with young people. There is the Service Theme which relates to the special status of teachers given for their performance of a unique mission in society. The Continuation Theme for those who become so attached to school, they do not want to leave. The Material Benefits Theme that includes an appropriate salary, especially based on working fewer days per year, and usually health and pension benefits. The Theme of Time Compatibility correlates to the special schedules teachers work. These schedules feature numerous holidays, which include summer vacation time, as well as the ability to finish work in mid-afternoons. Two other important benefits are social mobility and employment security.

The special mission of teachers gives their occupation a level of prestige that exceeds that which would be ascribed to their income levels. In addition, the teaching profession offers a significant measure of job security. Job security is based on benefits secured by union affiliations like tenure and seniority, and by a degree of insulation from market vagaries, such as layoffs during weakened production cycles. Also, as public sector employees, teachers are often given generous health care and pension benefits.[8]

Universally, teachers tend to become teachers because they like teaching children. In the United States it is popularly believed that teachers are born, not made. There is a perception that some individuals just have a knack with children. Teachers learn instructional theory and spend only a few months as student teachers. They are then responsible for their own classes. The lack of intensive training is not a recipe for success. By contrast, Asian teachers go through lengthy apprenticeships with master teachers. Lesson plans and classroom presentations are evaluated by a number of experienced teachers.

Teacher wages are another concern. In Japan, teacher salaries are higher than those in the U.S. Japanese teachers and university professors earn equivalent wages and have similar prestige.[9] In the United States an elementary school teacher earns approximately one-third the salary of a university professor. Part of the reason for lower U.S. teacher salaries may be that American students in colleges of education have lower college entrance scores than students in other departments. It would appear, therefore, that it is easier to gain acceptance into a college education department, which would create a cycle where those departments would tend to attract somewhat less qualified applicants.

Larger class sizes in Asia allow teachers to have a substantial percentage of nonclass time to prepare and compare notes with other teachers. Asian teachers usually spend no more than 60% of their time in front of a class. They spend about 20% more hours in school than U.S. teachers—9 hours per day compared to 7.3 hours. In addition U.S. teachers spend more time with students transitioning between activities. U.S. students work more on their own, rather than being instructed, and U.S. teachers spend more time with individual students attending to discipline issues.

Asian teachers have a considerably lower burn-out rate. This is attributed to a number of factors. The factors include a policy where teachers are rotated through different grade levels to expose them to new challenges. They are further motivated by the prospect of advancement. Principals in Asia are former teachers who have demonstrated particular skills. Principals are not chosen based strictly on administrative degrees as in the U.S. Asian students exhibit less pathological behavior which leads to fewer classroom problems. U.S. teachers maintain more teacher-centered classroom employing operant condition to maintain control. Asian teachers use classroom leaders to assist with disciplinary problems, thereby getting the whole group involved in addressing individual problems.

Despite a strong desire among teachers to teach, burnout as measured by the Maslach Burnout Inventory (MBI) is a persistent concern. The three dimensions of MBI are exhaustion, cynicism and inefficacy. Exhaustion is the first reaction to job stress. It is the feeling of being physically and emotionally overextended. This leads to cynicism where an individual assumes a detached attitude to insulate themselves from exhaustion and disappointment. Finally, inefficacy, or the feeling of being inadequate makes projects seem overwhelming. Teacher burnout, based on daily classroom anxiety, is a problem demanding growing attention.[10]

Good teachers are in limited supply. The most academically gifted candidates do not find their way to a classroom. The best teachers often leave after a short tenure. The three reasons offered by former teachers for giving up their jobs are workplace issues, low pay and low prestige. However, those becoming teachers are well aware of the three concerns going into the profession. These excuses are misleading. The real reasons for teacher turnover are the difficulties in maintaining classroom discipline.

In the not too distant past, teaching and nursing were the only professional jobs open to women. It was presumed that teachers would selflessly excuse the unpleasant conditions of their workplace. A range of common problems exist, from a lack of adequate resources to constant administrative interference. The response has been offering merit pay, expanded training and more teacher autonomy. Another problem endemic to teaching is that the relationship between teachers and parents is inherently antagonistic.[11] The relationship operates in many respects like the relationship between divorcing parents where children play one parent off the other for their personal advantage. Children may find it convenient to blame their bad behavior at home on a disagreeable school experience instead of confronting family issues.

Though teaching has both rewarding and undesirable aspects for teachers, their effectiveness is crucial with respect to the ability of students to learn. Research on the impact of teacher credentials and preservice training on the quality of instruction has yielded inconsistent results. However, it has been determined that instructional practices in the classroom do influence student performance. Specific teaching strategies and methods have been associated with learning gains. Thus, issues involving curriculum and instructional devices are important elements in the educational process. The ability to implement specific curricular and instructional approaches is predicated on classroom discipline and a competent pedagogical design.[12]

Although serious change is necessary, many impediments are in place. The obstacles to the implementation of school reform include, lack of sufficient teacher knowledge or guidance, beliefs or values held by teachers that differ from those of the reformers, the attitude or disposition of teachers that interferes with their ability to implement reforms and the teaching circumstances, wherein teachers are constrained from changing their practices.

Though teachers can prepare specific lesson plans for each class, everyday classroom situations require teachers to both establish a tranquil learning environment and deal with unexpected questions or comments. Other distractions include students arriving late, colleagues entering the classroom seeking information, changing classrooms, changing subject matter requiring the use of new material, fire drills, telephone calls and public announcements. The teaching process is not simply a matter of information delivery.

The responsibility for many of the problems related to student achievement has been placed squarely on the shoulders of the education establishment. One education observer has outlined specific teacher deficiencies that have led to poor student performance.

1. The licensing of teachers, what is known as certification, is a ritual without substance, requiring knowledge at the lowest possible level.

2. The curriculum used to teach our children is weak. Most public schools have virtually eliminated formal history and geography and are deficient in teaching composition, grammar, and spelling as well as mathematics and science.

3. Teacher training is lax. The undergraduate degree of most teachers, usually a bachelor of education, is less substantial than an ordinary liberal arts degree. The same hollowness is true of the master's degree obtained by teachers.

4. Tenure protects the most inadequate of our teachers.

5. Teachers' unions often operate as political organizations while masquerading as professional groups.

6. The American schoolhouse is heavily psychologized, beginning with educational psychology courses in teacher training up through the psychological testing and counseling of students.

7. Would-be teachers are usually self-selected from the bottom third of high school and university graduates.

8. Evidence indicates that there is no "profession" of education. Laypeople that enter the field with little or no training do as well as graduates of education schools, and often better.

9. More than any other field, education is top-heavy with administrators and bureaucrats.

10. The lack of separation between elementary and high school teachers, in salary and training, makes true scholarship in secondary schools difficult, if not impossible.

11. The doctor of education degree, the EdD held by most school superintendents and administrators, is inferior to the traditional PhD degree and requires little academic knowledge.

12. Many schools concentrate on weak students and resist enriching the education of gifted students, claiming that "tracking" is an "elitist" practice.

13. Highly educated college graduates without education establishment credentials are usually not permitted to teach in public schools, forcing them into private or college systems, losing superior talent.

14. The establishment dislikes traditional methods and continually develops new, unproven theories of education, none of which stand the test of time.

15. Parents are regularly fooled about their children's true abilities through blatant grade inflation, which is rampant in our schools.

16. Too many educators have low expectations for students, resulting in poor performance, especially among minority students.

17. By promoting concepts of "self-esteem," teachers create a false complacency among students, hindering their academic development.

18. Parents, the PTAs, and elected school board officials have abdicated their powers to the hired help, the education establishment.

19. State legislators, who have the ultimate power over public education, are generally ignorant about the subject, cowed by educators, and neglect their duty to parents and students. [13]

Many critics of education point to teachers' unions as an important source of student performance deficiencies. The National Education Association (NEA) has 2.6 million members with annual revenues totaling $1.25 billion. It was originally founded in 1857 as an association that included both teachers and administrators. However, in the 1960s the NEA discarded its administrator members and became a union representing teachers.

The smaller American Federation of Teachers (AFT) has 1.1 million members. The AFT was founded as a labor union in 1916 and was affiliated with the AFL-CIO. However, the AFT could not actually function as a labor union until the 1960s since public sector unions were illegal. It was not until 1961 that President Kennedy issued an executive order that permitted collective bargaining for federal employees. Subsequently, states began offering collective bargaining rights to their employees.[14]

Much of the success of the teachers' unions in promoting specific agendas has been based on their considerable political activities. For example, the first presidential candidate to receive the NEA's support was Jimmy Carter in 1976. At the union's request, Carter established the federal Department of Education. Union priorities include better wages and benefits for teachers, as well as smaller class sizes, which requires school districts to hire more teachers. Critic's primary point of contention with the teacher's union is largely based on the union's efforts to protect teachers and endorse self-serving policies that are not considered in the best interests of students and taxpayers. Some of these policies include offering tenure or indefinite job protection and better classroom assignments for underperforming teachers. In addition, unions continue to mount challenges to merit pay, school vouchers, charter schools and other school reforms popular with parents and legislators.

The AFT achieved national prominence during the 1960s under the leadership of Albert Shanker. Shanker orchestrated a number of teacher strikes during the mid-1960s in the country's largest school district—New York City. The strikes resulted in substantial raises and improved grievance procedures for teachers. Because the majority of teachers were white and the students, who were unable to attend school during the strike, were black, racial tensions became a significant part of the teacher vs. community dynamic. To address this important concern, the union promoted programs encouraging Black students to pursue teaching careers.[15]

Criticism of teachers unions and unions in general, includes concerns about the independence of union leaders from the rank and file that elected them. Traditionally it was believed that any democracy or collectivist association where strong leaders emerge will naturally develop a social order that includes a politically dominant class or persistently authoritarian group of oligarchs. The need to create a substantial bureaucratic organization to manage the affairs of the collectivity assures the evolution of a distinct political class. This is referred to as the "iron law of oligarchy."[16]

In order to obviate the imposition of a less than democratic rule, contemporary management theory proposes a flatter and more transparent organizational structure. Although many major corporations have adopted progressive management policies and structures, unions have generally resisted. An example of the consequences of an outmoded union management configuration was in evidence at a Chicago Teachers Union, an AFT affiliate, budget meeting. It was discovered that the union was facing a financial crisis. In 2004, when the new union president was elected, the union had $5.4 million in reserves. In the first 4 years of the president's tenure, the reserves had been reduced to $188,000 and the union had to borrow more than $2 million to continue to operate. Despite screaming and shoving at the meeting, the members were unable to get their leaders to provide information about loans or union officers' salaries.[17]

In recent years the level of U.S. union membership in private industry has dropped to about 7% or almost 80% lower than the membership rate 50 years ago. This number is barely sufficient to defend prior gains, let alone transform American society. In order for unions to reestablish their prominence, a sweeping reengineering of their leadership will be necessary.

The extent of the transformation must parallel the radical reengineering efforts that company leadership commenced in the 1980s. These widely popularized 80s solutions began with the discovery of the benefits of good production management during World War II. To assure timely delivery of high quality war material, the government employed many academics, statisticians, and scientists to study and improve mass production methods.

The eventual consequence of their many observations and recommendations was the development of a professional class of managers. These managers were formally trained in university graduate schools offering advanced degrees in business administration and management. Over the years libraries have been filled with literature designed for improving management techniques in production, finance, marketing, organizational behavior, economics and skills related to specific industries, and current and anticipated trends.

The propagation of this professional managerial class somehow bypassed the ranks of union leaders, who continue to insist on promoting senior line workers up through the management ranks. The result is a distinct cultural and intellectual mismatch between formally trained professional corporate managers and union managers skilled only in production line work. The problem is caused by inept union leadership.

There are a number of important reasons that are traditionally offered to account for the loss of union membership. They include:

Passage of the Taft-Hartley Act in 1947 which restricted union strength by prohibiting closed shops. Many Southern states quickly passed right-to-work laws interfering with union organizing. In enacting this legislation Southern states have been successful in depressing wages and benefits which attracted many large factory operations from the 50s through today.

The McClellan hearings of 1957 exposed unions like the Longshoremen's Association and the Teamsters, the largest American union at the time, as corrupt and subverted by criminals. The hearings uncovered collusion between employers and union officials, the use of violence and misuse of union funds by labor leaders. Prior to these hearings, 76% of Americans generally approved of unions. Immediately subsequent to the hearings' dramatic revelations, approval of unions slipped to 64%. The hearing lead to passage of the Landrum-Griffin Act in 1959. This Act specified extensive reporting requirements for labor organizations, in effect placing a stigma on all union operations.

Service industry employment surpassing number of manufacturing jobs. Union affiliation is generally associated with blue-collar factory work. As white-collar jobs increased and manufacturing jobs diminished due to increased labor saving capital investment union membership declined. Union affiliation has been shown to be more closely associated with jobs featuring greater degrees of autonomy where jobholders are more likely to embrace ownership of their positions, thus insisting on more voice. They also have more freedom to pursue organizing activities. However, newly enlightened management professionals were more responsive to the needs and rights of their employees and acted accordingly without third party intervention.

Corporations developed sophisticated anti-union strategies. Corporate management, particularly in the 90s and 00s, became fervently proactive in the elimination of a "union threat." One of the most antiunion companies is Wal-Mart. Because of their position, they have been specifically targeted by union organizers. In response Wal-Mart has its employees watch videos explaining how the company offers a feeling of family. The videos further state that union membership in America is declining because workers do not believe they are receiving any benefit from the monthly dues they are required to pay to union officials.[18] Wal-Mart also maintains an antiunion SWAT Team. When a store manager in Kentucky found a prounion sign hanging in a bathroom, he called corporate headquarters in Arkansas. They immediately dispatched a corporate jet with a SWAT Team to the store. Their purpose was to seek out incriminating evidence needed to get likely union supporters fired.[19] In another example, a Japanese auto manufacturer builds an auto assembly plant in the United States and seeks to avoid being organized by the United Auto Workers (UAW). The Japanese organized Quality Circles where workers are encouraged to make suggestions which promote meaningful workforce participation. Workers are also shown videos of laid-off UAW workers and closed Michigan factories. Workers are told they will lose income in the event of a strike and working hard will not enable an individual to keep their job if someone with more seniority wants it. The tag line is that if a company treats its workers properly, there is no reason to organize.[20] So far, the UAW has been unable to organize any of the dozens of Japanese-owned U.S. auto assembly transplants that began opening in the 1980s.

The PATCO Strike. In 1981 Robert Poli, president of the 13,000 member Professional Air Traffic Controllers Organization (PATCO), called for a strike against the Federal Aviation Administration (FAA). PATCO was seeking better wages, improved working conditions and shorter hours for its members, ostensibly, in the name of public safety. President Reagan declared the strike illegal and ordered the strikers back to work. The majority of strikers did not return to their jobs and were fired. Reagan's "busting" of the union received popular support when he cited the striker demands as placing an "unacceptable tax burden" on fellow citizens.[21]

The AFL-CIO failed to commit sufficient resources to organizing. The 2005 split between the more traditional high wage unions, like the UAW, steelworkers, machinists and communications workers, and a group of weaker lower paid unions, such as the SEIU, UFCW, UNITE-HERE and laborers was initiated in the name of a need for union membership expansion. The breakaway group had experienced considerable expansion in recent years in contrast to the declines occurring in old line industrial union membership. Despite any rhetoric to the contrary, the primary cause for this dissimilarity is the difference in job type increases. Employment in traditional manufacturing industries has dropped, whereas the number of low wage health care workers, janitors, retail clerks, food processors, and truck drivers has risen.

Seniority versus performance-based worker assessment. Historically, longevity was the most important asset an employee could attain. Longevity assured all-important job security and wage enhancements. Enforcement of layoff schedules and compensation based on seniority is a linchpin of union mandates. Presently, private, public, and governmental organizations insist on accountability based on specifically defined performance standards. This fundamental misalignment of priorities guarantees opposition to a union presence in all circumstances.

Leadership in the breakaway union amalgamation asserts an enlightened perception of the realities employers confront. However, the response to employer challenges is always defensive and generally results in concession and sacrifice by membership. Corporate reengineering of the 80s and 90s included infusing managerial ranks with academically polished administrators. Their formal MBA training was augmented with crucial platitudes disseminated in business popular literature.

The prevailing wisdom expressed the importance of: (1) resisting bureaucracy through the de-layering of organizations and blurring personnel distinctions; (2) embracing new ideas and change, rather than fearing them; (3) staying lean and agile in order to seize opportunities quickly; and (4) live quality-constantly measure, analyze, and improve.

Professional managers were responsible for leading established companies beyond the challenges of global competition, computerization, the Internet, and regulatory vicissitudes to name a few. During this same period, organized labor continued to implement strategies and structures that were developed in the 1930s and 40s. The result is the disappearance of American unions.

There is also concern about the disconnect between union leadership and the needs of its rank and file members. Union leadership tends to be decidedly entrenched. This leads to a lack of transparency, accountability and, more importantly, a paucity of new ideas. There is an inability to adapt to a rapidly changing macro-environment.

Since 1955 the AFL-CIO has had only three presidents (another served as acting president for only a couple of months). By contrast the United States has had 10 presidents since the mid-50s. Beginning more than a half century ago, AFL-CIO presidents served for 24 years, 16 years, and the current president, 13 years. Despite their long tenure, each president administered an organization that experienced both declining membership and a reduction in their constituents' wages and benefits. The union movement has lost 80% of its membership and worker wages have been steadily declining for the past 35 years.

In the case of the United Auto Workers (UAW), their most recent agreement called for wages and benefits that are less than half of those under the previous contract. Any truly democratic organization would have tossed these bosses well before their voluntary retirement. Just as corporate managers are accountable for increases in company profits and stock prices, the effectiveness of union leaders is measured by membership and member income enhancements. In 2005 the Change to Win Federation was formed precisely because the breakaway union leaders realized that it was not possible to remove the long-term leadership regardless of their ineptitude.

In order to compete in a rapidly changing environment, unions should employ professional managers. Bureaucratic layers must be removed and managers need to establish less fettered lines of communication with both the rank and file, and with employers. Like corporate managers, union managers have to be proactive—anticipating problems and working to avoid harmful confrontational bargaining and doomsday scenarios.

The unions' professional managers, serving at the discretion of an elected union board, would be at the disposal of union officers, union membership and company management. In addition to resolving and improving on day-to-day internal demands, professional managers would contend with extremely difficult issues like health insurance and pension funding. Thus, professional managers would operate on an equal footing with employers. Inasmuch as unions are still labor's only voice, they must become an equal voice.

Prior to the 1960s, the concerns faced by teachers were generally ignored because teachers were typically women. Salaries remained low since women's income was considered as only supplementary to their husband's salary. Education was less of a priority given that there was an acceptance of the need to educate only the top 15% of students who were likely to attend college and become professionals. The remaining 85% could find good jobs in manufacturing. The demands of principals were often arbitrary and capricious, with no teacher recourse. More experienced, higher paid teachers could be fired and replaced with newer lower paid teachers or cronies of school or political officials.

The tenure laws of the 1960s were teachers' only protection against these unjust activities. Teacher evaluation programs were instituted to prevent incompetent teachers from benefiting from tenure. Ostensibly, it is possible to remove unqualified teachers. Teachers' unions have consistently opposed merit pay on the basis that it is too subjective to be a long-term effective tool. Further, it has been tried and failed in the past.[22]

The purpose of unions formed in the late nineteenth century was to prevent the abuse of good workers from inept or vindictive managers. In the earlier stages of the industrial revolution managers came from the ranks of skilled workers. The problem was that the mechanical talents of tinsmiths, welders and woodworkers did not necessarily translate into superior managerial skills. Quite the contrary, these individuals were notorious for their odious treatment of underlings, particularly unskilled workers. As managers have become more enlightened through required professional management training, the popular perception of unions is that they serve only to protect bad workers from sound managers.

Teachers, unlike factory or retail employees, face extraordinary personal challenges each time they step on school property. The social and political upheaval of the 1960s has challenged settled assumptions about the nature of the classroom. Teachers are predisposed to bear their difficult responsibilities by learning to simply look away. That which could not be solved was named. Once named, the need for a solution loses its urgency. Students are defined as LD, BD, ADD, dyslexic, drug babies, at-risk, high poverty, and so forth. After they are labeled, expectations evaporate.[23]

The new methodology demanded education become integrated into the perspective of the child. This process can lead the learner to ecstasy. Discipline and mastery techniques do not have to stand in opposition to freedom and self-expression. It is as cruel to bore a child as to beat her/him. Artists and musicians are able to attain sublime moments only through mastery of technique. Existing classroom technique must undergo radical transformation in order to avoid boredom.

Each classroom has both an official and a hidden curriculum that are advanced by the teacher. The purpose of the official curriculum is the dissemination of academic content. The hidden curriculum, which demands a considerable amount of time, involves *crowds*, *praise*, and *power*. The *crowds* element relates to the general classroom setting. The classroom is a busy area. In elementary school classrooms teachers engage in more than 1,000 interpersonal interchanges daily. In addition to managing classroom dialogue, teachers must grant privileges, hand-out classroom supplies, run audio-video equipment, manage foot traffic, and deal with interruptions from students, administrators and other teachers. The crowded classroom conditions cause delay, denial, interruption, and social distraction. These circumstances must be met with exceptional patience.[24]

Praise is related to the pervasive spirit of evaluation that will dominate a student's school experience. Tests, quizzes, homework assignments, and subjective teacher evaluations provide constant judgments of the students' performance. The results are communicated both publicly and privately. These evaluations are supposed to measure student performance, but they also affect performance by shaping student attitudes and motivation—for better or for worse.

The unequal *power* relationship between teacher and student trains students early about the importance of acting to please those in authority. Students must learn to take orders from adults. Concepts of obedience and independence seem antithetical. However, preparing for adult challenges requires the integration of these two notions. Thus, training under the hidden curriculum is vital to the students' development. Teachers' classroom responsibilities are comprehensive. All of their professional resources are stretched thin trying to teach and provide administrative services.

Another approach, particularly in dealing with children in poverty refers to star teachers. Star teachers are not concerned with discipline. Although they are faced with horrendous problems in their classrooms from children being murdered to death threats, discipline is not a high priority. This is because they believe that problems are part of their job. They understand the circumstances that their students confront each day—the poverty and the violence. Generally, teachers are trained for "normal" children. However, teachers in "high-need student" classrooms shouldn't start with the assumption that some of the children shouldn't be there. Star teachers get to know their children on an individualized basis so they can anticipate definite problems from certain students and act in a proactive manner in dealing with their difficulties. Students are more likely to make problems for strangers. [25]

With fewer disciplinary problems, star teachers have more time to teach and develop relationships with their students. Star teachers do not engender hostility by giving assignments that students are unable to complete. They understand the competencies of each individual. If teachers are stressed, the students will behave in a similarly stressed manner. Teachers who are quitters and failures view discipline as an issue separate from teaching. However, learning activities are the basis for self-control. If students are learning, they discipline themselves.

Star teachers do not try to shape behavior through rewards and punishments. Interest, involvement and participation are key ideas in working with students. The main reason for avoiding punishment is that it doesn't work. Teachers cannot force anyone to learn. Many children in poverty become passive resisters after the primary grades—"stay out of trouble, but don't learn anything." Some students push the teachers to punish them in order to show they can control the teacher's behavior.

Homework has to be something students can do on their own and class time must be made for the students to share their individual work. It should not be left up to parents to make sure homework is done. Star teachers do not blame parents—many of whom are adolescents and uneducated themselves. They understand that most parents do care about their children and teachers must do their best to cooperate with them, including visiting their homes. Star teachers focus less on testing and grades than they do on individual assessments largely based on the effort expended by the student and how much progress they made. Star teachers do not use direct instruction as their primary method. They teach in units that frequently require group or collaborative learning. The goal is to work towards intrinsic motivation. Urban school districts have developed many vocational or school-to-work programs so kids can "get a job, and stay out of jail."

Star teachers want children to learn a wide variety of subjects. Children begin school intrinsically motivated. Teachers must keep them interested so kids remain motivated, and not just respond to a series of rewards and punishments. It is difficult to convince children in poverty that what they are learning is relevant and important. They must want to learn for the sake of learning. Learning is its own reward. Children will want to be in school if they believe that. Star teachers have to interest students in learning by modeling their own interests in learning. Star teachers learn to work within the school's mindless bureaucracy. They also set up support networks with colleagues.

Teachers can act as performance coaches. The role of a performance coach in education includes being a strategist, facilitator and psychotherapist. The coach must have high expectations for all students, view schools as a unit of coherence and change, and express the importance of adult learning and leadership. It is not feasible to teach all students in large junior and senior high schools as they are presently structured.

These schools are obsolete. Further, school and teacher incentives under NCLB are turning off students to learning. High stakes testing has increased drop-out rates for minority students. There are no educational benefits to using tests to retain students in the same grade. High stakes testing serves to narrow the curriculum to "teach-to-test." Student motivation is undermined. As a consequence, employers complain that graduates come with poor work habits, motivation, curiosity, and respect.

Students need "soft skills," such as written and oral communication capabilities and group problem-solving skills. "New Village Schools" have been suggested as an alternative to existing century old factory-model school. In the past 100 years everything has changed except schools. A return to teach-the-basics curriculum is complex since the definition of "basics" is not clear to school administrators and teachers. New Village Schools would be more effective in bringing students into the information age where information is constantly increasing and changing.

Good reasoning skills are necessary to sort all the available data. The incessant flow of new information must be integrated into a student's existing experience and knowledge base. This is accomplished through learners interacting with information. Achievement is not based solely on seat-time. It is more performance based. Students demonstrate the ability to use knowledge rather memorizing and regurgitating it.[26]

Teachers have to control for a variety of external influences on student behavior. Despite efforts to institute explicit behavioral initiatives designed to maintain classroom discipline, it is not possible to overcome the effects of the media. The primary function of the media is to sell things. Twenty-first century students are accomplished consumers. Exposure since birth to the brazen ubiquity of advertising and promotional gimmicks, children are shamelessly coddled by purveyors of all imaginable products and services. The intended result is a child as consumer king or queen. These minidivas fully expect the same royal treatment when they enter a classroom. Their unique preferences are sovereign. As a result, bad behavior abounds.

Teachers are not considered good if they do not entertain their classes. Entertainment can be a powerful tool. For example, In Aldous Huxley's *Brave New World* people come to love their oppression and the technologies that undo their capacity to think. Society is being ruined, not by oppressors inflicting pain, but by those inflicting distraction and pleasure.

The media metaphor shift from the printed word to television images has significantly impacted the content of discourse. The concept of truth is intimately linked to the biases of forms of expression.[27] Expressing concern about the effects of the growing popularity of radio and movies in the 1920s, one commentator noted, "No one in this world, so far as I know ... has ever lost money by underestimating the intelligence of the great masses of the plain people. Nor has anyone ever lost public office thereby."[28] The observer was noting the predisposal of these new mediums to make everything simple and orient productions to the lowest common denominator.

Television is a metamedium that directs, not only our knowledge of the world, but our way of knowing it. Thus, the images provided by television do not just shape our culture, they are our culture. Television is transforming our culture into one vast show business arena. In its use for advertising product, for example, the images it presents of the product are more important than the intrinsic value of that product in terms of encouraging people to buy it.

The classroom is still tied to the printed word. Through its storytelling, music, and dynamic images, television is relentlessly training and cultivating the minds of our youth. In doing so, it obliterates the school curriculum. It is necessary to be cognizant of the realities media impose in shaping student perceptions.

In addition, *New Kids* are predisposed to using hi-tech devices. Regardless of the educational potential evident by expanding the use of information and communication technology (ICT) in the classroom, the pedagogy of ICT cannot be implemented without increased levels of professional development for teaching staff.[29] Many teachers are disenchanted with a new emphasis on classroom e-learning. This reflects a generational digital divide. Only one-third of teachers reported being prepared to use ICT in the classroom. It is insufficient to simply offer teacher workshops to improve ICT expertise.

There are several barriers to technology adoption. They include time, support, faculty models, infrastructure, and culture. These barriers can be overcome using methods, such as tying incentives to desired outcomes, involving faculty in decision making to improve buy-in, use of faculty models, providing supplemental technical support with peer support, providing well-trained student assistants and offering administrative support.[30]

In addition, it has been discovered that in-service teacher self-efficacy on integrating the Internet into science and math curriculum can be improved over the long term with intensive summer workshop and supplemental online courses.[31] A new generation of teachers who grew up with computer and video game technology will be better prepared to relate their experience with that of the students. However, it will be decades before the current generation of teachers is fully replaced by those with better ICT competencies. Thus, it will be necessary to implement new instructional models that better enable old teachers to respond to the predilections of *New Kids*.

Curriculum

The purpose of a transmission in an automobile is to match the engine speed with road speed. Similarly, e-learning serves to mediate the rate of learning with student abilities. e-Learning offers the potential for epistemological pluralism. The child has a right to intellectual self-determination. Further, children have the ability to create knowledge rather than just consume it. They are able to achieve this outcome through the use of electronic games. However, the computer should not be used solely as a deluxe flashcard. Popular "skill and drill" applications largely underutilize the opportunities afforded by computers.[32]

Using a computer, students are able to create virtual worlds and environments wherein math and reading skills would have to be applied in order to achieve some specific objective, such as winning a race, erecting some type of structure or solving a puzzle or mystery. The video experience is fast-paced, compelling, and rewarding. Schoolwork is perceived as slow, boring, and out-of-touch.

The computer cannot be effectively injected into a curriculum as school programming is now conceived. The very nature of pedagogy must be modified to present knowledge as more interconnected. Knowledge is not simply the acquisition of facts from a series of disjointed disciplines. Knowledge is a system of categories that provide context for information acquisition. Putting information in context engenders its retention.

Unfortunately, many barriers will be encountered in an attempt to produce revolutionary change in education. These include, cost, politics, the power of vested interests in school bureaucracy and the lack of scientific research on new forms of learning. In addition, children are resistant to educational video games. They are automatically considered not fun. Teachers and administrators intuitively disapprove of video games, which they associate with violent and sexual content.

An electronic media-based school curriculum will look substantially different than the curriculum in today's classrooms. Electronic media-based studies provide a sophisticated learning environment. Students participating in a curriculum based on information and communication technology (ICT) tend to adopt flexible strategies, such as creating new ideas, risk-taking, improvisation, using trial and error methods for problem solving and rapid transition from one design to another. ICT projects also tend to foster the transfer of knowledge between students and cooperative development of ideas. By contrast, students working in a nonelectronic environment progress along a more linear path: planning, construction and troubleshooting.[33]

An unintended consequence of ICT utilization in the teaching of math, for example, is increased time-on-task. An instructional medium using an interactive system in math offers multiple pathways to the representation of mathematical concepts. By using audio, visual-graphics, and visual-text, problems are no longer static, as they would seem using a black and white text. Using electronic media to heighten student-control in a subject will result in more intense engagement by the student.[34]

Effective educational programming would include stimulating content that supports learner-centered, on-demand exploration, and problem solving. Learning by doing is fully implemented. Programs that induce question generation will play a central role. These programs promote active and reflective learning and construction of knowledge. Learners can create simulated environments, manipulate the learning experience and visualize results. There is a vast array of media and communication technologies, including pen-based interface, to produce a captivating learner experience.[35]

Recent education reformers in America have largely failed to take into consideration the dynamics of the classroom. The ideals promoted by reformers are for more rigorous and important content, more intellectual engagement and universal access to knowledge. The rigorous and important content, however, has to include a focus on meanings. For example, the causes and effects of the Civil War must be discussed along with significant names and dates. Mathematical concepts should be developed based on their usefulness in areas outside the discipline. Intellectual engagement relates to the manner in which students interact with the academic subject matter.

Presenting content so it is meaningful to the student will precipitate discovery learning. In discovery learning, the student's curiosity and imagination are utilized in the learning process. Providing universal access to knowledge is a reform ideal based on having academic knowledge available to all students who are attending school. Access to knowledge must not be limited to gifted students or those from a more economically privileged household.[36]

In the early part of the nineteenth century, Thomas Jefferson, and later, Horace Mann promoted compulsory education at the public's expense. Both Jefferson and Mann recommended dividing children into two programs. The first for those destined for labor. The second is for those intended for leisure and learning. Future laborers were to be sent into shops to work as apprentices. Those designated for learning were prepared for college.

It was not until 1916 that John Dewey recognized that in a democratic society all children have the same destiny and must be offered the same quality of schooling. According to Dewey, prospects for children were based on the demands of work, of citizenship and of learning. Achievement in each of these areas was the prerequisite of a fulfilling future.

One approach, developed in 1982, is the Paideia Program. Paideia seeks to address lifetime learning by teaching using a Socratic method. Teaching is done by questioning and conducting discussions of the answers extracted. This method of learning would be a useful tool throughout adulthood.[37] However, it is not sufficient to universalize schooling. At issue is accessibility of actual learning for all students.

New Kids possess a level of media sophistication and real-world knowledge that far exceeds the competencies of previous generations of students. Subjecting *New Kids* to learning models produced more than 100 years ago will assure behavioral problems. Electronic media, teachers and curriculum must be developed in a manner that will assimilate school design with twenty-first century student priorities.

The e-OneRoom Schoolhouse will address the need to adapt to current realities by offering inquiry-based programming using the most up-to-date graphic and computing capabilities. More importantly, the e-OneRoom Schoolhouse will provide an educational paradigm that will align student preferences with academic prerequisites.

An appropriate learning environment will lead to a student's comprehension of the interconnectedness of knowledge from all disciplines. The exploratory process follows the interconnected web of causality. This contrasts with linear or hierarchical programming that forces the learner into artificial linearized exploration which encourages compartmentalized or rote knowledge. Cross-disciplinary insights are necessary for deep understanding.[38]

Any barriers are a function of the broader perspective taken by the education establishment—politicians (since education is largely a publicly funded enterprise), administrators and teachers. The dominant viewpoint is based on an obsolete model. The fundamentals of that model, the 100+ year old egg-crate school, are entirely inconsistent with the prerogatives of contemporary students. Thus, the strategy has been to adapt the students to the model. This will continue to fail despite incessant tweaking.

Stanwood Cobb of the Association for Advancement of Progressive Education laid out an insightful statement of principles. The seven principles were:

1. *Freedom to develop naturally.* The pupil must have the full opportunity for initiative and self-expression.

2. *Interest—the motive of all work.* Interest in real world applications must be developed and satisfied.

3. *Teacher as guide, not task-master.* Teachers need professional training and should have latitude in developing student initiative and originality. Inspire and encourage students.

4. *Scientific study of pupil development.* Grading must include both objective and subjective reporting.

5. *Attention to child's physical development.* Bright, well-ventilated schools, playgrounds and school physician.

6. *Cooperation between school and home.* Intelligent cooperation between parent and teachers.

7. *Progressive school to be a leader in educational movements.* Should be laboratory for new ideas.[39]

These seven principles provide clear guidelines for bringing educational theory into the twenty-first century. They were proposed in 1918.

In the 1990s the federal government was once again becoming involved with public education by promoting the use of technology in classrooms. It provided $2 billion in grants for the Technology Literacy Challenge Fund to wire schools for computer and Internet use. However, insufficient teacher training and inadequate research and development in well-designed computer software and a tendency to maintain customary teaching practices resulted in a lack of progress in student performance.

Getting buy-in from teachers and administrators is critical to the success of any revolutionary changes in education. The buy-in cannot be achieved without teachers attaining a level of comfort and self-efficacy with the new technology. Adequate teacher training will have to accompany any introduction of technologically innovative educational solutions.

CHAPTER 7

GAMES

Serious Games

Serious games unite analytic concentration with the intuitive freedom of artistic and imaginative acts. Students often fail to understand how abstractions taught in school are relevant to the real world. However, increased emphasis on abstract knowledge is reflected in educational goals. These goals continue to rise in order to meet heightening demands of society. Games offer opportunities for action. Though games are primarily mental, they offer freedom, speed and reactive physical movements. Most important, games allow the possibility of winning or losing.[1]

Games have two components. First, games are rational and *analytic*. Second, games are *emotional, creative, and dramatic*. The *analytic* component includes the assumption of roles that an individual encounters in their customary activities. Role players compete to achieve specific objectives, though outcomes are uncertain and can be transitory. The *emotional and dramatic* component is based on risk. The action of the game becomes more important than the actual outcome. The complexity of decision-making creates a dynamic that generates suspense and surprise.

Games are played at many levels. Business, elections, international relations, and interpersonal connections are played with resources of power, skill, knowledge, and luck. Games are fun and highly motivating. Using games in formal learning will enhance learner interest and will assist in efficient communication. Games offer quick feedback and there

Education Redux: How to Make Schools Relevant to Our Children and Our Future,
pp. 129–160
Copyright © 2010 by Information Age Publishing

are immediate consequences for specific behavior. Games in school offer a reason for action.

For example, a game in which students engage in Civil War battlefield strategies would require that they research, either in a library or on the Internet, historical information that would aid in their problem solving. This creates an active learner. A game about an automobile assembly line would present problems where there are several sub-assembly lines and parts arriving from outside vendors that have to be scheduled for assembly. A competition involving both questions relating to production quality and quantity would require many mathematical calculations, as well as the need to address important personnel, energy use, allocation of resources, and finance issues. Decision-making under conditions of incomplete information or uncertainty will lead to intuitive problem solving.

Games should be designed to develop a sense of zero-sum (one wins and one loses) and non-zero-sum (everyone can win or everyone can lose) competition. Ideal problem-solving involves both analysis and intuition. Games will also help to produce social skills during cooperative problem solving.

Games stimulate conventional study. In an examination of the Constitution, for example, students would explore how, why and under what circumstances it was written, rather than just reading it. Teachers will spend more time observing students than directing them. Teachers will analyze and respond to student performance rather that attempt to control it. Scoring games is important to determine the relative effectiveness of play.

Games address a fundamental intellectual need. A state of optimal experience stands in stark contrast to the disagreeable condition of psychic entropy. Optimal experience is described as a state where information received by an individual is congruous with one's preferences and objectives. The result is an effortless flow of psychic energy based on a sense of self-efficacy—that one's skills are sufficient to manage immediate challenges.

Characteristics of optimal experience include intense concentration, a lack of self-consciousness and a distorted sense of time. Optimal experience yields a sense of gratification that enables individuals to act based on doing an activity for its own sake with minimal concern for specific rewards or regardless of the difficulty or potential danger. The primary function of these flow activities is to provide enjoyable experiences.[2] Games provide a tool for achieving optimal experience.

Video Games

There is a substantial gap between the exhilaration of video games that engage kids and the boring pace of learning in the existing classroom configuration. By engaging students, instruction is unforced and able to reach heretofore inaccessible young learners. Rules of the game are deduced by the participants through a process of trial and error. This makes it possible for children to learn entrepreneurial and risk-taking skills. It also enables children to collaborate with their peers.

When children attend school, it is necessary for them to "power down." Digital youth are accustomed to multitasking—video game playing, TV watching, and cell phone using. Their brains are programmed for speed and interactivity. In complex games, players must "level up" or constantly get better. Games have adaptivity meaning that they increase in difficulty more quickly for those that learn faster, and games make it easier to attain certain goals for those who are slower to follow. Feedback is always immediate.

Adding an entertainment dimension to problem-solving skills will engender a level of energy and enthusiasm that will keep students motivated. Under this arrangement there is a disintermediation where the teacher is no longer necessary to stand between the learner and the lesson content. The teacher will be a facilitator offering guidance and playing an empathy role.[3]

The video game industry began with the introduction of Pong in 1972. Pong was created in an electronics lab in 1958, but popularized by engineers who later produced the Atari console. Also in 1972, the board game, Dungeons and Dragons (D&D) was developed. The D&D board game sold 4.5 million copies.

In 1979, using ARAPNET, which was the forerunner of the Internet, Ultima, a D&D type computer game was launched. Ultima was a multiuser dragon (MUD) game where participants could compete over the net. In 2006, the video game industry generated $12.5 billion in U.S. software, hardware, and accessory sales.[4] This represents an increase of 19% over 2005. By contrast, Hollywood movie ticket sales dropped by 7.9% in 2005 to $9 billion annually.[5]

There are a number of specific elements necessary to compose a good video game. The game must begin with a good story.[6] The story must be simple and understandable. The story must have a theme, such as fantasy, adventure, or sports. It must also have a goal, such as get to the other side or find and retrieve.

The game must have good controls. They have to be intuitive—a joystick or keyboard directional signals, for example. There has to be technical enablers. These assure that all objects are treated in an efficient and unified manner. Room-to-room motion, chase/flee movements and tool objects must operate in a consistent form. The game world needs to be a good size. It has to be large enough to be interesting and small enough for the player to become familiar with it.

The different regions of the game have to be disjointed, but the objects and creatures and the way they interact must be permanent. The game display must have good color, animation, and sound effects. The game must have good playability. This includes progressively more difficult levels and time constraints. There must also be sufficient variety with random object placement and different routines for solving puzzles.

On their most basic level, games consist of two elements, eye candy (graphics) and game play. A fundamental component of game play is uncertainty. Uncertainty introduces the player to inquiry learning which requires experimentation and adaptivity. Games captivate because of their ability to appeal to an individual's inherent desire for rewards. Most games include fractal rewards and keep players informed of larger potential rewards. The desire for more rewards is a significant part of games' appeal. The pursuit of more rewards is highly challenging and the brain likes to be challenged.[7] Success at one level immediately enables the player to move to a higher level.

Having fun is the foundational element in the definition of games. Games are puzzles. They operate on the basis of prior knowledge and push the boundaries to test and expand that knowledge. Integrating new data into an existing knowledge base makes learning fun. The two game-play paradigms are, (1) get to the other side (Frogger and Donkey Kong), or (2) visit every location (PacMan).

Time limits add a third dimension. These aspects together with stimulating graphics allow games to offer fun (ability to master problem), aesthetics (which add to the enjoyment), the visceral reaction from successfully completing a task, and the positive self-image one attains from mastery. To be effective, it is necessary for games to, (a) have a variable feedback system; (b) deal with mastery issues for both expert players and struggling players and; (c) failure must have a cost so the player will prepare differently the next time. New patterns, which are unanticipated by game producers, may emerge. Players may engage in "modding," which is modifying the way the game is played.[8]

Video game technology can and should be used in schools. With games' broad availability, learning does not have to be confined to a school classroom with one teacher delivering a single lesson plan. Games are personalized for each user. They are interactive and engaging, and represent a constant challenge requiring new learning. Classroom learning is deliberately constrained to accommodate slower learners. Games are a better fit with children's high-tech world view.

Children experience situated cognition. This means that the process of learning is related to social and cultural prerequisites. Video games are also multimodal. They mix words with images. Literacy involves semiotic domains where meaning is created using symbols and representations.

Building meanings is an active process. The ability to critique and manipulate symbols and representations is necessary to develop critical thinking. The critical thinking engendered by video games will generate resources for future problem solving.[9]

The Net Gen population at 90 million Americans is larger than the Baby Boomer generation at 76 million people. Of kids from ages 2 to 17 years old, 92% have access to video games. Only 80% of children in that age range live in homes with a computer. For Net Gen children, video games define their reality. Games are based on skill, not following orders.

Video game revenue is greater than the amount people spend going to the movies. There are more than 145 million U.S. video game consumers. Nintendo has sold more than 1.4 billion video games. Younger boys like fast twitch games. Girls and older boys prefer puzzles, quiz, and game cards. Because of the action and the competitive nature of games, they absorb all of players' attention. Technical skills are rewarded and winning is important. Games increase players' ability to concentrate, multitask, and manage uncertainty.

Video games are available in a console variety that plug into a television and a PC version. The most popular console game genres are: action, 27%; sports, 18%; racing, 16%; role-playing, 9%; fighting, 6%; family, 5%; and shooter, 5%. PC game genres are: strategy, 27%; children, 15%; shooter, 12%; family, 10%; role-playing, 9%; sports, 6%; racing, 4%; adventure, 4%; and simulation, 4%.

Some of the valuable work attributes gamers develop include, being decision makers, but not acting in an authoritarian manner and accepting failure as part of the process; a willingness to share information with others—transparency; understanding of risk/reward tradeoff; self-educating through trial and error and using peer assistance. Gamers are team players, who also behave like heroes, in that, they believe that they can make things get better.[10]

An important obstacle to widespread support of the use of video games in education is the adult public's negative perception of them. Many of the more well-known games are based on violent premises. Violent video games came of age in the 1990s with titles like Mortal Kombat, Street Fighter, and Wolfenstein 3D. They contain aggressive and misogynistic images. The object of these games is to maim, wound, or kill opponents.

Wolfenstein 3D was one of the early first person shooter games. The controller views the world through the eyes of the character they are controlling. The object of the game is to kill everything that moves. Newer games, such as Duke Nukem, combine extreme violence with sex.

To address the violent content of some video games, a rating system has been instituted. In order to acquire M-rated games, the purchaser must be at least 17 years old. Games rated E are for everyone, but there are further descriptor categories. These include Mild Animated Violence, Mild Realistic Violence, Animated Violence, Realistic Violence, Animated Blood, and Realistic Blood. E-rated games prohibit Animated Blood and Gore, and Realistic Blood and Gore.

Research indicates that playing violent video games increases aggressive behavior and decreases prosocial behavior. School shootings in Paducah, KY, Jonesboro, AR, and Littleton, CO highlight the possible negative effects of kids playing violent video games.[11] Due to the popularity and the media attention given these games, many associate the violence with all video game play. Needless to say, this assumption is incorrect.

There are many types of video games. These include action, adventure, sports, strategy, puzzle, simulations, and role-playing.[12] The two most popular games in 2006 were "Madden NFL 07" for the PS2 with 2.8 million units sold, and "New Super Mario Brothers" for the Nintendo. There are also many games designed specifically for young girls. They include more character-centered plots, issues of friendship and social relationships. Gender preferences are not necessarily biological, but socially constructed. Girls prefer games featuring justice and collaboration over victory and competition. There are several popular Barbie video games. The average American girl owns nine Barbie dolls. Among U.S. girls 3 to 10 years old, Barbie has a 99% market share.[13]

Nintendo released the video game, Donkey Kong, in 1981. The main character in the original Donkey Kong game, designed by Shigeru Miyamoto, was named Mario. Mario was a plumber working in a major construction operation. The various game platforms included scenes taking place on large steel girders, construction elevators and conveyor belts with fires and construction material. In the game Mario is attempting to rescue a damsel in distress from a giant gorilla named Donkey Kong. Nintendo dominated the video game market throughout the 1980s and 1990s. Subsequent games featuring the Mario character largely contained jungle or forest scenes.

There is also a substantial genre of role-playing games (RPGs). Many of the RPGs involve elaborate story worlds where characters are created and stories are developed around them. RPGs are often played on computers through the Internet. Individuals involved in massively, multiplayer online role-playing games (MMORPGs or MMOs for short) typically spend 20-30 hours per week inside the fantasy world. In fact, 20% of those individuals claim the fantasy world is their real place of residence and the real world was where you went to eat and sleep. People migrate to MMOs because they think it is better than the real world.

These synthetic worlds overcome all physical limitations through the creation of an avatar, which is a representation of the player's physical being. There are more than 10 million users. Play money used in games is traded on eBay. The market for virtual items is $30 million annually. The more popular MMO's include Ultima Online, EverQuest, Lineage, Second Life, Dark Age of Camelot, Star War Galaxies, and World of Warcraft. RPGs or synthetic worlds foster the development of social capital through competition and cooperation. Good governance, rules of conduct, and a strong sense of community are essential to synthetic worlds. They encourage participants to become team players.[14]

Some negative effects have been identified for teens who have become video addicted. The result is behavior patterns such as staying in their rooms, ignoring friends and family, not eating or showering, grades dropping and increasing belligerence.[15] Although this type of severe behavior will require remediation by mental health care professionals, the existence of addictive behavior would suggest the attraction of video games for a variety of purposes including classroom use.

The current crop of *New Kids* learners have been infused with invaluable resources. Their level of sophistication with respect to all manner of electronic media and real-world savvy gleaned from television and the Internet should be exploited, not stultified. There is an overriding concern with dysfunctional classroom behavior. The behavior is treated as deviant rather than a function of an intrinsic mismatch between learners and their environment. Substituting the e-OneRoom Schoolhouse paradigm for the current egg-crate model will address the immutable discipline problems that prevent academic progress at all levels and support both an individualized learning curriculum and social development initiatives.

The e-OneRoom Schoolhouse paradigm will accomplish these objectives by:

- Offering advanced academic software that maintains a learner's interest using inquiry and exploratory programming, as well as state of the art graphics and story telling.
- Providing both single user and multiuser software to enhance the development of social capital.
- Enable teachers to be responsible for a larger number of students since their functions will be primarily limited to assistance and assessment.

A small number of teachers who are better trained in IT will allow for significantly improved teacher salaries. A simplified school format will enable a transfer of cost from building infrastructure to programming research and development.

In 1996 the federal government introduced a $2 billion Technology Literacy Challenge Fund (TLCF) to assure that every student in every school will be technologically literate.[16] The Fund had four goals, which were:

- All teachers will have training and support they need to help all students learn through computers and through the information highway;
- All teachers and students will have modern computers in their classrooms;
- Every classroom will be connected to the information superhighway; and
- Effective and engaging software and on-line resources will be an integral part of every school curriculum.

These programs were to be implemented with supplementary funds from state and local educational agencies. In addition, there are a number of public and private sector resources committed to these TLCF goals. Included are, Technology Innovation Challenge Grants, Universal Service Fund, Regional Technology in Education Consortia, Statewide Net-Day, Tech Corps, 21st Century Teachers, American Technology Honor Society, and private sector technology leaders chaired by Sumner Redstone of Viacom.

The educational establishment cannot continue to be oblivious to the on-going social maladies that are significantly more important than traditional diversity and tolerance issues. In order to perpetuate an American social agenda that benefits all citizens, it is necessary to adapt young people to perform with an eye toward their neighbor. There are severe negative consequences to an individual acting only based on his or her immediate self-interest. This information must be taught and learned.

Learning fundamentals such as, math science, reading, and the humanities, by using a combination of single-user and multiuser video games will address both the disciplinary and social capital expansion agenda. The substantial investment needed to create new educational games and to prepare teachers with extensive IT training will be more than offset with savings in current programs and administrative people, who are sadly functioning to perpetuate a thoroughly inept system.

From a broader perspective, it is necessary to produce a student population imbued with considerable human capital based on knowledge acquisition and social capital developed in an active group learning environment. This training will enable future generations to resolve the difficult societal and personal problems they will be forced to confront. Failure to make the revolutionary changes in our current educational system will assure growing economic inequality and social dysfunction.

e-OneRoom Schoolhouse (e-ORS)

One of the main reasons for e-ORS video games in the classroom is to train students in the art of manufacturing. The only association New Kids have with industrial production is through stories told to them by their grandparents. The manufacturing process adds value to raw material. It makes clothes from cotton, wool, and animal hides produced from agricultural products; makes cars, appliances, and electronic devices out of metals created from mined ore and coke; and makes plastic utensils, toys, and equipment housings derived from petroleum.

Manufacturing is not about doing mindless and repetitious manual assembly line work. Manufacturing requires the following set of skills: a strong entrepreneurial spirit to be responsible for creating a new enterprise; students must be trained to innovate so they have the ability to develop concepts for brand new or improved products; practical design and engineering skills are needed to make a product that works and can be produced in a cost efficient manner; an awareness of legal hurdles from patents to labeling; overcoming the intellectual challenge presented by production demands; financial demands including design costs, factory build-outs, machinery, and inventory costs; making use of available or developing new production technologies; marketing to appropriate demographic groups; advertising and promotional concerns on how to get the biggest response for each advertising dollar; and building an organization—getting the right people in the right jobs.

All of the training needed to provide a background in the different facets of manufacturing will be offered through a series of video games. Video games make manufacturing processes real to New Kids.

The popularity of video games among New Kids is unassailable. One of the most popular of recently released video games is Halo 3 which was developed for Microsoft's Xbox 360. Halo 3 is a first person shooter game (FPS). In an FPS game, the player watches the action down the barrel of the weapon they are firing. In a third person shooter game, the player can see the character they are manipulating. The standard version of the game retails for about $60.00. Halo 3 was released in September 25, 2007. In the first 24 hours it was available, sales totaled $170 million.

On average, a state-of-art video game takes 100 developers about two years to create. The cost runs into the $10+ million range. The Halo series was reputed to cost over $50 million to develop. Halo 3 is based on a story about an interstellar war between alien races in the twenty-sixth century. Like many earlier games that were built on the Dungeons & Dragons (D&D) model, the graphics are dark and menacing. Colors are usually various shades of gray, black, and blue.

D&D games, for example, include large, mostly empty castles, caves, and forests. There are armor plated characters, as well as creatures with dragon-like or bat-like features. First person shooter games feature a wide variety of weaponry from swords to advanced automatic rifles, shotguns and pistols firing bullets, rockets and laser beams. Flamethrowers, grenades and missile launchers can provide additional firepower. The object of first person shooter or third person shooter games is to shoot and kill anything moving. Graphic images of the blood and guts from slain enemies are an integral part of the video.

Another popular video game series is Grand Theft Auto. On April 29, 2008 the latest version, Grand Theft Auto IV (GTA4), was released. GTA4 was developed by Rockstar Games. First day sales of GTA4 were 3.6 million copies. By the end of the first week, GTA4 had sales totaling $500 million.[17]

GTA4 took 150 game developers almost 4 years to complete. It is a third person shooter and driving game allowing players to steal and drive a variety of vehicles including cars, boats, helicopters, and motorcycles. The content of the game is extremely violent and sales are limited to adults. The action in the game takes place in Liberty City, which does not attempt to disguise its resemblance to New York City.

The game is described as highly cinematic and realistic. The main character, Niko an Eastern European immigrant, has a number of adventures with other immigrant characters involved in criminal activities. The game offers a variety of targets to blow up and many people to kill. The game is immensely interactive. Not only do victims and vehicles respond to physical triggers, but personal relationships change based on specific events.[18]

An educational version of one of these popular games might be called something on the order of *Concept to Consumption (CtC)*. *CtC* would be based on a process of developing a new idea for a product, manufacturing the product, and bringing it to market. All of the action would occur in a factory setting.

A factory venue would enable the same dark and menacing look, which is an important tie-in to existing games. The game would feature cavernous old industrial buildings that contain heavy machinery, catwalks, cranes and power generating equipment. The building would be surrounded by alleys, railroad tracks, and truck loading docks that would be designed to add to the ominous character. Custom vehicles are a popular feature in games. The industrial need for large trucks and railroad trains, as well as small vehicles used by individual workers to get around inside the factories provides a basis for imaginative vehicular iterations.

The various machines inside the factory, including cutting, grinding, welding, stamping, and molding equipment would have intriguing forward-looking designs. The robotics throughout the plant, as well as the wiring, switches, and piping that run across ceilings, walls, and floors would be given special graphic treatment. Workers inside the factory would wear safety gear that could offer different and unique looks. The process of converting raw material into finished product entails cutting, forming, assembling and finishing. Each of these procedures required different machinery and tooling that have virtually endless design potential.

Industrial lasers have an important role in manufacturing operations. Lasers are used for cutting various materials, like metal and plastic. They are also used to guide computer controlled equipment used in cutting, welding and stitching. Though popularized in the James Bond movie, *Goldfinger* ("You expect me to talk? No Mr. Bond, I expect you to die."), for nefarious use, industrial lasers are both highly utilitarian and stimulating to employ due to their power and precision.

Another important type of manufacturing still in evidence in the United States is chemical production. Industrial chemicals fill vital everyday needs from processing food to making paint, plastic and diesel fuel. Many of the same chemicals are used in all of these products. For example, glycerin appears as a food additive for Twinkies and is used in the production of soap. Phosphates are used in Twinkie production, as well as for fertilizer and herbicides. Most chemicals begin with a mined substance or oil. Petroleum products are sent through cracking plants where the oil is superheated allowing molecules to be split off into a number of different substances. The plants consist of large towers and miles of pipes.[19] The plant configuration and the chemical reactions that occur in the production process could easily be simplified and simulated for game play.

Mining operations require huge custom machinery for drilling, transporting, and processing rocks of varying chemical composition. The initial rock removal is, of course, done underground. The equipment and underground locations offer many graphic and game play opportunities from manipulating heavy equipment to initiating chemical transformations.

The 1958 invention of the microchip or integrated circuit provided the technological basis for our computer culture. Microelectronics consolidates millions of parts into one by performing electronic activities on micro-miniature dimensions. Microchips are capable of making billions of decisions every second. They are made of tiny flakes of silicon, a mineral in rock. Development of microchip technology is a vital part of society's essential needs.

In the mid-60s, Gordon Moore, an early microchip engineer, suggested that chip density or the number of transistors per chip would double every 18 months while the price will diminish by half.[20] Continuing this rapid rate of progress will require training a vast number of competent engineers and scientists. Games will include design and performance components of microchips that can be inserted into machines to modify and enhance their performance.

Another course of study requiring significant preparation is biotechnology. Just as chemistry and physics were the engines behind the technologies of the twentieth century, biological and advanced material sciences will influence twenty-first century economic development. New products from bioterial technology will result from the exploration of the subatomic universe.

The objective is to produce both organic and inorganic "smart" materials. These smart materials will have their atomic architecture designed in a manner that will enable these substances to exhibit enhanced qualities. For example, biotech engineered textiles will be more durable, comfortable, fire-resistant and easier to assemble. Pharmaceutical development can focus on preventing illnesses, as well as treating them. It will be possible to regenerate body tissue to address a variety of conditions. Ceramic materials are being developed to improve the performance of airplanes and automobiles.[21] Video games will enable users to visualize and control subatomic reactions.

Story lines for the various games would revolve around the main characters that are charged with leading the numerous operations required to design, produce, market, and distribute finished goods. Designing and manufacturing exciting product using an assortment of machinery and tooling would be at the core of the games. The manipulation of manufacturing variables related to cost, productivity and quality would be an integral part of each character's responsibilities. The level of complexity of each process will be age and grade appropriate. Processes will become more involved in successive grades.

There are four reasons for using a manufacturing storyline in educational game development. The first is that manufacturing, which is the process of creating a finished saleable product from available raw materials, is an active, vital, and engaging pursuit that involves many types of activities—from design and production to marketing and distribution. It requires technical knowledge in an array of subjects and competent decision making capabilities.

Second, the manufacturing process requires the use of considerable expertise which may be generated both individually and through a group effort. To begin, one must introduce a marketable product. The new idea would be the outcome of a group consensus. Individuals within the group would also explore the various market segments into which the product would be sold and the numerous competitive forces the product would encounter.

Competitive forces include competition from within the industry— companies making similar product; the bargaining power of customers— a small number of large customers can dictate a market; the bargaining power of suppliers—a limited number of suppliers can set prices; the threat of new entrants (entry barriers may be high or low)—a business with a small capital requirements will be easy for others to enter; and the threat of substitute products. Product differentiation, price and quality will be part of the story line.[22]

The third reason for creating an industrial game context is to introduce factory production to young people. With the virtual disappearance of manufacturing in the U.S. students have limited knowledge of how products they purchase are made. The elaborate product delivery process from design to distribution is intricate and potentially fraught with peril. The nature of industrial product development engenders interest and excitement at each stage. Immersing children in a manufacturing context will offer the training and perspective necessary for children to pursue manufacturing entrepreneurial opportunities as adults.

Finally, video game manufacturing will enable students to address and improve on the important negative aspects of manufacturing, which include industrial pollution, inefficient energy consumption, and worker justice issues. American industrial history was and continues to be pressured by the dichotomous priorities imposed by the need for cities and towns to attract industry which generates good jobs, while at the same time having to address the lethal pollution responsible for widespread health problems and frequent premature death that those industries may produce. Reducing energy consumption and treating workers with dignity are subjects requiring awareness and training. The factory of the future will look different from those seen in the historical archives.

Environmental Protection Issues: In 1948 a small mill town, Donora, Pennsylvania located outside Pittsburgh, hosted a large integrated steel making plant and a factory producing zinc, which was used to coat the steel in order to prevent rust. Steel and zinc are manufactured using processes requiring the constant heating of mined materials to temperatures above 2,600° Fahrenheit. The temperature of the surface of the sun is 10,000° Fahrenheit. The sun is 93 million miles away. The heat is supplied by burning enormous amounts of locally mined coal. Gases emitted during these processes include sulfur, carbon, fluoride, nitrogen, and zinc. In large quantities these gases are extremely dangerous and have both long and short term negative health consequences for individuals working in or living near the plants. On a cold night in late October an air inversion trapped these fumes close to the ground creating a blinding fog. The incident resulted in 20 sudden deaths and caused 6,000 people to become ill. The 6,000 local residents would have continuing respiratory problems for the remainder of their lives.[23]

Many of these factories have been shuttered in the United States. However, they continue to operate in developing countries like China and India where the pollution and greenhouse gases produced is affecting all residents of the planet. The *CtC* games would require lessons in the use of alternative energy to power these factories and find ways to mitigate the noxious gas emissions created through the production process.

Alternative energy studies would include the utilization of the wind, sun and tidal power. Wind energy is harnessed using a wind turbine. Solar panels are used to capture and convert the energy of the sun to electrical power. The energy created from shifting sea tides is collected and transferred using undersea turbines or the construction of barrages, which is a type of dam, to convert the movement of the tides in a manner similar to the way hydroelectric power is created. Looking for clean ways to burn the coal that is abundant in the U.S. would be another important project to explore.

The electric grid, which moves electrical energy from power plants through a vast network of transmission lines into homes and businesses, also does not operate efficiently. As a result, a considerable amount of energy is wasted and environmental damage is greater than necessary. A smarter grid would save energy and cost.

Simple measures to improve efficiency would include both personal efforts and computer systems to adjust energy usage during peak periods. For example, when demand is unacceptably high, such as on a very hot day, electric users would get some type of warning from the electric company to slightly reduce their usage by decreasing cooling temperature or turning off other electrical appliances like washers and dryers. These simple conservation measures would reduce the need for huge generating capacity for relatively short high demand periods. A reduction of only 5% in high demand period usage would eliminate the need for 90 new coal fired plants to be built over the next 20 years.[24]

Worker Justice Issues: Worker treatment and social justice concerns will be addressed in a *CtC* program. In 1911 the Triangle Shirtwaist factory in New York City, which resulted in the deaths of 146 young women, was the worst industrial factory fire in American history. The factory owners, the city's business community, elected officials and governmental safety, and health enforcement agencies all shared responsibility for the tragedy. Immigrant working women sewing blouses for the burgeoning fashion industry forced to labor in sweatshop conditions making pitiful wages. Safety considerations were virtually nonexistent. A lack of fire escapes, defective drop ladders, defective sprinklers, a limited number of exits, locked exits, dark hallways, and obstructed approaches to fire exits were common in these facilities. When some loose fabric ignited on the eighth floor of the Triangle factory, its 500 employees went racing for exits. Only 354 of those workers made it out alive.[25]

Laboring 65 to 75 hour work weeks and often supplying their own needles and thread, immigrant women in New York City at the turn of the twentieth century were severely exploited and personally mistreated. Because of the large number of incoming Eastern European immigrants, workers were able to make few demands since they could be easily replaced. Regardless of the consequences, in 1909 members of Local 25 of the International Ladies Garment Workers Union called for a strike. Out of 32 thousand workers in 600 factories, more that 20,000 of the workers joined a citywide walkout. Despite harassment and arrest, the women walked the picket lines. Over a period of 2 weeks, employers consented to a 52 hour work week and provided 4 paid holidays. Workers no longer had to purchase their own tools and a grievance committee was established to negotiate future issues.[26]

Although these events occurred 100 years ago, many of the same issues persist in one form or another. Recent immigrants from Mexico have replaced those from Eastern Europe. Today, there exists a considerable measure of both federal and statewide legislation concerning minimum wages, payment of overtime, benefits, and health and safety standards. However, unlike their Eastern European counterparts, many of the Mexican immigrants entered the United States illegally. As result, there are employers who exploit these workers since the workers are reluctant to complain to the authorities for fear of being deported.

Another form of worker exploitation involves Chinese sourcing. Wal-Mart, the largest corporation in the world with annual sales approaching $400 billion, has been a significant contributor to the movement of American manufacturing to China. Corporately, Wal-Mart has a singular focus on buying at the lowest possible cost. To maintain its low cost strategic imperative Wal-Mart's treatment of suppliers, employees, and communities has received considerable negative attention.

Wal-Mart's treatment of suppliers has been held responsible for forcing a number of major consumer goods manufacturing companies to close U.S. production facilities and move their product manufacturing to China where workers are paid a fraction of U.S. wages. These actions have resulted in the loss of millions of well-paying American manufacturing jobs.

Between 1997 and 2004, 3.1 million U.S. factory jobs were lost.[27]Examples include, Huffy Corp, a bicycle maker, which was forced to close down plants in Celina, Ohio, Farmington, Missouri, and Southaven,

Mississippi putting 1,835 people out of work. L. R. Nelson, a lawn sprinkler maker in Peoria, Illinois laid off 1,000 workers in order to get the "China Price." Many other familiar brands like Rubbermaid, Black and Decker, Stanley Tools, Fedders air conditioners, Sunbeam mixers, Radio Flyer Wagons, Lakewood Engineering (portable fans and heaters), Etch-A-Sketch, and Pillowtex moved production to China where workers are paid 25¢ per hour.[28]

Wal-Mart's demand for the "China Price" precludes any consideration for American workforce prerogatives. In actuality, driving blue collar wages down serves Wal-Mart's need to expand since a growing low wage population is more likely to patronize Wal-Mart because of the shoppers' limited means.

Wal-Mart's treatment of its 1.6 million employees has also been taken to task. Aside from paying wages at a level where all of its nonexecutive status store employees are living below the poverty line, Wal-Mart has lost lawsuits for forcing employees to work extra hours without pay and paying women 5% to 15% less than men in the same positions. The annual employee turnover at Wal-Mart is close to 50%, necessitating the hiring of about 800,000 new employees each year. Wal-Mart also lost a lawsuit for locking in cleaning personnel at night in violation of fire safety standards. Further, the majority of these cleaning people were illegal immigrants.

Wal-Mart's community relations can also be described as abusive. Aside from being responsible for the closure of thousands of small family-owned businesses, Wal-Mart also exploits local taxpayers. For example, since only a miniscule portion of Wal-Mart employees qualify for any type of company health benefit, the company encourages its workers to take advantage of taxpayer funded facilities usually reserved for indigent residents, not full-time wage earners. Worker justice considerations would be and integral part of any entrepreneurial training.

Oil Shortage Issues: As China and India develop tens of millions of their own middle class citizens and vehicle ownership continues its rapid proliferation, the demand for petroleum products will likely push the cost of a barrel of oil substantially beyond its current $100+ price.

Oil consumption in China, with its 1.5 billion population, has risen 45% in just the past 5 years. In 2000 there were 16 million cars in China. By 2004, there were 27 millions cars, and it is estimated that in 2010 there will be 56 million cars and by 2020, 120 million cars. There are about 250 million cars in the United States. In 1992 China exported oil. In 2003, China became the second largest importer of oil behind Japan. By 2020 China's imports will have to quadruple. It is estimated that by 2025 China will import as much crude oil as the U.S. currently imports.[29]

About 60% of the oil consumed in the United States is used by the transportation sector. Recently, as oil climbed over $100 per barrel, serious discussions have occurred regarding the need to reduce American dependence on foreign oil. Since vehicles are the largest users of oil, it is most appropriate to consider radical conservation measures in that segment first. Reducing American reliance on oil will require both the adoption of individual conservation measures and the advent of a significant technological breakthrough. Pioneering advances in energy production have occurred in the past.

In 1942, during World War II, the first controllable chain reaction was accomplished in a nuclear reactor built underneath a sports stadium at The University of Chicago. From this successful experiment, the U.S. government determined it needed to develop an atomic weapon to win the war. The government was also concerned that Germany was developing a nuclear weapons capability which would have severely impacted the U.S. war effort. J. Robert Oppenheimer, a physicist born in New York City, was placed in charge of new government research facilities in Los Alamos, New Mexico and Oak Ridge, Tennessee. His objective was to produce an atomic bomb before Germany built one. The effort was called, The Manhattan Project. Oppenheimer was given all necessary technical and financial resources, including a workforce of 130,000 scientists, technicians, and support people to complete the project. He was able to build three atomic bombs by April, 1945 despite the challenges the brand new technology presented.

In 1712, Thomas Newcomen, a British blacksmith, built the first piston-driven steam engine. Steam was pumped into a cylinder and condensed using cold water to create a vacuum. The vacuum forced the piston downward. James Watt, a Scottish engineer considered the Father of the steam engine, made some critical improvements in 1763. Watt substantially increased the steam engine's efficiency by adding valves to the piston cylinder. The steam was created by heating water external to the piston cylinder.

In 1859 a French engineer, Lenoir, built the first continuously operating spark-ignition internal combustion engine. A few years later, in 1876, Nicolaus Otto, a German inventor, developed the first four-stroke internal combustion engine.

Today's automobile engines operate identically to those original piston-driven designs—using combustion to drive a vertically moving piston and transferring the vertical motion to a rotating shaft. The technology behind the contemporary internal combustion automobile engine is 300 years old. Many refinements have been made in metallurgy, computer-controlled injection systems, valve performance, and so forth. But, the engines still require burning fossil fuel, oil primarily, to work.

More than one-quarter of the world's proven oil reserves lie in one country—the Arab kingdom of Saudi Arabia which has a population of 24 million. Saudi Arabia is an absolute monarchy from which the U.S. imports about 2 million barrels of each day. At $100 a barrel, that amounts to $75 billion annually the U.S. alone pumps into their economy. The king of Saudi Arabia, Abd al Aziz of the ruling Al Saud family, is said to be descended from Muhammad ibn al Wahhab. In 1744 Wahhab founded the fundamentalist Muslim movement that reinforces parochial practices and called for jihad, or Holy War, against anyone not following strict Wahhabi teachings.

Today, all Saudi children are schooled in Wahhabism. These teachings include communally performed prayer five times a day and modest dress, especially by women. Wahhabism forbids use of alcohol, tobacco, and other stimulants. Music, dancing, laughing, and weeping have also been forbidden at times. Wahhabism maintains a community of morals enforcers to assure adherence to these rules.

Although slavery in Saudi Arabia wasn't abolished until 1962, as a result of pressure from the West, attitudes toward Western licentiousness and lack of values are inculcated in Saudis from childhood. It should not be surprising that the leaders of Middle Eastern terrorist organizations are all Saudis. They are funded by the billions of dollars we spend for their oil. How do you stop terrorism? Stop buying Saudi oil. How do you eliminate the need for oil? Replace the internal combustion engine.

Each year the federal government and local authorities spend more than a trillion dollars for defense. We spend almost $20 billion a year on NASA. While we are placing a high priority on defense systems and space exploration, the dollars spent on researching new battery technology, nitrogen fuel cell energy and even fusion experimentation is next to nothing by comparison.

The U.S. must establish a Manhattan Project Two to develop a new clean, non-fossil-fuel burning engine that eliminates the need for Middle Eastern oil. All resources necessary must be committed to this project. It shouldn't take 300 years to create a new engine. The U.S. depends on engine technology that predates the Revolutionary War.

An important part of the problem is the limited engineering resources, in terms of personnel and companies, capable of performing innovative solutions on the level required. The purpose of the *CtC* education curriculum would be to train large numbers of individuals with needed engineering competence and the ability to search for revolutionary solutions to critical problems.

The story line in the *CtC* video game would not require the use of destructive weaponry. Competition would be based on innovation. Innovative ideas would be developed throughout all aspects of the process. People would be assigned to research and design and individuals would be responsible for creating, administering, and maintaining a program to continually reduce cost and improve quality. This would include material control (purchase, deliver, and inventory control), quality assurance (establishing and meeting specifications), finance (allocating resources and preparing budgets), sales and marketing (advertising, customer relations, and new products), industrial relations (employee recruitment, training, evaluation, and salary administration), and plant engineering and maintenance (safety and limiting production interruptions).[30]

All aspects of engineering, production, and marketing require the use of varying levels of mathematics. Mastery of math skills would be developed on an individualized basis. However, the new material would be presented within the context of the larger problem of making and selling a product. This would increase the level of interest and address the issue of relevance. The specific math skills developed would apply immediately to a particular facet of the game. The ability to solve math problems both accurately and quickly would enable the individual's group to compete effectively.

Reading and writing skills would be introduced through the market research or other administrative requirements of the game. For example, appropriate demographic characteristics of various populations, either real or fictional, would be presented in paragraph form. Sentence analysis of this material would be completed at the group level. All instructions and research information would be offered in paragraph form. Individuals would then be required to prepare paragraphs critically addressing the issues presented. Sentence structure, spelling and concept clarity would be sorted out in the game. The game would not proceed with writing errors. Communication skills are vital to the enterprise.

To remove some of the mystery from reading, mathematics and literacy development, the following year by year curriculum in those subjects includes specific performance objectives that are age appropriate and properly sequenced. Learning reading, math, and literacy skills in Grade 1 through Grade 6 requires a precise progression of skill acquisition that is readily achieved using video game technology. The development of these skills would be woven into the game play of the *CtC* video challenges.

The arrangement of the reading, math, and literacy skill development process is described as follows:

1st Grade Reading Objectives

- Letter Recognition: ABCs. Learn sounds and names of letters.
- Vocabulary: Word recognition.
- Synonyms and Antonyms: Word games. Matching words that mean the same and words that are opposites.

- Words in Context: Word meanings in the context of sentences.
- Vowel Sounds and Rhyming: Rhyming sound exercises.
- Spelling: Practice spelling commonly used words.
- Grammar: Identify nouns and verbs.
- Capitalization and Punctuation: Capitalize beginning of sentences and names. Learn to use periods, question marks, commas, and exclamation marks.
- Word Usage: Learn when to use pronouns, such as "I" and "me." Learn plurals, verb tenses (present and past), and superlatives.
- Comprehension: Reading and listening to stories with short easy sentences. Follow story line, make predictions.[31]

1st Grade Math Objectives

- Patterns: Recognizing shapes.
- Sorting and Classifying: Recognizing shape sequences.
- Number Recognition and Counting: Learning numbers and number sequences. Associating a number with a group of objects.
- Ordinal Numbers: Ordering numbers-first, second, third, and so forth.
- Comparing Numbers: Understanding more than and less than.
- Addition: Adding together single digit numbers.
- Addition Story Problems: Solving word problems using addition skills.
- Subtraction: Subtracting single digit numbers, that is, put in x, take away $< x = y$.
- Subtraction Story Problems: Solving word problems using simple subtraction.
- Place Value: Identify hundreds, tens and ones, that is, 134 has 1 hundred, 3 tens, and 4 ones.
- Counting by Fives and Tens: Use groups of 5s and 10s to count to 100.
- Shapes: Identify square, circle, oval, triangle, and rectangle.
- Fractions: Show unequal equal and unequal parts, that is, half, third, quarter.
- Time: Tell time on analog clock.
- Money: Identify coins and make change.
- Measurement: Ruler used to measure in inches and in centimeters. Map distance reading.[32]

1st Grade Literacy Objectives

- *Literature:* Poetry; Aesop's Fables; Stories; Familiar Sayings.
- *History/Geography:* Ancient Middle East; Colonial American History; U.S. Geography.
- *Visual Arts/Music:* Portrait painting; Great Composers; Jazz; Folk Songs.
- *Science:* Forests; The Food Chain; Oceans; Human Body; Matter; Measurement; Electricity; Astronomy; Minerals; Scientists.[33]

2nd Grade Reading Objectives

- Vocabulary: Advanced word recognition.
- Words in Context: Word meanings in the context of sentences.
- Synonyms and Antonyms: Word games. Matching words that mean the same and words that are opposites.
- Spelling: Practice spelling commonly used words.
- Word Recognition. Compound words and contractions.
- Parts of Speech. Nouns, pronouns, verbs, adjectives.
- Breaking It Down. Identifying the main idea in a paragraph. Understanding sequencing and characters and settings in a story.
- Reading Comprehension: Predicting outcomes, drawing conclusions, and understanding cause and effect in stories.
- Literary Genres. Fact versus fiction. Reality versus fantasy. Biography. Poetry.
- Study Skills. Using a dictionary. Understanding alphabetical order. Understanding graphs and charts. Knowledge of the parts of a book—title page, table of contents, index, glossary.[34]

2nd Grade Math Objectives
- Sorting and Classifying: Identifying objects that are related to one another on a variety of levels, such as appearance, usage or origin.
- Addition: Adding together two and three digit numbers.
- Addition Story Problems: Solving word problems using two and three digit addition skills.
- Subtraction: Subtracting two and three digit numbers.
- Subtraction Story Problems: Solving word problems using two and three digit subtraction.
- Introduce Simple Multiplication Concept: For example, 3 times 7 equals $7 + 7 + 7$.

- Graphing and Charting: Make up charts and graphs to represent varying numbers of items.
- Review Fractions: Halves, thirds, quarters.[35]

2nd Grade Literacy Objectives

- *Literature:* Poetry; American Tall Tales; Ancient Greek Myths; Familiar Sayings.
- *History/Geography:* Asian Civilizations; Ancient Greece; U.S. Constitution, War of 1812, Civil War, Immigration; Geography of the Americas.
- *Visual Arts/Music:* Landscape painting; Sculptures; Abstract Art; Architecture; Musical Instruments; Musical Scale, Notes.
- *Science:* Cycle of Life and the Seasons; Insects, Water Cycle; Human Body—cells, tissues, organs, food pyramid, diet; Magnetism; Simple Machines—tools, levels, wheels, pulleys, planes, wedges, screws.[36]

3rd Grade Reading Objectives

- Vocabulary: Word recognition at proper Grade level.
- Synonyms, Antonyms and Homophones: Word games. Matching words that mean the same and words that are opposites at proper Grade level.
- Words in Context: Word meanings in the context of sentences at proper Grade level.
- Vowel Sounds and Rhyming: Rhyming sound exercises. Also consonant blends.
- Spelling: Practice spelling commonly used words at proper Grade level. Introduction to root words, prefixes and suffixes. Compound words.
- Grammar: Create sentences using various parts of speech—nouns, pronouns, verbs, adjectives.
- Capitalization and Punctuation: Learn use of apostrophes and quotation marks.
- Comprehension: Reading and listening to stories. Follow story sequence, identify characters and settings, make predictions and draw conclusions.
- Literary Genres: Fact versus Opinion. Reality versus Fantasy. Biography. Poetry.[37]

3rd Grade Math Objectives

- Addition: Adding together four digit numbers including regrouping.
- Addition Story Problems: Solving word problems using four digit addition skills.
- Subtraction: Subtracting four digit numbers including regrouping.
- Subtraction Story Problems: Solving word problems using four digit subtraction individually and combined with using addition.
- Place Value: Understanding ones, tens, hundreds, thousands, ten thousands, and so forth.
- Rounding: To the nearest 10, 100, 1,000, and so forth.
- Writing Numbers: Using words to represent numbers, such as two hundred thirty-one = 231.
- Mental Math: Introduce simple addition problems to be done without pencil and paper.
- Single Digit Multiplication: Learn multiplication tables for numbers one through nine.
- Multiplication Story Problems. Solving word problems using single digit multiplication.
- Division: Learn to divide larger numbers by smaller numbers.
- Division Word Problems: Use division to solve word problems.
- Fractions: Equivalents, that is, $2/4 = \frac{1}{2}$.
- Fractions: Division, that is, $\frac{1}{2}$ of $8 = 4$.
- Fractions: Numerators and denominators.
- Decimals: Turning fractions into decimals.
- Decimals: Addition and subtraction of numbers with decimals.
- Geometry: Shapes—triangle, square, pentagon, hexagon, and so forth.
- Geometry: Lines, line segments, and different types of angles—right, acute, obtuse, straight, perpendicular.
- Geometry: 3 dimensional shapes—cubes, cones, spheres.
- Geometry: Measuring 2 dimensional perimeters.
- Map Skills: Scaling—1 inch = 1 mile.
- Coordinates: Create graphs using coordinates.
- Measurements: Ounce and pound; inch and centimeter; foot, yard, mile and meter, kilometer.
- Roman Numerals: Converting roman numerals to numbers and numbers to roman numerals.

- Money: Adding and subtracting dollars and cents problems.
- Time: Adding and subtracting time intervals.[38]

3rd Grade Literacy Objectives

- *Literature:* Poetry; World Mythology; Ancient Greek and Roman Mythology; Stories—Biography, Autobiography, Fiction, Nonfiction; Familiar Sayings.
- *History/Geography:* Rivers of the World; Ancient Rome; The Vikings; Early North American Explorers; North American English Colonies.
- *Visual Arts/Music:* Lighting; Lines and Shapes; Reading and Writing Musical Notes and Rhythm; Great Composers.
- *Science:* Classifying Animals; Human Body—Skeletal and Muscular Systems, Brain and Nervous System, Light and Vision, Sound and Hearing; Astronomy—Planets; Ecology—Conservation; Scientists.[39]

4th Grade Reading Objectives

- Vocabulary: Word recognition at proper Grade level. Should understand meanings of words and be able to write longer and more complicated sentences.
- Words in Context: Word meanings in the context of sentences at proper Grade level. Should be able to infer word meanings in context, analyze story, characters, and outcomes. Can understand there are multiple meanings of words depending on context.
- Synonyms, Antonyms, Homophones and Homonyms: Word games. Matching words that mean the same and words that are opposites at proper Grade level. Skillful use of synonyms and antonyms to expand vocabulary.
- Spelling: Practice spelling commonly used words at proper Grade level. Use root words, prefixes, and suffixes to create words. Expand use of singular and plural words and compound words.
- Spelling: Use contractions.
- Grammar: Create sentences using various parts of speech—nouns, pronouns, verbs, adjectives. Understand concepts of tenses, masculine and feminine pronouns, plural and possessive pronouns.
- Comprehension: Reading and listening to stories. Follow story sequence, identify and analyze characters and settings, make predictions and draw conclusions.

- Reading Critically: Understand cause and effect relationships, identify motivations of characters, compare and contrast one story idea with another, predict outcomes and draw conclusions.
- Literary Genres: Students should be able to write in a variety of forms, including novels, poems, nonfiction periodicals and books, plays and myths.[40]

4th Grade Math Objectives

- Place Value: Understanding ones, tens, hundreds, thousands … millions.
- Rounding: To the nearest 10, 100, 1,000, and so forth.
- Estimating: Get approximate answers using rounded numbers.
- Skip Counting: Counting in multiples—twos, threes, fives, and so forth.
- Mental Math: Introduce simple addition problems to be done without pencil and paper.
- Multi Digit Multiplication: Learn multiplication skills multiplying two and three digit numbers using regrouping.
- Multiplication Story Problems. Solving word problems using multi digit multiplication with regrouping.
- Division: Learn to divide using multi digit divisors and dividends showing remainders in quotient.
- Division Word Problems: Use multi-digit division to solve word problems.
- Checking: Learn to check division problem answers using multiplication.
- Averaging: Learn to add two or more quantities and divide by the number of quantities.
- Averaging Word Problems: Solve word problems using averaging skills.
- Geometry: Shapes/angles—triangle, square, pentagon, hexagon, right, acute, obtuse.
- Geometry: Measuring circles—radius and diameter.
- Fractions: Comparing fractions— $\frac{1}{2} < \frac{3}{4}$.
- Fractions: Addition and subtraction using different numerators and denominators.
- Fractions: Addition and subtraction using mixed numbers—whole numbers and fractions.
- Decimals: Turning fractions into decimals.

- Decimals: Addition and subtraction of numbers with decimals.
- Graphing: Make bar charts, line charts, and pie charts using numbers and word problems.
- Coordinates: Create graphs using coordinates.
- Probability: Write probability ratios based on word problems.
- Probability: Learn about probability trees figuring possible combinations of two separate events.
- Measurements: Learn to measure fractions of an inch, foot, yard, mile, and so forth.
- Measurement Conversions: Convert inches to feet and yards, and inches and feet to centimeters and millimeters.
- Measurement: Learn to measure and calculate perimeter, area and volume of different shapes.
- Measurement: Learn weight conversions—ounces and pounds to grams and kilograms.
- Time Problems: Measuring speed and distance.
- Times Zones: Time problems involving travel through different time zones.
- Money: Adding and subtracting dollars and cents problems. Creating budgets and expense charts.[41]

4th Grade Literacy Objectives

- *Literature:* Poetry; Classical Stories and Fiction; Familiar Sayings.
- *History/Geography:* Maps; Hemispheres; Mountains; Europe in the Middle Ages; Rise of Islam; African Kingdoms; China Dynasties and Conquerors; American Revolution; Constitutional Government; Early U.S. Presidents; Reformers.
- *Visual Arts/Music:* Art of the Middle Ages, Islam, Africa, China and the U.S; Elements of Music; Listening and Understanding; Songs of the U.S. Armed Forces; Great Composers.
- *Science:* Human Body—Circulation and Respiration, Heart, Lungs, Blood Vessels; Chemistry—Atoms, Solutions; Electricity; Geology; Meteorology—Weather; Scientists.[42]

5th Grade Reading Objectives

- Vocabulary: Word recognition at proper Grade level. Should understand meanings of words and be able to write longer and more complicated sentences.

- Grammar: Subjects and predicates. Subjects and verbs. Complete sentences. Direct objects, indirect objects and prepositions. Create sentences using various parts of speech—nouns, pronouns, verbs, adjectives. Understand concepts—transitive and intransitive verbs, irregular verbs, and "be" as a helping or linking verb. Indefinite pronouns, interrogative and relative pronouns. Comparatives. Adjectives—demonstrative, indefinite, interrogative and possessive. Adverbs and adjective and adverb phrases. Conjunctions. Commands, requests and exclamations. Compound subjects and predicates. Using commas. Who, that and which clauses.
- Synonyms, Antonyms, Homophones and Homonyms: Word games. Matching words that mean the same and words that are opposites at proper Grade level. Skillful use of synonyms and antonyms to expand vocabulary.
- Spelling: Practice spelling commonly used words at proper Grade level. Use root words, prefixes and suffixes to create words. Break words into syllables. Learn about double consonants and verb forms. Practice proofreading.
- Similes, Metaphors and Analogies: Write sentences using similes, metaphors and analogies for comparison.
- Thesaurus: Learn to use thesaurus for synonyms.
- Comprehension: Using prior knowledge. Recall facts about music, art, animals and geography.
- Reading Skills: Skimming, map reading, following directions, labels, newspapers and schedules.
- Writing: Topic sentences, supporting sentences, building paragraphs, sequencing, purpose (inform, entertain, persuade). Descriptive and non-descriptive sentences, personal narratives, point of view, supporting your opinion. Writing a summary, a letter and news writing. Personifications, similes and metaphors. Writing a book report, and doing research. Taking notes, making an outline, editing and proofreading. Summarizing.
- Literary Genres: Students should be able to write in a variety of forms, including novels, poems, nonfiction periodicals and books, plays and myths.[43]

5th Grade Math Objectives

- Roman Numerals: Review.
- Place Value: Understanding ones, tens, hundreds, thousands … billions.

- Addition and Subtraction: How to check answers.
- Rounding: To the nearest 10, 100, 1,000, 10,000 and 100,000.
- Rounding and Estimating: Get approximate answers using rounded numbers. Use rounding and addition to estimate sums. Use rounding and subtraction to estimate differences.
- Prime Numbers: Positive whole number that can be divided evenly by itself and one.
- Multiples: Find least common multiple—smallest number that numbers in a set are divisible by.
- Factors: Numbers multiplied together to create a product. Factors of 12 are 4 and 3, 2, and 6, and 12 and 1.
- Add and Subtract Integers: Integer is a positive or negative whole number or zero. For example, 6 + (−2) = 4.
- Multiplying and Dividing Money: Using decimal point correctly.
- Calculator Basics: Learn to add, subtract, multiply, and divide using a calculator.
- Averages: Difference between mode, median, and mean.
- Fractions: Addition and subtraction using different numerators and denominators.
- Fractions: Addition and subtraction using mixed numbers—whole numbers and fractions.
- Fractions: Addition and subtraction using mixed numbers—whole numbers and improper fractions.
- Fractions: Multiplying and dividing fractions.
- Decimals: Turning fractions into decimals.
- Decimals: Addition and subtraction of numbers with decimals.
- Decimals: Multiplying and dividing decimals—proper movement of decimal point.
- Percents and Fractions: Convert fractions to decimals to percent.
- Percent: Find percent of a number with multiplication.
- Percent: Find percent by dividing the number given out of number possible.
- Ratios: Comparing two quantities.
- Proportions: Another way of writing a ratio.
- Lines, Geometric Figures and Angles: Learn to identify all types of lines and shapes and measure angles with a protractor.
- Circumference: Learn use of π (3.14).
- Triangles: Calculate area of a triangle.

- Graphing: Make bar charts, line charts and pie charts and circle charts using numbers and word problems.
- Temperature: Convert Fahrenheit to Celsius.[44]

5th Grade Literacy Objectives

- *Literature:* Poetry; Myths and Legends; Familiar Sayings and Phrases.
- *History/Geography:* The Seasons; Latitude and Longitude; Arctic and Tropical Zones; Lakes; Early American Civilizations; European Exploration; Renaissance and Reformation; England; Russia; Feudal Japan; U.S. Westward Expansion; Civil War; Reconstruction; Native American Cultures and Conflicts; U.S. Geography.
- *Visual Arts/Music:* Art of the Renaissance, Japan and the U.S; Elements of Music; Long and Short Notes; Sharps and Flats; Listening and Understanding; Songs About Western Expansion; Great Composers.
- *Science:* Human Body—Endocrine System; Human Growth Stages; Human Reproductive Systems; Chemistry—Matter and Change, the Elements, Molecules and Compounds; Classifying Plants; Photosynthesis; Life Cycles and Reproduction Scientists.[45]

6th Grade Reading Objectives

- Vocabulary: Word recognition at proper Grade level. Should understand meanings of words and be able to write longer and more complicated sentences.
- Grammar: Use possessive nouns, verbs, verb tense, and irregular verb forms. Subject/verb agreement, interrogative pronouns, pronoun/antecedent agreement, appositives, and dangling modifiers. Adjectives—positive, comparative and superlative. Adverbs—positive, comparative and superlative. Direct and indirect objects, conjunctions, affect and effect, among and between, amount and number, principal and principle, good and well, like and as. Colons, semicolons, dashes, quotation marks, apostrophes, plural possessive, and italics.
- Spelling: Practice spelling commonly used words at proper Grade level. Spell words using long and short vowels. Review rules for using ie, ei, sh, th, ch, ph, gh gn and silent letters. Use suffixes, ion, tion, ation, ment, ity, ship, ful, ist.
- Comprehension: Using prior knowledge. Recall facts about music, art, animals and geography.

- Reading Skills: Cause and effect, personification and symbolism. Generalizations, author's purpose, comprehension, recalling details, sequencing, and using prior knowledge.
- Writing: Analogies of purpose antonym analogies, partial analogies, action/object analogies, analogies of association, object/location analogies, cause/effect analogies and synonym analogies. Complete sentences, run-on sentences, four types of sentences, organizing and building paragraphs. Explaining with examples, creating word pictures, describing people, describing events, writing descriptive sentences, different points of view. Persuasive writing, setting the scene, creating a plot, and writing dialogue. Paraphrasing, summarizing, and outlining. Using right resources, reference books. Creating table of contents and indexes. Biographical research and friendly letters.[46]

6th Grade Math Objectives

- Place Value: Understanding whole numbers—ones, tens, hundreds, thousands … trillions. Understanding fractions—tenths, hundredths, thousandths.
- Addition and Subtraction: Use fractional place values with regrouping.
- Multiplying: Multiply using two and three digit numbers using zeros as place holders.
- Multiplying Integers: Multiplying positive and negative numbers.
- Division: Divide using two and three digit divisors showing remainders.
- Dividing Integers: Dividing positive and negative numbers.
- Equations: Value on both sides of = sign must be the same. Use combinations of addition, subtraction, multiplication, and division to solve problems.
- Add and Subtract Integers: Integer is a positive or negative whole number or zero. For example, $6 + (-2) = 4$.
- Multiplying and Dividing Money: Using decimal point correctly.
- Calculator Basics: Learn to add, subtract, multiply, and divide using a calculator.
- Averages: Difference between mode, median, and mean.
- Fractions: Addition and subtraction using different numerators and denominators.
- Fractions: Addition and subtraction using mixed numbers—whole numbers and fractions.

- Fractions: Addition and subtraction using mixed numbers—whole numbers and improper fractions.
- Fractions: Multiplying and dividing fractions.
- Decimals: Turning fractions into decimals.
- Decimals: Addition and subtraction of numbers with decimals.
- Decimals: Multiplying and dividing decimals—proper movement of decimal point.
- Logical Thinking: Use various mathematical skills to solve word problems.
- Area and Volume: Calculate area and volume of rectangles, triangles, polygons, circles and spheres.
- Metric Weights: Conversions using metric weights and pounds.
- Units of Capacity: Conversions using quarts, gallons and liters.
- Graphing: Make bar charts, line charts and pie charts and circle charts using numbers and word problems.
- Plotting Graphs: Using ordered pairs (x and y axis) to find points on a graph.[47]

6th Grade Literacy Objectives

- *Literature:* Poetry—Structure; Myths and Stories and Plays; Familiar Sayings and Phrases.
- *History/Geography:* World Geography—Deserts; Judaism and Christianity; Ancient Greece; Ancient Rome; The Enlightenment; the French Revolution; Industrialism, Capitalism, Socialism; Latin American Independence; Immigration to the U.S.; Industrialization and Urbanization; Reform.
- *Visual Arts/Music:* Classic Art—Ancient Greece and Rome; Gothic Art; The Renaissance; Baroque Art; Rococo Art; Neoclassical Art; Romantic Art; Realism Elements of Music; Beat, Scales, Chords; Listening and Understanding; Songs of Baroque, Classical and Romantic Periods; Great Composers.
- *Science:* Human Body—Diseases and Immune Systems; Energy, Heat and Energy Transfer; Plate Tectonics; Oceans; Astronomy—Gravity, Stars and Constellations.[48]

Learning reading, mathematics and achieving literacy is simply a matter of successfully progressing through the skill sets described above. Learning is not a random or amorphous procedure. Developing game software that corresponds with each stage of the knowledge acquisition process using an industrial frame of reference should not be an unusually difficult undertaking.

Games are created using middleware, which is game development software that can be readily purchased from online vendors. Two of the more popular programs are Maya and 3ds Max produced by Autodesk. Both programs simplify three dimensional work done on modeling and texturing in creating both background effects and animate characters. Various plug-in programs can be used for extending types of animation or graphic effects.[49]

Using middleware programs, storylines would consist of various characters being challenged to learn the reading and math lessons sequenced above. Each of the characters, placed in an industrial environment would have to master each skill level before proceeding to the next. The game and graphic context would make this process both exciting and relevant. The skills mastered would be used to further the development and production of a manufactured product.

CHAPTER 8

CONCLUSION

Truth can be defined as a point on a continuum between two diametrically opposed philosophical perspectives. The point, and consequently truth, is movable. Truth floats freely between the extremities. Much like an accounting balance sheet, truth can only be defined as a snapshot that freezes the assets and liabilities of a dynamic, continuously evolving endeavor at a precise moment in time. Truth, defined as the reigning norm, is not permanent.

The oppositional limits or thesis and antithesis of a socioepistemological metadialectic are personal responsibility and collective imperative. These limits are popularly described as Liberal versus Conservative, Capitalist versus Communist, and Democratic versus Republican. The truth or the accepted definition of reality always lies somewhere in between the poles. The point of truth (POT) moves back and forth, on the basis of the ability of people to perform. As individual performance capabilities increase, the POT moves in the direction of personal responsibility. As individual competence decline or the ability of an individual to determine personal outcomes diminishes, the POT moves towards collective action.

The American credo historically favored individualism. At the same time, it recognized the importance of assisting those in need. In order to increase the draw of the POT toward personal responsibility, it is necessary to improve individuals' human and social capital. This can only be achieved through effective education. The rugged individualism associated with America's frontier days did not require extensive skill sets since

Education Redux: How to Make Schools Relevant to Our Children and Our Future,
pp. 161–169
Copyright © 2010 by Information Age Publishing
All rights of reproduction in any form reserved.

most activity was related to agriculture and mining. As technology evolved over the past century and a half, those unable to keep up with its intellectual demands through education became more dependent on those who were able to stay on the cutting edge. Thus, an effective educational strategy will enable more people to participate as rugged individualists and entrepreneurs and eschew dependence on others.

Assisting the needy is funded through the collection of taxes from more successful individuals. The history of taxation in the United States is a reflection of the POT. Beginning in colonial times most taxes were collected in the form of tariffs on imports and exports. When the English Parliament imposed a tax on tea, the American Revolution began with the slogan, "taxation without representation is tyranny," since the colonists were not represented in the Parliament.

In the post-Revolutionary era, the federal government relied on tax contributions from the states which collected tariffs and property taxes. The imposition of an excise tax on liquor in 1794 led to the Whiskey Rebellion in southwestern Pennsylvania where Federal troops were sent in to overcome resistance to the tax by a group of farmers.[1]

To pay for the Civil War in the 1860s Congress passed a number of new excise taxes on items including playing cards, gunpowder, feathers, leather, pianos, yachts, billiard tables, and drugs. Congress also introduced the first income tax which was a 3% levy on annual incomes over $800. The income tax was abolished in 1872. The main source of government revenue until 1913 was the excise tax on alcohol and tobacco.

In 1913 a new income tax law was introduced with tax rates beginning at 1% of income. These tax rates began to rise dramatically with the need to cover the cost of World War I and, later, to cover shrinking revenues during the 1930's Depression. The Social Security Tax was added in 1935. Through World War II, the 1950s, 1960s and 1970s tax rates continued to rise up to a maximum rate of 87% of income for the top bracket. Beginning with the Economic Recovery Tax Act of 1981 through the Tax Relief and Reconciliation Act of 2001 the top tax bracket dropped to 33% of income. During that period of time, the U.S. National Debt rose from $800 billion to $9 trillion. Lowering taxes ostensibly meant the POT was moving toward personal responsibility. In reality the POT was moving in the opposite direction which required the assumption of massive debt to compensate for the budget shortfalls.

Other actions included passage of the Personal Responsibility and Work Opportunity Reconciliation Act of 1996 (PRWORA). It was intended to represent a significant movement from the collective imperative toward personal responsibility. Signed into law in August, 1996, the purpose of PRWORA is to serve as a welfare reform plan requiring work in exchange for limited welfare assistance.

Under PRWORA welfare recipients must work after 2 years on assistance. Work activities include, employment, on-the-job training, community service and vocational training. There will be a 5-year time limit for receiving any type of public assistance. Child support enforcement will be improved and there is a provision that unmarried minor parents live with a responsible adult. The law offers training, job subsidies, medical coverage, increased child care funding, and nutrition programs. However, assistance is only available to parents willing to work.[2]

From a realistic perspective, there are a couple of serious shortcomings in the PRWORA legislation. First, it is unlikely that any quick-fix workforce preparation lessons will provide welfare recipients with the prerequisite academic and life skills that eluded them throughout their many years of childhood and adolescence. Second, there are an increasingly diminished number of employment opportunities for individuals with substandard skill levels. The employment opportunities that may be available will guarantee the workers poverty level wages. Working 40 hours a week and living in poverty is not much of an incentive to get off welfare.

Problems engendered by living in poverty, such as the inability to purchase necessities and the social stigma attached to being poor, will assure the failure of PRWORA. Nevertheless, the politically appealing rhetoric of moving people from welfare to work will displace the reality of the program's lack of value.

Another problem with PRWORA has to do with de facto political leadership. In America's Black community where PRWORA was targeted, local neighborhood leaders are Christian preachers. Among Black Americans, 98% identify themselves as Christians. In a national survey conducted 25 years ago, 89% of Black Americans stated they were religiously affiliated.[3]

Unfortunately, there are Black preachers that promote a sense of entitlement, due to historically unjust treatment, over the importance of personal responsibility. Much was made in the press over sermons preached in a Black Chicago South Side church that was attended by a national presidential candidate.

The metadialectic or the battle between personal responsibility and the collective imperative rose to prominence at a number of significant junctures in U.S. history. For example, at the inception of America's Great Depression with unemployment doubling annually, President Hoover insisted America was a country of rugged individualists, and if people could not make their own way, it was their own fault.

In 1932 Americans elected Franklin Roosevelt as president. Roosevelt initiated the government program, Works Progress Administration (WPA). The WPA employed millions of people for the purpose of constructing public works projects including schools, bridges, dams, airports, courthouses, libraries, and arts projects. Despite providing earnings opportunities for 8.5 million workers, many questioned whether it was successful since it was not until the U.S. entered World War II in 1941 that there were enough jobs to end the Depression.[4] During the war effort, the country was run on deficit spending in the name of national defense.

Accountability is an adjunct to personal responsibility. The requirement wherein No Child Left Behind (NCLB) demands teachers shoulder virtually the entire burden of educational remediation represents a move toward personal responsibility. The problem here is also twofold. First, teachers do not have the ability or tools to overcome all the obstacles they must tackle in today's schools. Second, NCLB fails to consider student perspectives and concerns. Maybe the type of teachers students are offered do not serve their requirements.

Reliable educational opportunities are the only path to personal responsibility. Political legislation proposed to meet this obligation must be realistic and sensible. It is necessary to begin by getting to the root of the problem—addressing the basics, starting with the child's developmental process.

The rate at which a child advances through their cognitive stages may vary. However, the sequence is the same in all children. The development of a child's cognition transitions through four stages. The first level is sensori-motor. This stage begins at birth until age two. Sensori-motor intelligence is acquired through a process of stimulus-response and assimilation. The child constructs a complex system of schemes. Schemes are organizations of actions that are generalized by repetition in similar circumstances. Schemes organize reality in terms of spatial and causal structures.

The second stage from about the age of 2 until age 7 is called preoperational. The preoperational level is a prelogical stage. Although children are beginning to master symbols and words, they are unable to dissociate themselves from certain perceptions. They cannot make observations based on another person's point of view.

The third level is concrete operational which runs from ages 7 to 11. During this period schemes are developed that permit an understanding of logic-based tasks. However, operational thinking is still based on observations of objects that are actually present or that children have experienced directly or concretely. The ability to solve problems by generalizing from one set of circumstances to a similar set of circumstances does not yet consistently occur.

The final stage of development is formal operational which begins at age eleven. At this level of cognitive development the child is able to solve problems using abstract symbols, such as numbers, to represent real objects. Children are able to form hypotheses and sort out possible solutions.[5] These developmental stages are administered by parents and teachers. Improper supervision will reduce the capacity of the child's knowledge acquisition foundation.

The importance of establishing a knowledge acquisition foundation was addressed in a 1959 gathering of educators. Four themes were advanced that referred to teaching in schools. The first theme was to provide students with an understanding of the fundamental structure of the subjects to be taught in order to serve future learning. Learning can serve the future by enabling the transfer of knowledge from a proven ability to the completion of a similar task at another time. There can also be a nonspecific transfer or transfer of principles. Knowledge of general ideas enables future problem solving.

A second theme deals with intellectual development. Intellectual development refers to a process that begins in the early grades. Children learn to form thoughts early. A spiral curriculum would create continuity of knowledge development. The third theme relates to intuitive thinking. Intuitive thinking is the ability to leap to a tentative conclusion outside the formal analytic process. An exact definition of intuitive thinking within the context of observable behavior is difficult. Intuitive thinking refers to the act of grasping the structure of a problem without reliance on specific analytic mechanisms. The fourth theme is associated with the desire to learn and encouraging this desire. It is necessary for schools to engender an interest in learning by inculcating a set of attitudes and values with respect to intellectual activity.[6]

Children have an innate ability to procure and synthesize information from their natural environment. To maximize their learning experience, it is necessary to provide educational opportunities consistent with children's capacity to learn and formal instruction that will enable them to function successfully as adults.

There are two fundamental facets of formal training. The first is individual knowledge acquisition. The second is the inculcation of a sense of collective or community. Students have to be taught the importance of functioning as part as a group, not just as an individual. For example, the unremitting quest to buy more for less with funds created solely by wealth extractive activity will not ensure a sustainable economy. The consequences of the current flawed policy are visible to the *New Kids*.

Education, more than any other endeavor, is about the future, not the past or even the present. The form taken by educational institutions is as important as their substance—how subjects are taught is just as vital as what is taught. Schooling must reflect student predispositions in establishdding teaching methods and in offering a curriculum that is relevant to children's futures.

In the tradition of 1930s-style community and union organizers, the first stage in building an organization for change is developing an understanding of the population to be organized. Local organizations are an expression of the traditions and values of a community. Any new directions must be rooted in the experiences and preferences of the people.[7] Just as community values are the source academic development, a sense of the importance of community must be inculcated in students. A strong notion of community is inconsistent with most of the messages received by young people. Ubiquitous product marketing campaigns focus on individual needs and desires. A proper educational agenda has to change that perspective.

The public order has to provide the means for individuals to attain their aspirations. Otherwise, political violence or attacks on a political community will be made in response to unacceptable social conditions. The circumstances likely to precipitate a radical change include the level of intensity of shared discontents and the extent to which the political system is considered responsible for being the source of the discontents. Discontent arises as a result of relative deprivation. Relative deprivation is the perceived discrepancy between an individual's value expectations or the goods and conditions to which they believe they are entitled, and their value capabilities or the ability to attain these goods and conditions given the social means available to them. Deprivation induced discontent is a strong motivation to action.[8]

The caveat in this analysis is that the continued reduction of expectations will diminish the awareness of relative deprivation and, consequently, will minimize the likelihood of dramatic social or political change. Through the wonders of globalization with its access to virtually cost-free labor in underdeveloped countries, new branded clothing, shoes and the most sophisticated electronic products are inexpensive enough to be available to almost everyone. Just as Marx identified religion as the opiate of the masses, consumerism is now assuming that role.

Competent educational institutions are necessary to reduce the discontent created by relative deprivation. Nations, where students consistently demonstrate academic competence, are directed by centralized governmental education departments. By contrast, the U.S. educational system consists of more than 15,000 local school districts, 50 state boards of education and the federal Department of Education. In addition, there are innumerable stakeholder and interest groups. Included in this collection are parents, students, taxpayers, elected officials at many levels of government, teachers, administrators, unions, state and federal judiciaries, schools of education, researchers, universities, publishers of texts and tests, and journalists.

Because of the considerable number of interested parties, any major changes would require committing to an extensive amount of time and debate. Both the decentralized politics of American education and society's use of public education as an instrument of social policy fortify the barriers that impede significant change. The movement for national standards and assessments that resulted in the No Child Left Behind Act of 2001 began in 1989 as an agreement between the president and the nation's governors. Based on concerns about poorly educated young people, the ability of the nation to be competitive internationally, and growing income inequality, particularly among different racial and ethnic groups, the evolution of the standards movement began.[9]

Although NCLB has not lived up to expectations, this federally devised program may provide a basis for better programs in the future. Change will eventually occur based on the development of critical mass. A tipping model has been described using neighborhood migration as an example of the critical mass phenomenon.

When a few members of a minority group relocate into a homogenous neighborhood, some among the homogenous residents will leave or show signs of leaving. Their departure will create vacancies that would permit additional members of the minority group to enter. The increase in minority residents will, then, induce more of the original residents to relocate. Once a point of critical mass is reached where the original residents believe that they will have to panic sell their homes at lower prices, the earlier homeowners will all be expected to leave. The tipping model is about a process of conscious decisions and anticipations.[10] The tipping model is applicable o educational change.

In general, there is a high level of antipathy toward change. People tend to become comfortable with what they know—for better or for worse. Organizations, however, rarely accommodate this penchant. Organizations, by their nature, are in a constant state of flux. Organizations, institutions, corporations evolve. Their evolutionary character is a fundamental impulse based on the introduction of new methods of production and/or new markets. Qualitative change occurs as a consequence of freshly created situations. The result is creative destruction. Creative destruction is a requirement wherein the old is destroyed to make way for the new.[11] The introduction of the *New Kids* into a 100-year old educational bureaucracy is the catalyst for creative destruction. Despite a strong resistance to any significant challenges to the existing structures, the going configurations are unsustainable.

In the late 1950s a study of the comprehensive American high school was completed. Its purpose was to define the structure of education. High schools are comprehensive in the sense that they provide a student's entire secondary education under one roof and under one administration. It is responsible for educating the brightest and the most troubled. The mission of education is to provide equality of opportunity for all students. It is a development of the twentieth century.

The three primary objectives of the comprehensive high school are, (1) to provide a general education for all future citizens; (2) to offer elective programs for those needing skills to be used immediately on graduation, and; (3) prepare students for college. Is it reasonable to expect a comprehensive high school to be able to educate students of varying ability and backgrounds? This 1957 study made a number of recommendations which included: (a) Improving the counseling system so counselors can have an intimate knowledge of each student; (b) individualized programs since slotting students into specific academic categories is harmful to them; c) required programs for all; (d) ability grouping; (e) better special needs programs; (f) longer classroom periods; (g) summer school, and; (h) better science programs.[12] A half century later, many educational studies are expressing virtually the same prescriptions. The e-OneRoom Schoolhouse is responsive to these recommendations.

In the 1980s the percentage of high school graduates applying for college increased as a result of the growth of jobs for the cognitive elite— those individuals with exceptional cognitive abilities. These included accountants, social scientists, natural scientists, mathematicians and computer scientists, college teachers, engineers and architects, physician and attorneys. During the 1980s real wages began to climb for highly educated people, but fell for those with 12 or fewer years of education. This led to a form of partitioning where members of the cognitive elite were insulated and isolated by school, residence, and so forth. Since those with higher cognitive abilities became more valuable to employers, employers would seek out applicants in those partitioned sectors to the exclusion of others. Standardized testing became necessary to identify members of the cognitive elite.

Most faculty members at leading graduate schools of education are opposed to the entire standards based educational package. Testing has been described as an attack on intellectual freedom and that life scores based on living, not math scores should be an educator's concern. Biased cultural assumptions are built into standardized tests. This spells trouble in terms of equity.

Testing, however, is necessary to reveal the gap between Black and White students. Without testing the problems disadvantaged students face would not be visible. Three-quarters of White high school graduates in a National Education Longitudinal Study entered college and 36% completed a 4-year degree. Similarly 75% of Black high school graduates entered college, but only 16% finished. They did not have the prerequisite skills necessary to complete a college program.

Equalizing opportunity will be assisted by offering universal computer access. The computer industry is in the midst of a significant shift. Utility supplied computing will have the same dramatic effect on society as inexpensive electricity had more than 100 years ago. The current trend is to enable individuals and companies connect to an internet service that provides all the software and data storage capabilities now purchased individually. People will no long purchase a personal computer with a separate operating system, software and data storage. One will simply have a receptacle that plugs into an internet utility providing all of these assets for a less costly monthly fee. This development will make it extremely cost effective to purchase the receptacles for schools and have the necessary programming available for each student.[13]

In addition to universal computer access, better teaching is also necessary to close the achievement gap. The success of some charter schools is based on competent teaching. The right people were hired and their talents were nurtured. There was no lunch duty or paperwork. Teachers were given more than two hours per day of lesson planning time.

School classrooms, hallways, lunchrooms and bathrooms can be exceedingly dangerous. Kid's heads being shoved down toilets, books getting thrown out windows and teachers getting punched. To add to the incivility there are beepers going off, cell phone use during class, provocative clothing, desks turned over, throwing chairs, playing radios, yammering, singing, rude remarks to teachers, marijuana sold in bathrooms and graffiti suggesting trouble brewing. Successful schools have zero tolerance policy with regard to these types of behaviors. The successful charter schools also develop group or team based programs.

The e-OneRoom Schoolhouse will accomplish several important objectives. These include making students smarter, creating an interest in manufacturing, establishing a better sense of community, enabling better training of teachers and, finally, providing better school for less money.

NOTES

1: Introduction

[1] Rossi, R., & Ihejirika, M. (2008, Sept. 2). Rev. Meeks leads school boycott. *Chicago Sun-Times*.

[2] Downs, A. (1957). *An economic theory of democracy*. New York: Harper & Row.

[3] Slavin, R. (1989). PET and the pendulum. *Phi Delta Kappan, 70*(10), 752-758.

[4] Davis, D. (2007). *The secret history of the war on Cancer*. New York: Basic Books.

[5] Skinner, B. F. (1968). *The technology of teaching*. New York: Appleton-Century-Crofts.

2: The School Problem

[1] Ferkenhoff, E. (2004, July 6). Chicago to shutter most troubled schools. *The Boston Globe*.

[2] Rossi, R. (2006, April 21). 6.5% of CPS freshman finish college. *Chicago Sun-Times*.

[3] Whittle, C. (2005). *Crash course*. New York: Riverhead Books.

[4] Greene, J. P. (2005). *Education myths*. Lanham, MD. Rowman & Littlefield.

[5] National Commission on Excellence in Education. (1984) *A nation at risk*. Cambridge, MA: USA Research.

[6] Dickson, P. (1991). *Sputnik*. New York: Walker & Company.

[7] Jacoway, E. (2007). *Turn away thy son*. New York: Free Press.

[8] Marx, K. (1970). *A contribution to the critique of pure economy*. New York: International Publishers.

[9] Kohn, A. (1999). *The schools our children deserve*. New York: Houghton Mifflin.

[10] U.S. Department of Education. (2001). *Executive summary of No Child Left Behind Act*. Retrieved 04/06 from http://www.ed.gov/nclb/overview/intro/execsumm.html

[11] Wallis, C. (2008, June, 8). No Child Left Behind: Doomed to fail? *TIME Magazine*.

3: The Cause

[1] Postman, N. (1999). *Building a bridge to the eighteenth century*. New York: A. A. Knopf.

[2] Barber, B. (2007). *Con$umed*. New York: W. W. Norton.

[3] Weber, M. (1930). *The Protestant ethic and the spirit of Capitalism*. New York: Charles Scribner's Sons.

[4] Reich, R. (1991). *The work of nations*. New York: Alfred A. Knopf.

[5] Gillon, S. (2004). *Boomer nation*. New York: Free Press.

[6] Gordinier, J. (2008). *X Saves the World*. New York: Viking.

[7] Howe, N., & Strauss, W. (2000). *Millenials rising*. New York: Vintage Books.

[8]Schor, J. (2004). *Born to buy.* New York: Scribner.

[9]Marano, H. (2008). *A nation of wimps.* New York: Broadway Books.

[10]Cook, D. (2004). *The commodification of childhood.* Durham, NC: Duke University Press.

[11]Critser, G. (2003). *Fat land.* New York: Houghton Mifflin.

[12]Twenge, J. (2006) .*Generation me.* New York: Free Press.

[13]Klein, A. (2007). *A class apart.* New York: Simon & Schuster.

[14]Lasch, C. (1979). *The culture of narcissism.* New York: W. W. Norton.

[15]Greene, J., & Forster, G. (2004). *Sex, drugs and delinquency in urban and suburban public schools.* Manhattan Institute for Policy Research. ERIC (ED483335)

[16]Williams, B. (2006, December 25). But enough about you... *TIME Magazine.*

[17]Halpern, J. (2007). *Fame junkies.* New York: Houghton Mifflin.

[18]Boorstin, D. (1987). *The image.* New York: Atheneum.

[19]Keen, A. (2007). *The cult of the amateur.* New York: Doubleday/Currency.

[20]Gerth, H., & Mills, C. W. (1958). *From Max Weber.* New York: Oxford University Press.

[21]Tapscott, D., & Williams, A. (2006). *Wikinomics.* New York: Portfolio.

[22]Gilder, G. (1981). *Wealth and poverty.* New York: Basic Books.

[23]Bru, E. (2006). Factors associated with disruptive behavior in the classroom. *Scandinavian Journal of Educational Research*, *50*(1), 23-43.

[24]Bandura, A. (1997). *Self-efficacy: The exercise of control.* New York: Freeman.

[25]Stout, M. (2000). *The feel-good curriculum.* MA: Perseus Books.

[26]Kahneman, D., Knetsch, J., & Thaler, R. (1986). Fairness as a constraint on profit seeking. In D. Kahneman & A. Tversky (Ed.), *Choices, values and frames.* New York: Cambridge University Press.

[27]Kamenetz, A. (2006). *Generation debt.* New York: Riverhead Books.

[28]Baldacci, L. (2004). *Inside Mrs. B's classroom.* New York: McGraw-Hill.

[29]Eaton, S. (2006). *The children in room E4.* Chapel Hill: Algonquin Books.

[30]Steinberg, L. (1996). *Beyond the classroom.* New York: Simon & Schuster.

[31]Rideout, V., Roberts, D., & Foehr, U. (2005). *Generation M: Media in the Lives of 8-18 year-olds.* Retrieved September, 2006 from www.kff.org

[32]McDaniel, T. (1983). *The teacher's dilemma.* Washington, DC: University Press of America.

[33]LeFever, G., Arcona, A., & Antonuccio, D. (2003). ADHD among American Schoolchildren. *The Scientific Review of Mental Health Practice*, *2*(1).

[34]Kozol, J. (1991). *Savage inequalities.* New York: Crown.

[35]Kozol, J. (2005). *The shame of the nation.* New York: Crown.

[36]Coleman, J. (1990). *Equality and achievement in education.* Boulder, CO: Westview Press.

[37]Herrnstein, R., & Murray, C. (1994). *The bell curve.* New York: The Free Press.

[38]Cuban, L. (2001). *Oversold & underused.* Cambridge, MA: Harvard University Press.

[39]Thernstrom, A., & Thernstrom, S. (2003). *No excuses.* New York: Simon & Schuster.

[40]National Research Council. (1993). *Losing generations.* Washington, DC: National Academy Press.

[41]Williams, J. (2006). *Enough.* New York: Crown.

[42]Anderson, E. (1990). *Streetwise*. Chicago: The University of Chicago Press.

[43]U.S. Dept. of Education. (n.d.). Retrieved August 2007, http://nces.ed.gov/nationsreportcard/states/profile.asp

[44]Buck, P. (2001). *Worked to the bone*. New York: Monthly Review Press.

[45]Lowen, J. (2005). *Sundown towns*. New York: Simon & Schuster.

[46]U.S. Census Bureau. (n.d.). Retrieved September 2007, from http://www.census.gov

[47]Valencia, R., & Black, M. (2002). "Mexican Americans Don't Value Education!"—On the basis of the myth, mythmaking, and debunking. *Journal of Latinos and Education, 1*(2), 81.

[48]Ross, E. (2004). *Slaves to fashion*. Ann Arbor: University of Michigan Press.

4: Futile Responses

[1]Sadovi, C. (2008, Sept. 11). Earn an A? Here's $50. *Chicago Tribune*.

[2]Biehler, R., & Snowman, J. (1990). *Psychology applied to teaching*. Boston: Houghton Mifflin.

[3]Skinner, B. F. (1968). *The technology of teaching*. New York: Appleton-Century-Crofts.

[4]Wolfe, T. (1979). *The right stuff*. New York: Farrar, Strauss and Giroux.

[5]Lewis, R., Romi, S., Qui, X., & Katz, Y. (2005). Teachers classroom discipline & student misbehavior. *Teaching and Teacher Education, 21*(6), 729.

[6]Kohn, A. (1993). *Punished by rewards*. New York: Houghton Mifflin.

[7]Stevenson, H., & Stigler, J. (1992). *The learning gap*. New York: Summit Books.

[8]Sacks, P. (1999). *Standardized minds*. Cambridge, MA: Perseus.

[9]Oakes, J. (1985). *Keeping track: How Schools structure inequality*. New Haven, CT: Yale University Press.

[10]Bracey, G. (1995). *Final exam*. Bloomington, IN: Technos Press.

[11]Tyler, R. (1949). *Basic principles of curriculum and instruction*. Chicago: University of Chicago Press.

[12]Wiener, N. (1950). *The human use of human beings*. New York: Avon Books.

[13]Deming, W. E. (1982). *Out of the crisis*. Cambridge, MA: MIT.

[14]Drucker, P. (2006). *Concept of the corporation*. Edison, NJ: Transaction Publishers. (Original work published 1946)

[15]Hirsch, E. D. (1988). *Cultural literacy*. New York: Vintage Books.

[16]Hirsch, E. D. (2006). *The knowledge deficit*. New York: Houghton Mifflin

[17]Beniger, J. (1986). *The control revolution*. Cambridge, MA: Harvard University Press.

[18]Ouchi, W. (2003). *Making schools work*. New York: Simon & Schuster.

[19]Perelman, L. (1992). *School's out*. New York: William Morrow.

[20]Liker, J. (2004). *The Toyota way*. New York: McGraw-Hill.

[21]Rothstein, R. (1998). *The way we were?* New York: The Century Foundation Press.

[22]Dewey, J. (1938). *Experience and education*. New York: Collier Books.

[23]Newman, F., & Holzman, L. (1993). *Lev Vygotsky: Revolutionary scientist*. New York: Routledge.

[24]Gardner, H. (1993). *Frames of mind*. New York: Basic Books.

[25]McLaren, P. (1989). *Life in schools*. New York: Longman.

[26]Freire, P. (1970). *Pedagogy of the oppressed*. New York: The Seabury Press.
[27]Ilich, I. (1970). *Deschooling society*. New York: Harper & Row.
[28]Neill, A. S. (1960). *Summerhill*. New York: Hart.
[29]Bloom, A. (1987). *The closing of the American mind*. New York: Simon & Schuster.

5: Relevance

[1]Conlin, M. (2008, January 9). Youthquake. *Business Week*.
[2]Kingsbury, K. (2008, June 18). Pregancy boom at Gloucester High. *TIME Magazine*.
[3]Durkheim, E. (1951). *Suicide: A study in sociology*. Glencoe: Free Press.
[4]Nathan, J. (2004). *Japan unbound*. Boston: Houghton Mifflin.
[5]Economic Policy Institute. (2007). Retrieved August 2007, from http://epinet.org
[6]Lynch, D. (2008, March 20). Does tax code send U.S. jobs offshore? *USA Today*.
[7]Adler, W. (2000). *Mollie's job*. New York: Scribner.
[8]Kuhn, T. (1962). *The structure of scientific revolutions*. Chicago: The University of Chicago Press.
[9]Bell, D. (1973). *The coming of post-industrial society*. New York: Basic Books.
[10]Durkheim, E. (1984). *The division of labor in society*. New York: The Free Press.
[11]Riesman, D. (1961). *The lonely crowd*. New Haven, CT: Yale University Press.
[12]Pulliam, J., & Van Patten, J. (2007). *History of education in America* (9th ed.). Princeton, NJ: Pearson Prentice Hall.
[13]Ornstein, A., & Hunkins, F. (1998). *Curriculum: Foundations, principles and issues*. Boston: Allyn & Bacon.
[14]Bowers, F., & Gehring, T. (2004). Johann Heinrich Pestalozzi. *Journal of Correctional Education*, *55*(4).
[15]Federal Reserve Consumer Balance Sheet. (n.d.). Retrieved August 2007, from http://www.federalreserve.gov/releases/Z1/
[16]Kolb, R. (2003). *Futures, options, and swaps*. Malden, MA: Blackwell.
[17]Thornton, E. (2007, May 7). Roads to riches. *Business Week*.
[18]O'Brien, T. (1998). *Bad bet*. New York: Random House.
[19]Welte, J., Barnes, G., Wieczorek, W., Tidwell, M., & Parker, J. (2002). Gambling participation in the U.S. *Journal of Gambling Studies*, *18*(4), 313.
[20]Clotfelter, C., & Cook, P. (1989). *Selling hope*. Cambridge, MA: Harvard University Press.
[21]Keating, P. (1996, May 1). Lotto fever: We All Lose! *MONEY Magazine*.
[22]Goodman, R. (1995). *The luck business*. New York: The Free Press.
[23]Committee on Indian Affairs. United States Senate. (1999). *National gambling impact study. Commission final report*. S.HRG 106-117. Washington, DC: U.S. Government Printing Office.
[24]Phillips, K. (2008). *Bad money*. New York: Viking.
[25]Scurlock, J. (2007). *Maxed out*. New York: Scribner.
[26]Bensinger, K. (2007, Dec. 30). New cars that are fully loaded-with debt. *Los Angeles Times*.
[27]Kuttner, R. (2007). *The squandering of America*. New York: Alfred A. Knopf.
[28]Fox, J. (2008, Sept. 15). Lehman's collapse. *TIME Magazine*.

[29]Herszenhorn, D. (2008, October 4). House approves bailout on second try. *The New York Times*.

[30]Ritter, P. (2008, June 10). Jeeves 2.0. *TIME Magazine*.

[31]Editors. (2006, October 23). The Best B-Schools of 2006. *Business Week*.

[32]Harvard Business School. (2007). Making a case: The birth of the HBS Case Study. *Enterprise Newsletter*. Retrieved March 1, 2008, from www.hbs.edu/corporate/enterprise/case.html.

[33]Tenenbaum, S. (1965). *The wise men of Chelm*. New York: Thomas Yoseloff.

[34]Venkatesh, S. (2006). *Off the books*. Cambridge, MA: Harvard University Press.

[35]Shiller, R. (2005). *Irrational exuberance*. Princeton, NJ: Princeton University Press.

[36]Editors. (2008, May 23). Double, oil and trouble. *The Economist*.

[37]Galbraith, J. (1979). *The Great Crash 1929*. Boston: Houghton Mifflin.

[38]Kotlikoff, L., & Burns, S. (2004). *The coming generational storm*. Cambridge, MA: MIT Press.

[39]Hacker, J. (2006). *The great risk shift*. New York: Oxford University Press.

[40]Piore, M., & Sabel, C. (1984). *The second industrial divide*. New York: Basic Books.

[41]U.S. Census Bureau. (2007). Retrieved from http://www.census.gov

[42]Schlosser, E. (2001). *Fast food nation*. Boston: Houghton Mifflin.

[43]Mitchell, S. (2006). *Big-box swindle*. Boston: Beacon Press.

[44]Galbraith, J. (1952). *American Capitalism*. Boston: Houghton Mifflin.

[45]Dine, P. (2008). *State of the unions*. New York: McGraw-Hill.

[46]Florida, R. (2002). *The rise of the creative class*. New York: Basic Books.

[47]Blinder, A. (2007). *How Many Jobs May Be Offshorable*. Retrieved August, 2007, from http://www.princeton.edu/~ceps/workingpapers/142blinder.pdf

[48]Associated Press. (2008, Feb. 14). U.S. trade deficit down in 2007. *CNN.com*.

[49]Gifford, R. (2007). *China road*. New York: Random House.

[50]Yardley, J. (2005, Jan. 31). Fearing future, China starts to give girls their due. *New York Times*.

[51]Lim, L. (2008, May 21). Parents blame Chinese officials for school collapse. *NPR.All Things Considered*.

[52]Cheng, T. (2007, December 7). The heavy price of China's mega-dam. *Al Jazeera*.

[53]Wong, E. (2008, July 24). China presses hush money on grieving parents. *New York Times*.

[54]Barboza, D. (2008, Sept. 23). China's quality watchdog chief steps down. *New York Times*.

[55]Harney, A. (2008). *The China price*. New York: The Penguin Press.

[56]Kingston, M. (1989). *The woman warrior*. New York: Vintage Books.

[57]Shirk, S. (2007). *China: Fragile superpower*. New York: Oxford University Press.

[58]Editors. (2008, May 1). Angry China. *The Economist*.

[59]Barboza, D. (2008, May 1). Child Labor Cases Uncovered in China. *New York Times*.

[60]Roberts, D., Engardio, P., Bernstein, A., Holmes, S., & Ji, X. (2006, Nov. 27). Secrets, lies & sweatshops. *Business Week*.

[61]Chan, M. (2008, March 14). Red tape battle for China migrants. *Al Jazeera*.

[62]Aversa, J. (2008, March 5). Fed says economy has weakened this year. *Yahoo News.*

[63]McCormack, E. (2007). Worldwide competition for students heats up. *Chronicle of Higher Education, 54*(12).

[64]Burrows, E., & Wallace, M. (2000). *Gotham.* New York: Oxford University Press.

6: Solution: The e-OneRoom Schoolhouse

[1]Jameson, F. (1991). *Postmodernism.* Durham, NC: Duke University Press.

[2]Usher, R., & Edwards, R. (1994). *Postmodernism and education.* London: Routledge.

[3]Tapscott, D. (1998). *Growing up digital.* New York: McGraw-Hill.

[4]Bloom, B. (1956). *Taxonomy of educational objectives.* New York: Longman.

[5]Putnam, R. (2000). *Bowling alone.* New York: Touchstone.

[6]Tönnies, F. (1957). *Community and society.* East Lansing, MI: Michigan State University Press.

[7]Boone, L., & Kurtz, D. (1980). *Contemporary marketing.* Hinsdale, IL: The Dryden Press.

[8]Lortie, D. (1975). *Schoolteacher: A sociological study.* Chicago: University of Chicago Press.

[9]Stevenson, H., & Stigler, J. (1992). *The learning gap.* New York: Summit Books.

[10]Maslach, C., & Leiter, M. (1997). *The truth about burnout.* San Francisco: Jossey-Bass.

[11]Johnson, S. (1990). *Teachers at work.* New York: Basic Books.

[12]Guarino, C., Hamilton, L., Lockwood, J., Rathbun, A., & Hausken, E. (2006). Teacher qualifications, instructional practices, and reading and mathematics gains of kindergartners. *National Center for Educational Statistics, U.S. Dept. of Education.*

[13]Gross, M. (1999). *The conspiracy of ignorance.* New York: HarperCollins.

[14]Brimelow, P. (2003). *The worm in the apple.* New York: HarperCollins.

[15]Kahlenberg, R. (2007). *Tough liberal.* New York: Columbia University Press.

[16]Michels, R. (1915). *Political parties.* Glencoe, IL: The Free Press.

[17]Rossi, R. (2008, June 5). Teachers union meeting turns into Springer show. *Chicago Sun-Times.*

[18]Ehrenreich, B. (2001). *Nickel and dimed.* New York: Henry Holt & Co.

[19]Greenhouse, S. (2008). *The big squeeze.* New York: Alfred A. Knopf.

[20]Graham, L. (1995). *On the line at Subaru-Isuzu.* Ithaca, NY: Cornell University Press.

[21]Round, M. (1999). *Grounded: Reagan and the PATCO crash.* New York: Garland.

[22]Cameron, D. (2005). *The Inside story of the teacher revolution in America.* Lanham, MD: ScarecrowEducation.

[23]Leonard, G. (1968). *Education and ecstasy.* Berkeley, CA: North Atlantic Books.

[24]Jackson, P. (1990). *Life in classrooms.* New York: Teachers College Press.

[25]Haberman, M. (1995). *Star teachers of children in poverty.* W. Lafayette, IN: Kappa Delta Pi.

[26]Wagner, T. (2002). *Making the grade.* New York: RoutledgeFalmer.

[27]Postman, N. (1986). *Amusing ourselves to death.* New York: Penguin Books.

[28]Vidal, G. (1991). Forward. In M. Rodgers (Ed.), *The impossible H. L. Mencken.* New York: Doubleday.

[29]Beastall, L. (2006). Enchanting a disenchanted child: Revolutionising the means of education using information and communication technology and e-Learning. *British Journal of Education, 27*(1), 97.

[30]Brzycki, D., & Dudt, K. (2005). Overcoming barriers to technology use in teacher preparation programs. *Journal of Technology and Teacher Education, 13*(4), 619-641.

[31]Watson, G. (2006). Technology professional development: Long-Term effects on teacher self-efficacy. *Journal of Technology and Teacher Education, 14*(1), 151-165

[32]Papert, S. (1993). *The children's machine.* New York: Basic Books.

[33]Barak, M. (2005). From order to disorder: The role of computer-based electronics projects on fostering ofhigher order cognitive skills. *Computers and Education, 45,* 231-243.

[34]FitzPatrick, S. (2001). Students' experiences of the implementation of an interactive learning system in their eighth grade mathematics classes. *ERIC* (ED470137).

[35]Van Dam, A., Becker, S., & Simpson, R. (2005, March/April). Next-Generation Educational Software. *EDUCAUSE.*

[36]Kennedy, M. (2005). *Inside teaching.* Cambridge, MA: Harvard University Press.

[37]Adler, M. (1984). *The Paideia Program.* New York: MacMillan.

[38]Van Dam, A., Becker, S., & Simpson, R. (2005, March/April). Next-Generation Educational Software. *EDUCAUSE.*

[39]Cremin, L. (1961). *The transformation of the school.* New York: Vintage Books.

7: Games

[1]Abt, C. (1970). *Serious games.* New York: Viking Press.

[2]Csikszentmihalyi, M. (1990). *Flow.* New York: Harper & Row.

[3]Prensky, M. (2006). *Don't bother me mom, I'm learning.* St. Paul: Paragon House.

[4]Ortutay, B. (2007, January 12). Video Game Sales a Record $12.5 Billion. *Southeast Missourian Newpaper.*

[5]King, B., & Borland, J. (2003). *Dungeons and dreamers.* New York: McGraw Hill.

[6]Wolf, M., & Perron, B. (Ed.). (2003). *The Video Game Theory Reader.* New York: Routledge.

[7]Johnson, S. (2005). *Everything bad is good for you.* New York: Riverhead Books.

[8]Koster, R. (2005). *A theory of fun for game design.* Phoenix, AZ: Paraglyph Press.

[9]Gee, J. (2003). *What video games have to teach us about learning and literacy.* New York: Palgrave MacMillan.

[10]Beck, J., & Wade, M. (2004). *Got game.* Cambridge, MA: Harvard Business School Press.

[11]Anderson, C. (2003). Video games and aggressive behavior. In D. Ravitch & J. Viteritti (Ed.), *Kid stuff.* Baltimore: Johns Hopkins University Press.

[12]Herz, J. (1997). *Joystick nation.* Boston: Little, Brown & Co.

[13]Cassel, J., & Jenkins, H. (1998). *From Barbie to Mortal Kombat.* Cambridge, MA: MIT Press.

[14]Castronova, E. (2005). *Synthetic worlds.* Chicago: University of Chicago Press.

[15]Associated Press. (2007, June 21). Video game addiction: A new diagnosis? *New York Times*.

[16]Riley, R. (1996). *Application for State Grants under the Technology Literacy Challenge Fund—November, 1996*. Retrieved March 11, 2007, from http://www.ed.gov/Technology/TLCF/ltr.html

[17]Richtel, M. (2008). A $500 Million Week for Grand Theft Auto. *New York Times*. May 7, 2008.

[18]Miller, G. & Goldstein, H. (2008). Grand Theft Auto IV Hands-On. *IGN.com.* . Retrieved February 28, 2008, from http://xbox360.ign.com/articles/855/855555pl.html

[19]Ettlinger, S. (2007). *Twinkie, deconstructed*. New York: Hudson Street Press.

[20]Zygmont, J. (2003). *Microchip*. Cambridge, MA: Perseus.

[21]Oliver, R. (2000). *The coming Biotech Age*. New York: McGraw-Hill.

[22]Porter, M. (1980). *Competitive strategy*. New York: Free Press.

[23]Davis, D. (2002). *When smoke ran like water*. New York: Basic Books.

[24]Bergstein, B. (2008). Smarter electric grid could be key to saving power. *Yahoo News*. Retrieved May 4, 2008, from http://news.yahoo.com/s/ap/20080504/ap_on_bi_ge/future_of_electricity

[25]Stein, L. (1962). *The triangle fire*. Ithaca, NY: Cornell University Press.

[26]Sachar, H. (1992). *A History of the Jews in America*. New York: Alfred A. Knopf.

[27]Fishman, C. (2006). *The Wal-Mart effect*. New York: The Penguin Press.

[28]Bianco, A. (2006). *The bully of Bentonville*. New York: Doubleday.

[29]Margonelli, L. (2007). *Oil on the brain*. New York: Doubleday.

[30]Lindbeck, J., Williams, M., & Wygant, R. (1990). *Manufacturing technology*. Englewood Cliffs, NJ: Prentice Hall.

[31]Maack, M. (2001). *Get Reading for Standardized Tests, Reading, Grade 1*. New York: McGraw-Hill.

[32]School Specialty Publishing. (2004). *Total Math.Grade 1*. Ohio: American Education Publishing.

[33]Hirsch, E. D. (Ed.). (1997). *What your first grader needs to know*. New York: Dell.

[34]Ulrich, L. (2001) *Get Reading for Standardized Tests, Reading, Grade 2*. New York: McGraw-Hill.

[35]School Specialty Publishing. (2004). *Total Math.Grade 2*. Ohio: American Education Publishing.

[36]Hirsch, E. D. (Ed.). (1998). *What your second grader needs to know*. New York: Dell.

[37]Baker, J. (2001). *Get Reading for Standardized Tests, Reading, Grade 3*. New York: McGraw-Hill.

[38]School Specialty Publishing. (2004). *Total Math.Grade 3*. Ohio: American Education Publishing.

[39]Hirsch, E. D. (Ed.). (2001). *What your third grader needs to know*. New York: Bantam Dell.

[40]Callahan, K. (2001). *Get Reading for Standardized Tests, Reading, Grade 4*. New York: McGraw-Hill.

[41]School Specialty Publishing. (2004). *Total Math. Grade 4*. Ohio: American Education Publishing.

[42]Hirsch, E. D. (Ed.). (2004). *What your fourth grader needs to know*. New York: Bantam Dell.

[43]School Specialty Publishing. (2004). *Total Basic Skills. Grade 5*. Ohio: American Education Publishing.

[44]School Specialty Publishing. (2004). *Total Math. Grade 5*. Ohio: American Education Publishing.

[45]Hirsch, E. D. (Ed.). (2005). *What Your Fifth Grader Needs to Know*. New York: Bantam Dell Publishing.

[46]School Specialty Publishing. (2004). *Total Basic Skills. Grade 6*. Ohio: American Education Publishing.

[47]School Specialty Publishing. (2004). *Total Math. Grade 6*. Ohio: American Education Publishing.

[48]Hirsch, E. D. (Ed.). (2006). *What your sixth grader needs to know*. New York: Doubleday.

[49]Irish, D. (2005). *The Game Producers Handbook*. Boston: Thomson Course Technology.

8: Conclusion

[1]U.S. Department of the Treasury. (n.d). *History of the U.S. Tax System*. Retrieved April 2008, from http://www.ustreas.gov/education/fact-sheets/taxes/ustax.shtml

[2]U.S. Department of Health & Human Services. (n.d.). *The Personal Responsibility and Work Opportunity Reconciliation Act of 1996*. Retrieved April, 2008, from http://www.acf.dhhs.gov/programs/ofa/prwora96.htm

[3]Johnson, B. (2001). The role of African-American churches in reducing crime among Black youth. *CRRUCS Report*. University of Pennsylvania Manhattan Institute.

[4]Taylor, N. (2008). *American-made*. New York: Bantam Books.

[5]Piaget, J., & Inhelder, B. (1969). *The psychology of the child*. New York: Basic Books.

[6]Bruner, J. (1960). *The process of education*. New York: Vintage Books.

[7]Alinsky, S. (1969). *Reveille for radicals*. New York: Vintage Books.

[8]Gurr, T. (1970). *Why Men Rebel*. Princeton, NJ: Princeton University Press.

[9]Ravitch, D. (1995). *National Standards in American Education*. Washington, DC: The Brookings Institution.

[10]Schelling, T. (1978). *Micromotives and macrobehaviors*. New York: W. W. Norton.

[11]Schumpeter, J. (1942). *Capitalism, Socialism and Democracy*. New York: Harper & Row.

[12]Conant, J. B. (1958). *The American high school today*. New York: McGraw-Hill.

[13]Carr, N. (2008). *The big switch*. New York: W. W. Norton.

ABOUT THE AUTHOR

Eli Fishman grew up and lives in Chicago. His education credentials include an MBA from Northwestern University's Kellogg Graduate School of Management in Evanston, IL and an MA in Sociology from The University of Chicago where he completed his doctoral coursework. Fishman's professional career included owning a seat on the Chicago Board Options Exchange, where he was actively engaged in futures trading, and 20 years of factory ownership. One factory, located on Chicago's Near West Side, employed over 30 people in plastic injection molding and steel fabricating processes. A second factory that employed up to 70 people was located in Cape Girardeau, MO. That operation produced men's and women's work shoes and boots. The employees were members of the United Auto Workers union. Fishman has been an advocate for worker justice issues including the support of American manufacturers. He has written regular columns for publications in St. Louis, Cape Girardeau, and Southern Illinois. Fishman has also been the subject of stories in the *Wall Street Journal, St. Louis Post-Dispatch, Southeast Missourian, Southern Illinoisan,* and others.

INDEX

9 781607 524045